COLUMBIA CRITICAL GUIDES

Toni Morrison

Beloved

EDITED BY CARL PLASA

Series editor: Richard Beynon

COLUMBIA UNIVERSITY PRESS ◣ NEW YORK

Columbia University Press
Publishers Since 1893
New York
Editor's text copyright © 1998 Carl Plasa

First published in the Icon Critical Guides series in 1998
by Icon Books Ltd.

Library of Congress Cataloging-in-Publication Data
Toni Morrison, Beloved / edited by Carl Plasa.
    p.   cm. — (Columbia critical guides)
    Includes bibliographical references and index.
    ISBN 0–231–11526–1 (cloth : alk. paper). —
    ISBN 0–231–11527–x (pbk. : alk. paper)
    1. Morrison, Toni. Beloved.   2. Historical fiction, American—
History and criticism.   3. Afro-American women in literature.
4. Infanticide in literature.   5. Slaves in literature.   6. Ohio—In
literature.   I. Plasa, Carl, 1959–   .   II. Series.
PS3563.08749B436   1998
813'.54—dc21   98-39506

∞

c 10 9 8 7 6 5 4 3 2 1
p 10 9 8 7 6 5 4 3 2 1

Contents

This chapter begins with a brief overview of Toni Morrison's work as it has developed in the course of the last three decades and shows how, since the publication of *Beloved* in 1987, Morrison has become a kind of literary and cultural 'superstar'. It goes on to address broadly some of the questions raised by Morrison's fiction – from the politics of reading to the politics of critical theory itself as a means of approaching texts such as *Beloved* and African-American writing in general. The chapter concludes by summarising the main concerns of the criticism on *Beloved* contained in the Guide, with particular reference to issues of intertextuality, the supernatural, the body and history.

'An Extraordinary Act of Imagination': Reviews of *Beloved* and Interviews with Toni Morrison

This chapter is divided into two sections, the first of which registers the immediate critical impact of *Beloved* in both Britain and America in the shape of reviews by A.S. Byatt, Thomas R. Edwards and the controversially negative Stanley Crouch. The chapter's second section consists of interviews with Morrison in which she discusses and reflects upon the project of writing *Beloved* with Marsha Darling and the prominent black British theorist, Paul Gilroy.

'Trying to Fill in the Blanks': *Beloved*'s Intertexts

This chapter explores *Beloved* from an intertextual perspective. Beginning with discussion and analysis of one of the historical documents on which Morrison drew in writing *Beloved*, the chapter moves on to consider the complex relations of dialogue and revision between Morrison's text and the African-American slave narrative tradition. The importance of this tradition to Morrison's work is illustrated both in an extract from 'The Site of Memory', a lecture delivered by Morrison around the time of *Beloved*'s publication, and in the essay by Marilyn Sanders Mobley with which the chapter concludes.

INTRODUCTION

■ It seems to me that the best art is political and you ought to be able to make it unquestionably political and irrevocably beautiful at the same time. □

Toni Morrison[1]

TONI MORRISON'S *Beloved* (1987) is perhaps the most important text to have emerged out of the African-American literary tradition in recent years. The novel powerfully meets the criteria outlined in the epigraph above, fusing, as it does, a brilliant formal and linguistic complexity with a wider vision in which questions of slavery, race, gender and the dilemmas of historical memory are compellingly posed. This critical Guide brings together a generically varied selection of materials designed to provide students with a clear framework through which to approach and engage with Morrison's text. Beginning with reviews of *Beloved* and interviews with its author, the book goes on to include one of the historical documents on which Morrison drew in the course of writing *Beloved*, together with an extract from a lecture in which she discusses her relation to the nineteenth-century slave narratives that constitute the origins of black writing in America. The bulk of the book consists of nine essays (given either in full or as extracts of varying length) that demonstrate the ways in which a range of critics have responded to Morrison's call for a fully politicised aesthetic. Despite the differences in the theoretical models they deploy (Bakhtinian, feminist, post-structuralist, post-colonial, psychoanalytic), the critical analyses the Guide explores are uniformly marked by a careful attention to textual detail that is fully attuned, simultaneously, to the larger historical and cultural contexts in which Morrison's novel is implicated.

Over the last three decades, Morrison's work has come steadily to assume an increasing critical stature and cultural prominence and, in the period since the event of *Beloved*'s publication, has developed in a number of new directions. First and foremost, of course, Morrison is best known as a novelist and to date has produced seven fictional works – *The Bluest Eye* (1970), *Sula* (1973), *Song of Solomon* (1977), *Tar Baby* (1981), *Beloved* (1987), *Jazz* (1992) and *Paradise* (1998). She is also the author of

Dreaming Emmett (1986), a play based on the murder of fourteen-year-old Emmett Louis 'Bobo' Till for allegedly whistling at a white woman. At the same time she has held several university positions as a teacher of literature and, from 1989, has been Robert F. Goheen Professor, Council of Humanities, at Princeton. In 1992 she published *Playing in the Dark: Whiteness and the Literary Imagination*, a major work of literary criticism that examines the shaping role of African-Americans in the development of the American literary tradition and has been influential in the formation of critical debates concerning the multiculturalism of literary texts in America. In addition, Morrison has edited and co-edited, respectively, two works of cultural criticism engaging with recent high-profile media events in America. The first of these is *Race-ing Justice, En-gendering Power: Essays on Anita Hill, Clarence Thomas, and the Construction of Social Reality* (1993) and the second, in collaboration with Claudia Brodsky Lacour, is *Birth of a Nation'Hood: Gaze, Script and Spectacle in the O. J. Simpson Case* (1997).

The productivity of Morrison's activities as writer, critic and cultural commentator is matched by the extent of the critical interest that her work has generated, especially following the appearance of *Beloved*. By any standards, this is quite phenomenal: the simple action of keying Morrison's name into the MLA bibliography alone calls up well over 400 entries for the post-*Beloved* period, approximately one-third of which focus either exclusively or in part on this particular text. Such interest is mirrored and paralleled in the numerous forms of institutional recognition with which Morrison has been regaled in the course of her career. Of these, the most prestigious have been the National Book Critics' Circle Award for *Song of Solomon* in 1978, the Pulitzer Prize for *Beloved* in 1988 and the Nobel Prize for Literature – awarded to an African-American writer for the first time – in 1993. Morrison's pre-eminence – her status as 'superstar', to use Trudier Harris's word[2] – has not caused her to lose touch with a popular audience, however: she recently appeared on the Oprah Winfrey Show, filmed attending a small dinner party at which she was guest of honour and read and discussed passages from *Song of Solomon* with a group of women, both black and white.[3]

It would be misleading to isolate *Beloved* from the rest of Morrison's work (the novel, after all, is the first part of a trilogy, of which *Jazz* is the second and *Paradise* the third). Yet at the same time, there is no doubt that, above all others, *Beloved* is the text that has secured Morrison's reputation. Though international in scope and reach, this reputation is strongest, of course, in America where, in the wake of *Beloved*, as Nancy J. Peterson comments:

■ 'Toni Morrison' has become the name around which debates of considerable significance to American literature, culture, and ideology have amassed – these include debates about multicultural curricula; about the relation of slavery to freedom; about the degree of determinism and/or free will African Americans might experience; about the possibility of creating literature that is both aesthetically beautiful and politically engaged; about the interlocking relation of racism, sexism, and classism; about the ability to construct meaningful dialogues across entrenched differences; about the possibility of laying claim to our lives and imaginations from within a postmodern, capitalist society.[4] □

Morrison is thus indeed, to cite Peterson again, '*the* American and African American (woman) writer to reckon with'.[5]

Who, however, should conduct such a reckoning: white readers, black readers or both? The question of the politics of reading is one that has prompted a good deal of recent critical debate, in relation not only to Morrison's work but that of other 'non-white'[6] writers also and is directly addressed by Catherine Belsey in *Desire: Love Stories in Western Culture* (1994). As the title of this book implies, Morrison's *Beloved* is a text that does not feature within it: the concern is with love stories in a Western rather than African-American cultural tradition. Yet at the same time, as *its* title implies, the love story is one of the genres that *Beloved* incorporates and transforms.[7] This is most noticeably so in terms of Sethe's relation both to Paul D, 'the last of the Sweet Home men' as he is repeatedly called, and Beloved herself, whom Sethe kills – precisely – out of love. While Belsey considers the possibility of reading Morrison's text, she steps back from it, in the end, nonetheless:

■ I should dearly have liked [. . .] to discuss the brilliant account in *Beloved* [. . .] of the imbrication of the deadly past of slavery in a present which cannot in consequence realize the possibilities of life. [. . .] but I have a fear of appearing to colonize [Morrison's] work, or at least of seeming to pre-empt the work of African-American critics. The problem is not that Morrison's work 'belongs' to them, or indeed to anyone. But what she writes about includes the white expropriation of black experience and I am afraid to repeat that process.[8] □

Belsey's sense of 'inhibition'[9] as a white feminist reader of an African-American feminist text is well-grounded, both historically and politically, and can only be redoubled for those critics of *Beloved* who – like this editor – are not only white but also male. Yet it is questionable whether reading and writing on *Beloved* from a white perspective, whether as male or female, is likely, in 1994, to 'pre-empt' a black critical response to *Beloved*, since such a response had already been underway for some considerable time prior to that date and is, indeed, impressively evident in a number of essays collected in the Toni Morrison Double Issue of *Modern Fiction Studies* (Fall/Winter 1993) that appeared in recognition of Morrison's Nobel Prize award.

Belsey's reflections on the politics of reading stand in stark contrast to the position delineated by Gayatri Chakravorty Spivak in *The Postcolonial Critic: Interviews, Strategies, Dialogues* (1990). For Spivak, reading across the lines of gender and racial difference is positively to be encouraged, entailing hazards that are worth negotiating for the potential shifts in perception – of self and other – that they bring. The detailed example she gives, in the course of an interview with Sneja Gunew, is taken from her own practice as a teacher of 'Third World' texts in the classrooms of First World universities:

■ I will have in an undergraduate class, let's say, a young, white male student, politically-correct, who will say: 'I am only a bourgeois white male, I can't speak.' In that situation – it's peculiar, because I am in the position of power and their teacher and, on the other hand, I am not a bourgeois white male – I say to them: 'Why not develop a certain degree of rage against the history that has written such an abject script for you that you are silenced?' Then you begin to investigate what it is that silences you, rather than take this very deterministic position – since my skin colour is this, since my sex is this, I cannot speak. [. . .] From this position, then, I say you will of course not speak in the same way about the Third World material, but if you make it your task not only to learn what is going on there through language, through specific programmes of study, but also at the same time through a *historical* critique of your position as the investigating person, then you will see that you have earned the right to criticize, and [. . .] be heard. [. . .] In one way you take a risk to criticize, of criticizing something which is *Other* – something which you used to dominate. I say that you have to take a certain risk: to say 'I won't criticize' is salving your conscience, and allowing you not to do any homework.[10] □

These two stances on the politics of reading are clearly opposed to one another. While this Guide implicitly aligns itself with Spivak's position rather than Belsey's, the central point to underscore is that the question of 'who reads' has itself become a contentious issue in current criticism and theory, taking on a set of historical and political implications from which it is usually thought to be wholly removed.[11]

Questions concerning the politics of reading rapidly open into larger questions about the politics of critical theory itself as a means of addressing African-American texts. Given the importance of the role played by theory in many of the critical readings of *Beloved* collected in this Guide, it is perhaps worth dwelling on these questions. They can initially be broached in terms of the distinction between 'separatist' and 'syncretist' models of African-American literature formulated by Linden Peach.[12]

In the separatist model, African-American literature is to be located emphatically within an African cultural context. Such an approach is at the same time marked by a certain resistance to and suspicion of theory, which – as a result of its Euro-American provenance – is deemed to be inevitably complicit with the very structures and histories of racial domination that black writing seeks to interrogate and dismantle.[13] In the context of critical work on *Beloved*, the possibilities of viewing Morrison's novel from a specifically African perspective have been discussed by Barbara Christian in 'Fixing Methodologies: *Beloved*', an article published in 1993. Christian on the whole acknowledges the usefulness of Western theoretical methods – particularly feminist psychoanalysis, Marxism and formalism, along with intertextual approaches – as ways of reading Morrison's text. Yet at the same time she remains 'perturbed by the attention, by the *kind* of critical attention *Beloved* has tended to receive, or to put it in our current literary critical language, by the critical discourses that [. . .] are beginning to appropriate this complex novel'.[14] It is not that Christian wishes to reject these developments out of hand. Her concern, rather, is to register their failure to engage with – even efface – *Beloved*'s own engagement with 'African belief systems'[15] and to show how these are inscribed in the text.

Conversely, proponents of the syncretist model argue that African-American writing is more productively viewed as a culturally hybrid form. As Jacqueline de Weever argues, it is 'a literature in which African and African-American traditions are blended. Neither completely African nor completely Euro-American, this new blend is just as firmly American as the novels previously defined as American because this flower can bloom nowhere else'.[16] Several critics have considered *Beloved* in these terms: Caroline M. Woidat and Charles Lewis have brought Morrison's text provocatively into dialogue with Nathaniel Hawthorne's *The Scarlet Letter* (1850),[17] while Richard C. Moreland and Sylvia Mayer chart the intersections and tensions between *Beloved* and Mark Twain's *Adventures of Huckleberry Finn* (1885).[18] In another example of the critical production of *Beloved* as culturally hybrid text, Kari J. Winter has argued that it not only spectacularly combines white and black literary traditions – Euro-American female Gothic, on the one hand, and African-American slave narratives, on the other – but also 'reconstructs and illuminates' both at the same time.[19]

These readings take their place within a larger critical and theoretical project, currently ongoing in America, directed at reading across the 'color-line'[20] and viewing it, moreover, as the site where cultural identities are not irreducibly divided from one another but mutually transformative. As Kenneth Warren puts it:

■ Staring at one another across the void of American identity, African and European Americans have been constructing themselves and each other, each side trying to lay claim to an unchallenged cultural legacy and each failing (to paraphrase Twain) to prove unambiguous title. As each side tries to construct a *sui generis* account of its own heritage, the Other insists upon emerging in unexpected and embarrassing places.[21] □

From this culturally hybridised perspective, readings of *Beloved* (and/or African-American writing in general) that are informed by Western theory become less problematic, because the texts on which they operate are themselves produced, to greater or lesser degrees, in relation to a Western cultural context – albeit in ways that are frequently far from 'cordial, peaceful, or fraternal'.[22] Indeed, some black writers found themselves unable to celebrate Morrison's Nobel Prize award on the grounds that her work was, precisely, too Euro-American.

Chapter one of this Guide is divided into two sections, the first of which is dedicated to initial reviews of *Beloved* by A.S. Byatt, Thomas R. Edwards and the right-wing commentator, Stanley Crouch. Those by Byatt and Edwards are fully in step with the general acclaim that Morrison's text first elicited and offer a provisional working out and assemblage of many of the themes, concerns and emphases to be developed by subsequent criticism. The extract from Crouch, by contrast, is a denunciation of *Beloved*/Morrison, as vehement as it is both scurrilous and wrong-headed. Running thoroughly counter to the overwhelmingly positive critical reaction to *Beloved*, it is included here less in the interests of some spurious critical balance than as an illustration of just how highly charged debates about Morrison's work can sometimes be. Attention is given also, in this section of the chapter, to the ways in which other critics – Paul Gilroy most notably – have unpicked and critiqued Crouch's position, still maintained, incidentally, in Crouch's 1995 claim that Morrison is a writer with 'no serious artistic vision or real artistic integrity'.[23] In the chapter's shorter second section the focus shifts towards Morrison's own reflections on some of the projects underlying *Beloved* and their relevance for a contemporary African-American cultural politics. These issues are discussed in extracts taken from two interviews with Morrison conducted by Marsha Darling and Gilroy himself, a few months after *Beloved* was published.

In chapter two the main concern is with *Beloved*'s intertextual dimensions. It begins with a newspaper account written by the Reverend P.S. Bassett that records his meeting with Margaret Garner, the historically real '*cause célèbre*'[24] on whom the Sethe of Morrison's text is based. (This account is first alluded to in *Beloved* in the conversation that takes place between Paul D and Stamp Paid just after the novel's midpoint has been reached.[25] Though criticism frequently notes the importance of the historical documents that Morrison reworks in the shaping of

Beloved, they are rarely directly cited and certainly not in any great detail. Following this, the chapter moves towards consideration of the complex dialogue between *Beloved* and the tradition of the African-American slave narrative. The centrality of this tradition for Morrison's writing is demonstrated in an extract from her own discussion of the topic in 'The Site of Memory', a lecture given in the year of *Beloved*'s publication. It is further examined in the essay by Marilyn Sanders Mobley with which the chapter ends. Framing her discussion of *Beloved* with the theoretical insights of Mikhail Bakhtin, Mobley reads Morrison's text as a 're-accentuation' of earlier writings geared to the excavation of aspects of slavery – both personal and collective – that those texts could not originally accommodate. In this way, Mobley shows how, in the words of Henry Louis Gates, Jr., *Beloved* invents and articulates 'a language that gives voice to the unspeakable horror and terror of the black past'.[26] Together with these concerns, the chapter discusses the ways in which the category of history has itself been problematised in the work of recent critical theorists and assesses the implications of this development for those – such as African-Americans – whose history has been repeatedly denied and negated by a dominant white culture. In this respect, the chapter looks forward to the fuller examination of questions of history in *Beloved*, which occurs in chapter five.

Chapter three takes as its main subject what might be called the 'supernatural' elements of Morrison's text. The first two extracts – from essays by Deborah Horvitz and Elizabeth B. House – offer two mutually exclusive interpretations of the eponymous figure at *Beloved*'s mysterious heart. For Horvitz, as for numerous other critics, Beloved is indeed what Sethe assumes her to be – the ghost of her dead child returned in bodily form, while at the same time symbolising all those mothers and daughters lost to the Middle Passage from Africa to America. For House, on the other hand, Beloved is neither ghostly nor symbolic but human and literal and, as such, to be read as one who has suffered and survived the Middle Passage in her own person. The chapter does not set out to resolve these interpretative conflicts and conundrums, but sees them, rather, as sign and symptom of a deliberate indeterminacy on *Beloved*'s part as it collapses the experiences of death and the Middle Passage into one another. The main piece in this chapter is Pamela E. Barnett's 'Figurations of Rape and the Supernatural in *Beloved*', published in May 1997. Barnett concurs with Horvitz on the ghostly status of Beloved, but connects her, via psychoanalytic theories of trauma, to questions of memory and repression relating specifically to rape. The essay's principal critical innovation consists in the argument it makes about the ways in which *Beloved* reinscribes and historicises rape itself: rapist and victim are not necessarily synonymous with male and female in this novel, Barnett suggests, but rather with white and black. Because the essay is so recent, the critical response to it is yet to be forthcoming.

Barnett's concern with rape presupposes an emphasis on the body that is developed in the material presented in chapter four, much of which relies, either implicitly or explicitly, on post-structuralist and post-modernist ideas about the role of language in the construction of subjectivity. For David Lawrence and April Lidinsky, for example, male and female bodies are not only literally enslaved in *Beloved* but also subjugated alike to regimes of discourse that come to be internalised, even as, for both critics, such processes are gradually unravelled in the course of the novel. Kristin Boudreau similarly explores the nexus of relations between language, selfhood and embodiment in *Beloved*, using the work of Elaine Scarry on pain as a starting point from which to read the text. Boudreau's essay additionally looks back to the intertextual emphasis of chapter two by situating Morrison's text in relation to but also against traditions of Euro-American Romanticism and African-American blues. *Beloved*, she argues, precisely departs from these traditions by seeing pain not as something that humanises but something that – because it is unrepresentable – works in fact to dehumanise or 'unmake' the subject.

The Guide concludes, in chapter five, with extracts from essays by Sally Keenan and Peter Nicholls that are overtly theoretical, Keenan's being post-colonial (as well as feminist) and Nicholls's psychoanalytic in perspective. Such differences of approach are offset, however, by a shared concern with the problem of historical memory, which itself threads a path throughout this Guide. Keenan is in part indebted to Horvitz and the importance of both their readings of *Beloved* resides mainly in the expanded frame of reference that they bring to the text, showing that *Beloved* is not just a narrative about American slavery but one that opens out, crucially, towards the ruptures of the Middle Passage – 'the past which no one talks about – the slave ships'[27] – and the African diaspora as a whole. While Keenan expresses reservations about the use of psychoanalysis in the reading of *Beloved*, the extract from Nicholls makes the counter-argument that psychoanalysis provides a significant critical resource. Invoking Freud's insights into the ways in which traumatic memories are in a sense created after the fact and relating this to post-modern theories of time and history, Nicholls shows how such processes of psychic deferral are at work within Morrison's text. His analogous and more provocative suggestion is that the advent of *Beloved* is itself a kind of trigger for the eruption into late twentieth-century American and African-American consciousness of dimensions of history long excluded. Morrison's novel, for Nicholls, is in every sense a 'shocking' text.

With its narrative disjunctions, secretions and indeterminacies and the disturbing nature of its content, *Beloved* is by no means a light read: it is a demanding novel. Yet it is also demanding in another sense, insisting that its readers, whether black or white, attend to and acknowledge the historical weight of the stories that it tells so hauntingly, as Beloved herself makes growing claims upon Sethe – for love, remembrance, recognition – perhaps even seeking retribution for damage done. This Guide illustrates some of the ways in which critics have sought to negotiate the demands of this colossal text, offering a diverse set of increasingly sophisticated readings and responses that will, it is to be hoped, be developed in future scholarship.

CHAPTER ONE

'An Extraordinary Act of Imagination': Reviews of *Beloved* and Interviews with Toni Morrison

FOLLOWING ITS publication in September 1987, *Beloved* was widely reviewed and – with one important exception – widely praised, both as Morrison's 'best' novel to date and one of the most significant literary achievements of the postwar period. However, critical acclaim for *Beloved* soon became mixed with controversy when the novel failed to win the National Book Award for the year in which it was published. To the intelligentsia of black America this represented something of a scandal that was at the same time quite predictable, one more instance of the marginalisation and neglect of black writing by a predominantly white literary establishment. The sense of affront occasioned by these events culminated in an open letter, published in the *New York Times Book Review* in January 1988. Signed by forty-eight prominent black writers and critics (from Maya Angelou and Alice Walker to Henry Louis Gates, Jr. and Hortense Spillers), the letter celebrated Morrison's writings, up to and including *Beloved*, while protesting against the fact that she – like the recently deceased James Baldwin before her – had never been honoured with either the National Book Award or the Pulitzer Prize, those 'key-stones', as the letter called them, 'to the canon of American literature'.[1]

For Walter Goodman, the letter was a form of 'Literary lobbying'[2] (and indeed *Beloved* did go on to win the Pulitzer in March 1988). For John Wideman, one of the letter's signatories, its purpose, by contrast, was 'not to mount a public relations campaign for Toni Morrison, but merely to point out that sometimes the pie doesn't get shared equally'.[3] However the letter is read, its implications are clear: *Beloved* – like Morrison's work as a whole – does not inhabit a purely aesthetic space but is enmeshed, rather, in a larger cultural politics. For some critics, indeed, even the recognition and canonisation of Morrison's work that has taken place since *Beloved* are problematic, hovering ambiguously, in Richard Todd's view, between 'innocent or disinterested acceptance', on the one hand, and 'an appropriation undertaken in the name of "Political Correctness"', on the other.[4] Morrison herself is fully attuned to the ways in which questions of a text's canonicity must be addressed from the perspective of the racialised society in which that text is produced. 'Canon building', she comments:

■ is Empire building. Canon defense is national defense. Canon debate, whatever the terrain, nature and range (of criticism, of history, of the history of knowledge, of the definition of language, the universality of aesthetic principles, the sociology of art, the humanistic imagination), is the clash of cultures. And *all* of the interests are vested.[5] □

It is in this vexed and conflictive context that the following three reviews of *Beloved* (comprising the main part of this chapter) are situated.

Reviews

■ To review Morrison [. . .] is to take risks, the risk that you will be read by people who know her work, that you will be publicly perceived as wrong – wrong because your view is clearly political, or wrong because it is not; wrong because the importance of her issues make [*sic*] artistic assessment difficult, or wrong because her artistic brilliance may make her ideas, her psychological insights, seem more original, more true, than they are. One is afraid of being seduced by rhythmic prose, provocative images, and easy, warm, answers. And yet all types of reviewers take the plunge and respond to a work like *Beloved*. □

Marilyn Judith Atlas[6]

The first review included here (and given in full) is A.S. Byatt's 'An American Masterpiece', which appeared in the *Guardian* for 16 October 1987 and provides an indication of the immediate critical impact made by *Beloved* in Britain. Like Morrison, Byatt is herself both novelist and critic and responds to what she calls 'the exact beauty of [Morrison's] singing prose' with her own precise lyricism, so that, at times, she seems indeed to undergo the kind of readerly seduction described above. The review touches on a number of issues that later criticism takes up, develops and theorises in much greater detail: from motherhood and memory to the role of language as an instrument of domination under slavery and, perhaps above all, the question of *Beloved*'s relation to American literature and culture at large.

■ *Beloved* begins: '124 was spiteful.' 124 is a house in Cincinnati in 1873, inhabited by Sethe, once a runaway slave from the horribly named 'Sweet Home' Kentucky farm, and her daughter, Denver. The house is spiteful because it is haunted by the terrible fury of a baby whose throat was cut to make her safe from repossession after the infamous Fugitive Slave Act.

This sad ghost, possessed by infant rage and an infant's absolute and peremptory need for love, manages to materialise herself just as Sethe is cautiously attempting to come to terms with the affection offered by Paul D, the only survivor of the five 'Sweet Home men' who worked with her and loved her. Beloved – as she names herself after the one word on her pink tombstone – exacts love and payment in a wholly credible and comically disastrous way from her mother, her sister and the generous and dignified Paul D. In the early days Sethe suggested to Baby Suggs, her mother-in-law, that they move. 'What'd be the point?' asked Baby. 'Not a house in the country ain't packed to its rafters with some dead Negro's grief.'

If Beloved represents the terrible pain and suffering of a people whose very mother-love is warped by torture into murder, she is no thin allegory or shrill tract. This is a huge, generous, humane and gripping novel.

In the foreground is the life of the black people whose courage and dignity and affection is felt to be almost indomitable. Their names are the no-names of non-people and are as alive as jazz with their quiddity and idiosyncrasy. Baby Suggs's owner has always believed her to be called 'Jenny' but never asked Baby herself. The Sweet Home men are Paul D Garner, Paul F Garner, Paul A Garner, Halle Suggs and Sixo the wild man. (Garner was their owner's name; all the acknowledged individuality of Paul D – one of the most convincing gentle adult men I have met in a book for years – resides in his D). They do not love, or almost do not, the land whose beauty they respond to, which is not theirs, where they are not at home, though they try to make families and keep their pride.

This is an adult book, but all the characters have the essential *virtue* of fairy-tale heroes and exact our primitive affection unquestioningly. Toni Morrison's love for her people is Tolstoyan in its detail and greedy curiosity; the reader is *inside* their doings and sufferings.

The world of the whites by contrast, is almost wholly distanced – rising to the surface of consciousness only as and when the blacks can briefly bear to contemplate what it has done to them. The Civil War slips by almost without mention. Those whites who might think of themselves as good or kind are judged by Sethe's dismissive and patient acceptance of their obtuseness and ignorance about the essentials of her life. Those who whipped and tortured and hanged are judged implacably by the brief accounts of reminiscences the blacks cannot suppress however they try to numb themselves.

The emotional condition of all the people of this story is deliberate limitation of memory. Dying, Baby Suggs thinks 'Her past had been like her present – intolerable – and since she knew death was anything but forgetfulness, she used the little energy left her for pondering color.' The women do not remember the children they have borne to be sold away like fatstock, because it would hurt too much. Paul D and Sethe, meeting after terrible years, do each other the essential courtesy of sparing themselves from their worst things, which they pass over vaguely. They do not speak of the bits and collars they have been forced to wear.

But the past rises up and cries for blood, like Beloved. Paul D, witched into making love to this beautiful dead thing, finds his heart, which he thinks of as a tobacco tin rusted shut, is red and alive. This living redness connects him to Baby Suggs's sermon to the black people in which she exhorts them to love their own living bodies – neck and mouth and skin and liver and heart – since *they* will not.

The book is full of the colours whose absence distresses the defeated Baby Suggs so that she hungers for yellow, or lavender, or a pink tongue even. It is also – and connectedly, through the name, coloured people – full of marvellous descriptions of the brightness and softness of black bodies – pewter skins of women skating in the cold, Sixo's indigo behind as he walks home naked after meeting his girl. Beloved perceives whites as skinless. Sethe, full of rage and distress, turns on Paul D 'a look like snow'.

Another profound and patterning metaphor is related to Sethe's horror when the two brutal and inhuman nephews of her schoolmaster owner write – with ink she has made for them – 'a list of Sethe's animal characteristics'. When Paul D discovers what she did and attempted to do to her children in her desperation, he reproaches her; – 'You got two feet, Sethe, not four.'

This image works subtly in all ways. During her escape Sethe *crawls* towards the river, pregnant, desperate to reach her other unweaned baby (already in Ohio), ripped open by whipping, reduced to an animal level by white men's beastliness. The child she is trying to get to – Beloved – is always described as 'crawling-already?', moving on all fours and aspiring to walk straight.

The slaves whose stories lie behind Toni Morrison's novel were thought by whites at this time to be in some way animal. The case for slavery was argued on these grounds. What Toni Morrison does is present an image of a people so wholly human that they are almost superhuman. It is a magnificent achievement.

Toni Morrison has always been an ambitious artist, sometimes almost clotted or tangled in her own brilliant and complex vision. *Beloved* has a new strength and simplicity. This novel gave me night-mares and yet I sat up late, paradoxically smiling to myself with intense pleasure at the exact beauty of the singing prose. □

Despite its somewhat clipped and aphoristic style, Byatt's reading of *Beloved* remains suggestive, especially in its final paragraph, where the focus shifts from textual detail to a much broader reflection on the relations between Morrison's novel and the canonical texts of the mid nineteenth-century period in which that novel is situated:

■ It is an American masterpiece, and one which, moreover, in a curious way reassesses all the major novels of the time in which it is set. Melville, Hawthorne, Poe, wrote riddling allegories about the nature of evil, the haunting of unappeased spirits, the inverted opposition of blackness and whiteness. Toni Morrison has with plainness and grace and terror – and judgment – solved the riddle, and showed us the world which haunted theirs. □

The reassessment of the American literary past brought about by the advent of *Beloved* is indeed 'curious'; not least because its logic appears to be close to that which informs the model of textual relations outlined by T.S. Eliot (another dead white American male writer and vigorous defender of canons) in 'Tradition and the Individual Talent' (1919). Just as the literary past, for Eliot, is 'altered by the present as much as the present is directed by the past',[7] so *Beloved*, for Byatt, transforms and resolves the 'riddling allegories' produced by Melville, Hawthorne and Poe, illuminating slavery as their hidden ground.

Byatt's closing remarks reward further consideration, for they are strangely prescient of one of the directions taken by Morrison's work subsequent to the writing of *Beloved*. For the reframing of the American literary tradition that Byatt sees as the indirect effect of *Beloved* is precisely – and overtly – the project of *Playing in the Dark: Whiteness and the Literary Imagination*, a critical work that Morrison published in 1992. The central aim of this text, as Morrison explains in its opening pages, is to challenge and dismantle the conventional assumption that the American literary canon 'is free of, uninformed, and unshaped by the four-hundred-year-old presence of, first, Africans and then African-Americans in the United States'.[8] This she does, in a series of brilliant readings of texts by authors ranging from Edgar Allan Poe to Willa Cather and Ernest Hemingway, by demonstrating that the 'characteristics' of America's national literature are less the signs of a mysteriously free-standing '"American-ness"' than mediated responses to the 'overwhelming presence of black people'[9] that must constantly be negotiated by America's white imagination.

The second review (reprinted almost in its entirety) is Thomas R. Edwards's 'Ghost Story', published in the *New York Review of Books* on 5 November 1987. It is much fuller in its engagement with *Beloved* than Byatt's piece and perhaps should even be classified as a review-essay. Like Atlas in the epigraph that introduces this section of the chapter, Edwards begins by recognising the difficulties and demands that *Beloved* imposes upon its potential reviewer/reader, commenting on how customary resources are rendered irrelevant both by the harrowing nature of the novel's subject and the compelling manner in which it is handled. Notwithstanding such difficulties, Edwards grapples valiantly with Morrison's novel, offering, in particular, some stimulating if also problematic insights regarding *Beloved*'s use of the supernatural.

■ A novel like Toni Morrison's *Beloved* makes the reviewer's usual strategies of praise and grumbling seem shallow. [. . .] One can only try to suggest something of what it is like to find one's way through an extraordinary act of imagination while knowing that one has missed much, that later reading will find more, and that no reader will ever see all the way in.

Beloved is unlike anything Morrison has done before. Where her previous novels [. . .] dealt with the experience of black people, especially black women, in modern America, this one goes back into history, and behind history into the materials of myth and fantasy that sober history usually thinks it is duty-bound to rationalize or debunk or ignore. Before the Civil War, on a Kentucky farm called Sweet Home, a group – a family, in a sense – of slaves lived more or less contentedly under the fairly enlightened rule of reasonably humane masters, the Garners. Mr. Garner conversed with his field hands, consulted their views about their work, treated them as men, not implements. Mrs. Garner managed the female house servants kindly and helped them with what they didn't know. Still, institutional if not personal inhumanity remained – even Mrs. Garner was amused by her girl Sethe's hope that her union with Halle Suggs might be dignified by a marriage ceremony, and while Garner readily agreed to free Halle's crippled mother, Baby Suggs, he charged Halle far more in future Sunday labor than her market value justified. As Edens go, Sweet Home had its flaws – 'It wasn't sweet and it sure wasn't home', one of its inmates recalls. But Sethe's response to this witticism – 'But it's where we were. . . . All together. Comes back whether we want it to or not' – states a need for connection with the past that the book will dwell upon.

Sweet Home fell apart in the 1850s when Garner died and the farm was taken over by a theorizing sadist, called schoolteacher by the slaves – he was a great one for measuring heads and keeping notes –

whose brutality to his human livestock drove them to attempt mass escape. Sethe managed to smuggle her three young children across the Ohio to Baby Suggs and, after an epic birthing in the fields, got there finally herself. But the men were killed, tortured, imprisoned, scattered by their bid for freedom.

This is the story's background, told in flashbacks. Now it is 1873, the war is long over, slavery has been abolished. Sethe lives in Baby Suggs's house outside Cincinnati, where she cooks in a restaurant; Baby herself is dead, as is Sethe's older daughter; her sons ran away in early adolescence, not to be heard of again. She lives in seclusion with her daughter Denver, the child she bore during her escape, who is thought 'simple' by others and fears to leave the house alone. Sethe and Denver are avoided by their black neighbors, evidently because their house is haunted by the troubled, violent spirit of the daughter who died, known only as Beloved from the pathetically brief inscription on her tombstone.

Beloved thus proposes to be a ghost story about slavery, and Morrison firmly excludes any tricky indeterminacies about the supernatural. This ghost of the elder daughter is no projection of a neurotic observer, no superstitious mass delusion. Various sensible characters witness its manifestations and accept their reality; and unlike most writers of reasonably serious supernatural fiction – Dickens, Wilkie Collins, Sheridan Le Fanu, M.R. and Henry James – Morrison provides us no cozy corner from which to smile skeptically at the thrills we're enjoying. If you believe in *Beloved* at all you must accept the ghost in the same way you accept the other, solidly realistic figures in the story.

The ghost is violently exorcised by one of the men from Sweet Home, Paul D, who finds his way to Cincinnati after years of imprisonment and wandering to offer Sethe love and release from her history of suffering. But then Morrison, with even more daring indifference to the rules of realistic fiction, brings to Sethe's house a lovely, history-less young woman who calls herself Beloved and is unquestionably the dead daughter's spirit in human form. Beloved moves right in, drives the male recalcitrance of Paul D out of the house, captivates Denver, and begins her conquest of Sethe's own troubled heart.

This new Beloved is no mere apparition. She is solidly physical, indeed she perfects her humiliation of Paul D by seducing him. At one extraordinary moment we see her struggling to keep body and soul together:

> Beloved looked at the tooth and thought, This is it. Next would be her arm, her hand, a toe. Pieces of her would drop maybe one at a time, maybe all at once. Or on one of those mornings before

Denver woke and after Sethe left she would fly apart. It is difficult keeping her head on her neck, her legs attached to her hips when she is by herself. Among the things she could not remember was when she first knew that she could wake up any day and find herself in pieces.

This is the grotesque comedy of certain moods of folklore, in which figures of extrahuman potency and menace are partly humanized by assuming some of our own vulnerability; though they try to conceal it, they do speak our language after all. But of course they mostly don't – their sketchy familiarity is in fact what makes them so dangerous, and Beloved is not finally a beneficent intruder. □

Edwards is certainly correct in his contention that the effectiveness of Morrison's text is largely dependent upon the reader's capacity to 'accept' the ghost who is at its enigmatic centre, whether figured as the poltergeist whom Paul D eventually vanquishes from Sethe's home or in the reincarnated shape of the 'historyless young woman who calls herself Beloved'. Yet, in one important respect, Morrison's use of the supernatural is ultimately both trickier and more indeterminate than Edwards allows. Even as he notes the differences between the supernaturalism of *Beloved* and that which characterises a Euro-American Gothic tradition running from Dickens to Henry James, that tradition remains unquestioned as a point of reference from which to read Morrison's text. The results of this are enabling and disabling at the same time. On the one hand, *Beloved* would indeed appear to exploit many of the conventions that mark the Gothic tradition Edwards invokes: indeed, Kate Ferguson Ellis's description of the characteristics of Gothic novels – with their 'houses in which people are locked in and locked out' and concern with a 'violence done to familial bonds that is frequently directed against women'[10] – is extremely germane to *Beloved*. On the other hand, however, the exercise in comparison and contrast that Edwards conducts could be said to entail a certain ethnocentrism that obscures *Beloved*'s status and functioning as a specifically African-American text. For Barbara Christian, the figuration of Beloved as 'an embodied spirit, a spirit that presents itself as a body'[11] removes Morrison's novel from the contexts of Euro-American Gothic and the 'classical folklore' to which Edwards later alludes, resituating it in relation to 'the African traditional religious belief that Westerners call ancestor worship'.[12] Christian thus proposes a perspective on *Beloved*

■ that acknowledges the existence of an African cosmology, examines how that cosmology has been consistently denigrated in the West, and explores its appropriateness for texts that are clearly derived from it.

Since *Beloved*, as a sign of a continually developing African cosmology, is as much about the period when Africans were forcibly displaced from their Motherland as it is about slavery in North America, it would seem logical for critics to consider how African belief systems might illuminate this text.[13] □

It is not a question, though, of choosing between these radically different approaches. As Christian herself states, 'because of its richness of texture, *Beloved* does and should generate many and various, even contending, interpretations'.[14] The point, rather, is to recognise that reading is never a politically innocent or neutral activity.

■ To speculate about why Morrison should have created such a character and what she means to her, it may be well to stand back a bit. Black experience in America of course originates in slavery, which is to say that it begins with the behavior of white people. The whites in the book – the people without skin, Beloved calls them – are good, bad, or indifferent, but this is almost irrelevant [. . .]. For many blacks, however sadly, the issue may not be so much what exactly they have suffered from racism as how they can survive it. And survival points to the heart of this book, the question of memory.

Sethe's 'serious work', she reflects while kneading bread in the restaurant, is 'beating back the past', but of course the past is not simply an enemy but the source of our present selves. She vividly remembers the horrors she fled from at Sweet Home, but she does not often willingly remember a later horror, of which she was not just a victim but also an agent. After her escape, while living with Baby Suggs, she once beat back the past by trying and, except in one case, failing to kill her children when the sadistic schoolteacher appeared with the sheriff to claim his lost property and take Sethe and her children back to Kentucky. (In the event, he judged her to be damaged goods and went home without her.) This tragedy, barely hinted at until the book is half over, puts a new light on things. It explains why Baby Suggs's tough spirit failed late in her life, why Sethe's boys always slept holding hands until they were old enough to flee, why Denver is afraid of going out and so mistrusts visitors like Paul D, why Sethe is avoided by her neighbors. Most important, it explains why the spirit of Beloved, the child Sethe did kill, so yearns for acceptance and love.

Beloved's demand is to be remembered, to regain some form of life in the love of her tormented mother. Men are not very responsive to such an appeal; the boys run away, Paul D drives out the ghost and contends less successfully with the reincarnated Beloved in his hope of convincing Sethe to live in 'the world'. That world includes his serious love for her, but it also includes schoolteacher, the Klan, the prison Sethe served time in after the murder, and other white horrors. By remembering Beloved, cherishing her in her newfound flesh, Sethe avoids 'life' in a way that her life's own nature amply justifies, but hers is also, the book seems to say, a response to experience that may be most tempting, and dangerous, to women and especially to mothers.

Here Morrison's understanding and sympathy come into admirably intricate play. She knows and respects what slavery does to men, how dreadfully it wounds what for better or worse defines the manhood that most men cherish – physical capacity, pride of dominance, freedom of will and action. But she knows that it can do something subtler and perhaps worse to women, something that here centers on the figure of Baby Suggs, dead now but an abiding presence in the minds of her daughter-in-law Sethe and her granddaughter Denver, though significantly not so in the mind of Beloved, who died too young to have known her grandmother's power. Baby knew what life in the world was like, that 'Being alive was the hard part', as Sethe says later; she knew that some of the worst horrors of slavery are small and specific, like not seeing your children grow up – as seven of her children, by different fathers, died or were sold away before maturity – or having, like Sethe, to be told by white women how to nurse and care for your own babies. She tried to persuade Sethe that the past is better accepted than fought against: 'Lay em down, Sethe. Sword and shield. . . . Both of em down. Down by the riverside. . . . Don't study war no more. Lay all that mess down.' Or, more tersely, 'Good is knowing when to stop.'

Baby Suggs is the matriarch, the goddess of home; after she was freed, her body broken, she made 'a living with . . . her heart' as a lay preacher around Cincinnati, conducting Saturday services in the woods at which children laughed, men danced, and women wept, and then all laughed and danced and wept together until they were exhausted and ready for Baby's offer of 'her great big heart'. Her gospel was love, but not a kind that white religion has much to say about:

> 'Yonder they do not love your flesh. They despise it. They don't love your eyes; they'd just as soon pick em out. No more do they love the skin on your back. Yonder they flay it. . . . Love your hands! Love them. Raise them up and kiss them. Touch others with them, pat them together, stroke them on your face 'cause they don't love that either. *You* got to love it, *you*! . . . No, they don't love your mouth. You got to love it. This is flesh I'm talking about here. Flesh that needs to be loved. . . . And all your inside parts that they'd just as soon slop for hogs, you got to love them. The dark, dark liver – love it, love it, and the beat and beating heart, love that

too. More than eyes or feet. More than lungs that have yet to draw free air. More than your life-holding womb and your life-giving private parts, hear me now, love your heart. For this is the prize.'

None of Morrison's people have entire access to truth, and Baby's eloquent celebration of the flesh and its affections seems to her a lie when she is dying, shaken (we later understand) by Sethe's violation of her own children's flesh. Once she preached that the only grace her people could have was 'the grace they could imagine. That if they could not see it, they would not have it.' But she ends by thinking, 'There was no grace – imaginary or real – and no sunlit dance in a Clearing could change that.' But it's to Baby's remembered comfort that Sethe returns in her later tribulations, and Baby's doctrine of the body as the seat of love and grace that identifies the wrenching ambiguity of Beloved herself. Beloved yearns to exist and be loved in the flesh by the mother who, driven frantic by memory, violated that flesh so grievously. But finally it seems clear to Beloved, so imperfectly lodged in her improvised new body, that 'we are all trying to leave our bodies behind'; her desire, as with certain creatures of classical folklore, is not to exist as a separate, integral self but to fuse with her mother in a single 'hot thing' that yet preserves her self as object as well as subject: 'I want to be there in the place where her face is and to be looking at it too'.

This impossible desire leads the novel to its catastrophe and resolution, a kind of reprise of the original tragedy in which Beloved is dismissed, though not exactly defeated, and Sethe uncertainly begins to see that she herself, and not Beloved, may be her own 'best thing'. And Beloved's thwarted desire points back toward what I take to be the story's center. 'To be there . . . and to be looking at it too' is the terrible paradox of memory, of history itself, the hopeless yet necessary wish still to be a part of what we can understand only because it and we no longer are what we were, or think we may have been. At the simplest, most personal level, Sethe wants to preserve her memories – in effect, herself – against the distractions of living in the present, in the 'world', that Paul D's love, and in a way Baby Suggs's too, offer as compensation. In an important way Sethe is right to want this: her history matters; her own children can know nothing of slavery except through the stories she tells them, and her people (in Morrison's own longer view) will be imaginatively cheated, their dignity cheapened, if stories like hers are lost.

Yet memory, isolated from immediate life, is terribly dangerous. It permits guilt and self-loathing and hatred of others (however well deserved) to batten on themselves. Beloved is *all* memory – hers seems to be a collective racial memory whose 'personal' contents mingle with recollections of the Middle Passage from Africa. She loves both sweets and her mother's stories too well, and as she grows obese and insatiable in her domination of the household, Sethe herself becomes increasingly demoralized, loses her job, begins to starve. Stories are important – they are in fact all we have of the past – yet at the end the voice that tells Beloved's story insists that hers is 'not a story to pass on', even though that voice has been passing it on for 275 pages. It should not be told, it *will* be told – the paradox is unresolvable. The memory – personal, political, poetical – of a social horror of such magnitude may distort or cancel living possibilities: but living possibilities, pursued without regard for such memories, are pretty sure to be trivial, empty possibilities in the end.

Though it is hard for a white, male reader to be sure about this, I would suppose that in *Beloved* Morrison means to help thoughtful black people, especially women, to create or re-create an imagination of self that 'white history' or 'male history' has effectively denied them, even while showing them how easily such an imagination can become self-defeating. What I am sure about is that this book will convince any thoughtful reader, of any sex or color, that Toni Morrison is not just an important contemporary novelist but a major figure of our national literature. She has written a work that brings to the darkest corners of American experience the wisdom, and the courage, to know them as they are. □

The self-consciousness with which Edwards begins his discussion of *Beloved* resurfaces in these final comments. But here it is also explicitly inflected by the question of race, as Edwards signals the awkwardness of his position as a 'white, male reader' of a text that has very few complimentary things to say either about whiteness or masculinity or the 'history' written in their name. While such reflexiveness can often seem like an empty gesture in the direction of political correctness – a kind of narcissistic piety – it would appear, in this instance, to work as a respectful decentring, on Edwards's part, of his own critical authority.

The profound admiration for *Beloved* so clearly and eloquently expressed by Byatt and Edwards stands in stark contrast to the response of Stanley Crouch in 'Aunt Medea', another long review, initially published in *New Republic* on 19 October 1987 and subsequently reprinted in Crouch's ominously entitled *Notes of a Hanging Judge: Essays and Reviews, 1979–1989* (1990). In the first half of the review (not included here) Crouch sees *Beloved* and Morrison's work *per se*, together with that of other black feminist writers (Toni Cade Bambara, Gayl Jones and Alice Walker), as deriving from the Baldwinian vision of black suffering as a source of potential liberation and enlightenment for white and black alike. At the same time, Morrison *et al* are viewed as the proponents of a glib and divisive feminist ideology, emergent in the 1970s, which enables them to appropriate 'the martyr's belt that had been worn so long by the black man',[15] precisely by unmasking the patriarchal oppression that he inflicts upon the black woman. But Morrison is not only regarded as dangerously feminist by Crouch; she is additionally accused, as Nancy J. Peterson notes in her analysis of Crouch's review, of 'capitalizing on the desire of white readers to consume black women's tales of being abused by black men'.[16]

Crouch is equally 'vitriolic',[17] to use Peterson's phrase, in the second half of the review, which focuses specifically on *Beloved*. As if to compromise his own critical authority still further, Crouch commences his discussion of Morrison's text with the following sentence:

■ *Beloved*, Morrison's fourth novel, explains black behavior in terms of social conditioning, as if listing atrocities solves the mystery of human motive and behavior. □

This is a serious gaffe: *Beloved* is not, of course, Morrison's 'fourth novel' but her fifth. Crouch proceeds undaunted nonetheless:

■ It is designed to placate sentimental feminist ideology, and to make sure that the vision of black woman as the most scorned and rebuked of the victims doesn't weaken. Yet perhaps it is best understood by its italicized inscription: '*Sixty Million and more*'. Morrison recently told *Newsweek* that the reference was to all the captured Africans who died coming across the Atlantic. But sixty is ten times six, of course. That is very important to remember. For *Beloved*, above all else, is a blackface holocaust novel. It seems to have been written in order to enter American slavery into the big-time martyr ratings contest, a contest usually won by references to, and works about, the experience of Jews at the hands of Nazis. As a holocaust novel, it includes disfranchisement, brutal transport, sadistic guards, failed and successful escapes, murder, liberals among the oppressors, a big war, underground cells, separation of family members, losses of loved ones to the violence of the mad order, and characters who [. . .] have been made emotionally catatonic by the past.

That Morrison chose to set the Afro-American experience in the framework of collective tragedy is fine, of course. But she lacks a true sense of the tragic. Such a sense is stark, but it is never simpleminded. For all the memory within this book, including recollections of the trip across the Atlantic and the slave trading in the Caribbean, no one ever recalls how the Africans were captured. That would have complicated matters. It would have demanded that the Africans who raided the villages of their enemies to sell them for guns, drink, and trinkets be included in the equation of injustice, something far too many Afro-Americans are loath to do – including Toni Morrison. In *Beloved* Morrison only asks that her readers tally up the sins committed against the darker people and feel sorry for them, not experience the horrors of slavery as they do.

Morrison, unlike Alice Walker, has real talent, an ability to organize her novel in a musical structure, deftly using images as motifs; but she perpetually interrupts her narrative with maudlin ideological commercials. Though there are a number of isolated passages of first-class writing, and though secondary characters such as Stamp Paid and Lady Jones are superbly drawn, Morrison rarely gives the impression that her people exist for any purpose other than to deliver a message. *Beloved* fails to rise to tragedy because it shows no sense of the timeless and unpredictable manifestations of evil that preceded and followed American slavery, of the gruesome ditches in the human spirit that prefigure all the injustice. Instead, the novel is done in the pulp style that has dominated so many renditions of Afro-American life since *Native Son*.

As in all protest pulp fiction, everything is locked into its own time, and is ever the result of external social forces. We learn little about the souls of human beings, we are only told what will happen if they are treated very badly. The world exists in a purple haze of overstatement, of false voices, of strained homilies; nothing very subtle is ever really tried. *Beloved* reads largely like a melodrama lashed to the structural conceits of the miniseries. [. . .]

Beloved means to prove that Afro-Americans are the result of a cruel determinism:

> [that's] what Baby Suggs died of, what Ella knew, what Stamp saw and what made Paul D tremble. That anybody white could take your whole self for anything that came to mind. Not just work, kill, or maim you, but dirty you. . . . Dirty you so bad you forgot who you were and couldn't think it up.

This determinism is also responsible for the character of Sethe, the earth mother heroine who might be called Aunt Medea. Mistakenly thinking that they will be sent back to slavery, Sethe gathers her four children for slaughter, and kills one daughter before she is stopped. When the novel opens it is 1873. The ghost of the dead daughter has been haunting Sethe's home for years, frightening off neighbors, shaking, rattling, and rolling the house.

The book's beginning clanks out its themes. Aunt Medea's two sons have been scared off: there is the theme of black women facing the harsh world alone. Later on in the novel, Morrison stages the obligatory moment of transcendent female solidarity, featuring a runaway indentured white girl, Amy Denver, who aids pregnant Sethe in her time of need:

> A pateroller passing would have sniggered to see two throw-away people, two lawless outlaws – a slave and a barefoot whitewoman with unpinned hair – wrapping a ten-minute-old baby in the rags they wore. But no pateroller came and no preacher. The water sucked and swallowed itself beneath them. There was nothing to disturb them at their work. So they did it appropriately and well.

Woman to woman, out in nature, freed of patriarchal domination and economic exploitation, they deliver baby Denver. (Amy is also good for homilies. While massaging Sethe's feet, she says, 'Anything dead coming back to life hurts.' When Sethe quotes the girl as she tells Amy's namesake the story of her birth, Morrison writes, 'A truth for all times, thought Denver.' As if that weren't gooey enough, there's the fade-out: 'Sethe felt herself falling into a sleep she knew would be deep. On the lip of it, just before going under, she thought, "That's pretty. Denver. Real pretty."')

Then there is the sexual exploitation theme, introduced in a flashback in the opening pages: for ten minutes of sex, the impoverished Sethe gets the name 'Beloved' put on the gravestone. This theme in particular is given many variations. One of the most clumsy comes in an amateurishly conceived flashback designed to reveal that even Sethe's mother had a touch of Medea:

> Nighttime. Nan holding her with her good arm, waving the stump of the other in the air. "Telling you. I am telling you, small girl Sethe," and she did that. She told Sethe that her mother and Nan were together from the sea. Both were taken up many times by the crew. "She threw them all away but you. The one from the crew she threw away on the island. The others from more whites she also threw away. Without names, she threw them. You she gave the name of the black man. She put her arms around him. The others she did not put her arms around. Never. Never. Telling you. I am telling you, small girl Sethe."

It doesn't get much worse, or the diction any more counterfeit.

Baby Suggs, Sethe's mother-in-law, is philosophical about the house ghost, and introduces the stoicism theme when it is suggested that they move away. 'Not a house in the country ain't packed to its rafters with some dead Negro's grief. We lucky this ghost is a baby', she tells Sethe. 'My husband's spirit was to come back in here? or yours? Don't talk to me. You lucky. You got three left. Three pulling at your skirts and just one raising hell from the other side. Be thankful, why don't you? I had eight. Every one of them gone away from me. Four taken, four chased, and all, I expect, worrying somebody's house into evil.' Through Baby Suggs we will eventually learn how right Paul D is to conclude that 'for a used-to-be slave woman to love . . . that much was dangerous, especially if it was her children she had settled on to love. The best thing, he knew, was to love just a little bit; everything, just a little bit, so when they broke its back, or shoved it in a croaker sack, well, maybe you'd have a little love left over for the next one.'

Morrison is best at clear, simple description, and occasionally she can give an account of the casualties of war and slavery that is free of false lyricism or stylized stoicism:

> Sethe took a little spit from the tip of her tongue with her fore-finger. Quickly, lightly she touched the stove. Then she trailed her fingers through the flour, parting, separating small hills and ridges of it, looking for mites. Finding none, she poured soda and salt into the crease of her folded hand and tossed both into the flour. Then she reached into a can and scooped half a handful of lard. Deftly she squeezed the flour through it, then with her left hand sprinkling water, she formed the dough.

Or Paul D remembering the people he saw on the road after making his escape from slavery, people

> who, like him, had hidden in caves and fought owls for food; who, like him, stole from pigs; who, like him, slept in trees in the day and walked by night; who, like him, had buried themselves in slop and jumped in wells to avoid regulators, raiders, paterollers, veterans, hill men, posses, and merrymakers. Once he met a Negro fourteen years old who lived by himself in the woods and said he couldn't remember living anywhere else. He saw a witless colored woman jailed and hanged for stealing ducks she believed were her own babies.

But Morrison almost always loses control. She can't resist the tempta-tion of the trite or the sentimental. There is the usual scene in which the black woman is assaulted by white men while her man looks on; Halle, Sethe's husband, goes mad at the sight. Sixo, a slave who is captured trying to escape, is burned alive but doesn't scream: he sings 'Seven-O!' over and over, because his woman has escaped and is preg-nant. But nothing is more contrived than the figure of Beloved herself, who is the reincarnated force of the malevolent ghost that was chased from the house. Beloved's revenge – she takes over the house, turns her mother into a servant manipulated by guilt, and becomes more and more vicious – unfolds as portentous melodrama. When Beloved finally threatens to kill Sethe, 30 black women come to the rescue. At the fence of the haunted property, one of them shouts, and we are given this: 'Instantly the kneelers and the standers joined her. They stopped praying and took a step back to the beginning. In the beginning there were no words. In the beginning was the sound, and they all knew what that sound sounded like.'

Too many such attempts at biblical grandeur, run through by Negro folk rhythms, stymie a book that might have been important. Had Morrison higher intentions when she appropriated the conventions of a holocaust tale, *Beloved* might stand next to, or outdistance, Ernest Gaines's *The Autobiography of Jane Pittman* and Charles Johnson's *Oxherding Tale* [. . .]. Yet to render slavery with aesthetic authority demands not only talent, but the courage to face the ambiguities of the human soul, which transcend race. Had Toni Morrison that kind of courage, had she the passion necessary to liberate her work from the failure of feeling that is sentimentality, there is much that she could achieve. But why should she try to achieve anything? The position of literary conjure woman has paid off quite well. At last year's PEN Congress she announced that she had never considered herself American, but with *Beloved* she proves that she is as American as P. T. Barnum. ☐

The hostility of this assessment of *Beloved* is without parallel among the numerous reviews that the text has generated and it is tempting to dismiss Crouch as he dismisses Morrison. Yet such a temptation is one that has been productively resisted by those who have responded to Crouch's position. Atlas argues that Crouch's review is 'self-protective'.[18] By trivialising the Middle Passage into a 'trip across the Atlantic' and generally reducing the magnitude of Morrison's novel to the scale of a television 'miniseries' or 'portentous melodrama', Crouch evades and disavows the painful confrontations that, for most readers, *Beloved* forces: as Peterson suggests, the Morrison whom Crouch constructs in 'Aunt Medea' 'seems to be the projection of personal and cultural anxieties that have very little to do with the power and merit of *Beloved*'.[19]

Perhaps the most sustained and searching critique of Crouch's arguments is provided by Paul Gilroy in the concluding pages to *The Black Atlantic: Modernity and Double Consciousness* (1993). Gilroy begins by flatly rejecting Crouch's description of *Beloved* as 'above all else, a blackface holocaust novel [. . .] written in order to enter American slavery into the big-time martyr ratings contest'. He goes on, however, to pose a 'restrained counter-question to Crouch's acid polemic' that forms the basis of his own discussion of *Beloved*:

■ What would be the consequences if [Morrison's] book had tried to set the Holocaust of European Jews in a provocative relationship with the modern history of racial slavery in the western hemisphere? Crouch dismisses without considering it the possibility that there might be something useful to be gained from setting these histories closer to each other not so as to compare them, but as precious resources from which we might learn something valuable about the way that modernity operates, about the scope and status of rational human conduct, about the claims of science, and perhaps most importantly about the ideologies of humanism with which those brutal histories can be shown to have been complicit.[20] □

This passage lays bare the irony by which 'Aunt Medea' is fractured. With its essentialist vision of 'the human spirit that prefigures all injustice' and castigation of *Beloved* for revealing 'little about the souls of human beings', Crouch's review shows itself to be shaped by the very humanist ideology with which, for Gilroy, the Holocaust and slavery are alike 'complicit': for a writer such as Morrison, humanism is not the solution but part of the problem. If reviewing Morrison involves risks, it is clear from the material covered above that some reviewers negotiate those risks more successfully than others.

Interviews

■ They always say that my writing is rich. It's not – what's rich, if there is any richness, is what the reader gets and brings him or herself. That's part of the way in which the tale is told. The folk tales are told in such a way that whoever is listening is in it and can shape it and figure it out. It's not over just because it stops. It lingers and it's passed on. It's passed on and somebody else can alter it later.

Toni Morrison[21] □

This chapter's briefer second section features extracts from two interviews given by Morrison shortly after *Beloved*'s publication, between which there is an inevitable degree of overlap. While the extracts seem to bring the student of Morrison into direct contact with an authorial presence, they should not be regarded as providing access to the 'truth' of *Beloved*. As recent critical theory has demonstrated, the notion of authorial intention is highly problematic, laden with all kinds of questionable assumptions about subjectivity and language and the relations between them, and should not be allowed to set a limit to interpretation.

Though Morrison does indeed discuss her intentions in the writing of *Beloved* (particularly in the first extract), her comments function neither to fix nor to exhaust the signifying possibilities of the text: as the epigraph above suggests, the 'richness' of Morrison's work is as much an effect of what the reader 'gets and brings' to the text as of the text itself. That said, however, any analysis of *Beloved* that is not informed by Morrison's complex and provocative reflections on her own work is likely to be seriously impoverished.

The first extract is from Marsha Darling's 'In the Realm of Responsibility: A Conversation with Toni Morrison', which originally appeared in *Women's Review of Books* in March 1988 and has subsequently been anthologised in Danille Taylor-Guthrie's edited collection, *Conversations with Toni Morrison* (1994). Here the issue of responsibility that gives the interview its title takes two principal forms. First, there is the responsibility of the African-American writer towards history or, more exactly, that aspect of history – the Middle Passage – which constitutes, in Christian's words, a 'monumental collective psychic rupture'[22] for African-Americans. Secondly, there is the responsibility of the African-American mother towards her children as it is determined by the slave experience, culminating in an act of infanticide, which, as Morrison puts it and *Beloved* shows, is as 'understandable' as it is 'excessive'.

■ MD: What are our responsibilities to the living and the dead? What are the boundaries between the living and the dead? For instance, who – what – brings the baby spirit Beloved to 124 Bluestone Road? Is she summoned? Does she come because of some higher law that has not been reckoned with? Reading *Beloved* got me thinking about cause, effect – what are those boundaries, whose responsibilities? Do you want to suggest that it is Sethe accounting to herself that summons the spirit? Does Beloved bring herself? Does Sethe bring Beloved?

TM: I will describe to you the levels on which I wanted Beloved to function. That may answer the question in part. She is a spirit on one hand, literally she is what Sethe thinks she is, her child returned to her from the dead. And she must function like that in the text. She is also another kind of dead which is not spiritual but flesh, which is, a survivor from a true, factual slave ship. She speaks the language, a traumatized language, of her own experience, which blends beautifully in her questions and answers, her preoccupations, with the desires of Denver and Sethe. So that when they say 'What was it like over there?' they may mean – they do mean – 'What was it like being dead?' She tells them what it was like being where she was on that ship as a child. Both things are possible, and there's evidence in the text so that both things could be approached, because the language of both experiences – death and the Middle Passage – is the same. Her yearning would be the same, the love and yearning for that face that was going to smile at her.

The gap between Africa and Afro-America and the gap between the living and the dead and the gap between the past and the present does not exist. It's bridged for us by our assuming responsibility for people no one's ever assumed responsibility for. They are those that died en route. Nobody knows their names, and nobody thinks about them. In addition to that, they never survived in the lore; there are no songs or dances or tales of these people. The people who arrived – there is lore about them. But nothing survives about . . . that.

I suspect the reason is that it was not possible to survive on certain levels and dwell on it. People who did dwell on it, it probably killed them, and the people who did not dwell on it probably went forward. They tried to make a life. I think Afro-Americans in rushing away from slavery, which was important to do – it meant rushing out of bondage into freedom – also rushed away from the slaves because it was painful to dwell there, and they may have abandoned some responsibilities in so doing. It was a double-edged sword, if you understand me.

There is a necessity for remembering the horror, but of course there's a necessity for remembering it in a manner in which it can be digested, in a manner in which the memory is not destructive. The act of writing the book, in a way, is a way of confronting it and making it possible to remember.

MD: One of my questions was going to be – and I think you've just answered it – where's the healing? There's a healing in the memory and the re-memory. Yes, each character tells her or his story, and through that there are confrontations with each other; there are a lot of things that go on, yet there's a healing in bringing it into 1873.

TM: And no one speaks, no one tells the story about himself or herself unless forced. They don't want to talk, they don't want to remember, they don't want to say it, because they're afraid of it – which is human. But when they do say it, and hear it, and look at it, and share it, they are not only one, they're two, and three, and four, you know? The collective sharing of that information heals the individual – and the collective. [. . .]

MD: I wanted to ask you about your sense of Sethe as mother, woman. There is a way that she loves that is intense. And I'm not sure where I see you locate her *self*. She tells us at one point that she is not separate from these children; she is these children and these children are her. Could you talk some about that? That is a real powerful part of the book and very controversial, in that she takes responsibility for the very breath in their bodies.

TM: Under those theatrical circumstances of slavery, if you made that claim, an unheard-of claim, which is that you are the mother of these children – that's an outrageous claim for a slave woman. She just *became* a mother, which is becoming a human being in a situation which is earnestly dependent on your not being one. That's who she is. So to claim responsibility for children, to say something about what happens to them means that you claim all of it, not part of it. Not till they're five or till they are six, but *all* of it. Therefore when she is away from her husband she merges into that role, and it's unleashed and it's fierce. She almost steps over into what she was terrified of being regarded as, which is an animal. It's an excess of maternal feeling, a total surrender to that commitment, and, you know, such excesses are not good. She has stepped across the line, so to speak. It's understandable, but it is excessive. This is what the townspeople in Cincinnati respond to, not her grief, but her arrogance.

MD: Is that why they shun her? They go away, they leave, they just abandon her.

TM: They abandon her because of what they felt was her pride. Her statement about what is valuable to her – in a sense it damns what they think is valuable to them. They have had losses too. In her unwillingness to apologize or bend . . . she would kill her child again is what they know. That is what separates her from the rest of her community.

MD: And what they punish her for.

TM: Oh, very much. [. . .] One of the things that's important to me is the powerful imaginative way in which we deconstructed and reconstructed reality in order to get through. The act of will, of going to work every day – something is going on in the mind and the spirit that is not at all the mind or the spirit of a robotized or automaton people. Whether it is color for Baby Suggs, the changing of his name for Stamp Paid, each character has a set of things their imagination works rather constantly at, and it's very individualistic, although they share something in common. So it's important to me that the interior life of each of those characters be one that you could trust, one that felt like it was a real interior life; and also be distinct one from the other, in order to give them – not 'personalities', but an interior life of people that have been reduced to some great lump called slaves. [. . .]

MD: [. . .] the women characters you create are intense, strong, active presences. In this novel they talk to us from the nineteenth century.

But you are obviously saying things about the here and now and about women here and now. Could you elaborate on that?

TM: The story seemed to me to yield up a persistent struggle by women, Black women, in negotiating something very difficult. The whole problem was trying to do two things: to love something bigger than yourself, to nurture something; and also not to sabotage yourself, not to murder yourself. [. . .] I'll say it this way. This story is about, among other things, the tension between being yourself, one's own Beloved, and being a mother. [. . .] One of the nicest things women do is nurture other people, but it can be done in such a way that we surrender anything like a self. You can surrender yourself to a man and think that you cannot live or be without that man; you have no existence. And you can do the same thing with children.

It seemed that slavery presented an ideal situation to discuss the problem. That was the situation in which Black women were denied motherhood, so they would be interested in it – everybody would be interested in making, holding, keeping a family as large and as productive as it could be. Even though there are greater choices now, an infinite variety of choices, the propensity for self-dramatizing seems to me to be just as great. I'm curious about it, that's all. For me it's just an examination of what on earth is going on, what is all this about? And the thread that's running through the work I'm doing now is this question – *who is the Beloved*? □

The second extract is from Gilroy's 'Living Memory: A Meeting with Toni Morrison.' Published in Gilroy's *Small Acts: Thoughts on the Politics of Black Cultures* (1993), this is a slightly expanded version of an interview that first appeared in *City Limits* for 31 March–7 April 1988. Though the shortest piece in this chapter, it is in many ways the most suggestive: as well as re-exploring the forms of historical and maternal responsibility discussed in the previous extract, Gilroy's exchange with Morrison ranges far beyond the precincts of *Beloved*, offering a series of additional speculations that are nonetheless directly pertinent to the concerns of the text. With the minor exceptions of two phrases in the first and penultimate paragraphs, all of the comments included in quotation marks are Morrison's.

■ Black women's experiences and, in particular, the meanings they attach to motherhood, are central themes in *Beloved*. For Morrison, these issues cannot be divorced from a different, deeper contradiction: the tension between the racial self and the racial community. This is explored in the book through a profound examination of infanticide. The story is loosely based on the real case of Margaret Garner, a young woman who killed her children rather than let the slave-catchers take them back to bondage. When arraigned for their murder, she simply repeated: 'They will not live as I have done.'

'It occurred to me that the questions about community and individuality were certainly inherent in that incident as I imagined it. When you are the community, when you are your children, when that is your individuality, there is no division . . . Margaret Garner didn't do what Medea did and kill her children because of some guy. It was for me this classic example of a person determined to be responsible.' □

The terms of Morrison's discussion of Garner of course recall Crouch, though only further to undermine him: Garner – on whom the Sethe of *Beloved* is modelled – is precisely not, for Morrison, a Medea-figure, killing 'her children because of some guy'.

■ The Garner story illustrates more than the indomitable power of slaves to assert their humanity in restricted circumstances. It encapsulates the confrontation between two opposed philosophical and ideological systems and their attendant conceptions of reason, history, property and kinship. One is the product of Africa, the other is an expression of Western modernity. Morrison sees the intensity of the slave experience as something that marks out blacks as the first truly modern people, handling in the nineteenth century dilemmas and difficulties which have become the substance of everyday life in our own time.

'Well, the people that we call the true modernists in painting knew the pitfalls of direct representation. . . . The so-called modernist writers of the nineteenth century registered the impact of industrialization in literature – the great transformation from the old world to the new. Africa was feeling the same things. Can you imagine what it would have been like if they had left that continent untampered with? It's not simply that human life originated in Africa in anthropological terms, but that modern life begins with slavery. . . . From a woman's point of view, in terms of confronting the problems of where the world is now, black women had to deal with "post-modern" problems in the nineteenth century and earlier. These things had to be addressed by black people a long time ago. Certain kinds of dissolution, the loss of and the need to reconstruct certain kinds of stability. Certain kinds of madness, deliberately going mad in order, as one of the characters says in the book, "[. . .] not to lose your mind". These strategies for survival made the truly modern person. They're a response to predatory Western phenomena. You can call it an ideology and an economy, what it is is a pathology. Slavery broke the world in half, it broke it in every way. It broke Europe. It made them into something else, it made them slave masters, it made them crazy. You can't do that for hundreds of years and it not take a toll. They had to dehumanize, not just the slaves but themselves. They have had to reconstruct everything in order to make that system appear true. It made everything in World War II possible. It made World War I necessary. Racism is the word that we use to encompass all this. The idea of scientific racism suggests some serious pathology.' □

This passage is remarkable, not least for its abrupted style, which breaks 'the world in half' in half a sentence and shatters 'Europe' in three words. It also reintroduces and rearticulates the 'counter-question' – of the relation between the Holocaust and slavery – that Gilroy himself articulates above in answer to Crouch, seeing the one as the effect, ultimately, of the other.

Perhaps most important, however, is the related argument Morrison makes about the 'post-modern'. In traditional accounts, post-modernism (as a mode of cultural production) and post-modernity (as a cultural condition) are located historically in the wake of the Holocaust and seen as resulting from a disillusion with the 'grand narratives' of progress and enlightenment that it inevitably brought about. Yet if it is indeed the case that slavery 'made everything in World War II possible', such accounts turn out to be limited, inadequate and, crucially, Eurocentric. Morrison's suggestion it seems, amid these heady speculations, is that post-modernism and post-modernity need to be rethought, as it were, along the axis of a black feminist politics. To do so is to recognise that the so-called 'post-modern condition' has its advent long before the moment usually assigned to it: it is already something with which 'black women had to deal [. . .] in the nineteenth century and earlier'. From this perspective, *Beloved* may well prove to be the post-modern text *par excellence*.

■ With *Beloved*, Morrison aimed to place slavery back in the heart of Afro-America's political and literary culture.

'Slavery wasn't in the literature at all. Part of that, I think, is because, on moving from bondage into freedom which has been our goal, we got away from slavery and also from the slaves, there's a difference. We have to re-inhabit those people.'

The book is not a historical novel in the sense of *Roots* or *Jubilee*, but it deals directly with the power of history, the necessity of historical memory, the desire to forget the terrors of slavery and the impossibility of forgetting. 'The struggle to forget, which was important in order to survive is fruitless and I wanted to make it fruitless.' Morrison savours the irony that black writers are descending deeper into historical concerns at the same time that the white literati are abolishing [them] in the name of something they call 'post-modernism'. 'History has become impossible for them. They're so busy being innocents and skipping from adolescence into old age. Their literature and art reveals this great rent in the psyche, the spirit. It's a big hole in the literature and art of the United States.'

So why have she and other Afro-American novelists made this decisive turn to history? 'It's got to be because we are responsible. I am very gratified by the fact that black writers are learning to grow in that area. We have abandoned a lot of valuable material. We live in a land where the past is always erased and America is the innocent future in which immigrants can come and start over, where the slate is clean. The past is absent or it's romanticized. This culture doesn't encourage dwelling on, let alone coming to terms with, the truth about the past. That memory is much more in danger now than it was thirty years ago.' [. . .] □

CHAPTER TWO

'Trying to Fill in the Blanks': *Beloved*'s Intertexts

■ History is [. . .] an ongoing tension between stories that have been told and stories that might be told. □

Lynn Hunt[1]

THE QUESTION of *Beloved*'s intertextuality – the relations of dialogue and revision into which it enters with other texts – forms the interpretative framework for numerous analyses of Morrison's novel. The kind of intertextual reading that occurs most frequently is one that situates *Beloved* in relation to the tradition of the African-American slave narrative and is succinctly represented here in the essay by Marilyn Sanders Mobley with which this chapter closes.[2] Like other critics adopting such an approach to Morrison's text, Mobley takes her cue from Morrison herself, who extensively discusses the importance of the slave narratives to her work, together with the problems that they pose, in 'The Site of Memory', from which the second extract in the chapter is taken.

The chapter begins, however, with an account of the historically real figure of Margaret Garner, whose story – critics agree – forms the basis of Morrison's own.[3] The account is that provided by the Reverend P. S. Bassett, and takes the form of a newspaper article appearing in *American Baptist* for 12 February 1856. This document – as Mobley notes – is included in *The Black Book* (1974), a kind of cultural history of black 'oppression, resistance and survival' in America stretching back to the seventeenth century, which Morrison edited for Random House.

A Visit to the Slave Mother Who Killed Her Child

■ Last Sabbath, after preaching in the city prison, Cincinnati, through the kindness of the Deputy Sheriff, I was permitted to visit the apartment of that unfortunate woman, concerning whom there has been so much excitement during the last two weeks.

I found her with an infant in her arms only a few months old, and observed that it had a large *bunch* on its forehead. I inquired the cause of the injury. She then proceeded to give a detailed account of her attempt to kill her children.

She said, that when the officers and slave-hunters came to the house in which they were concealed, she caught a shovel and struck two of her children on the head, and then took a knife and cut the throat of the third, and tried to kill the other, – that if they had given her time, she would have killed them all – that with regard to herself, she cared but little; but she was unwilling to have her children suffer as she had done.

I inquired if she was not excited almost to madness when she committed the act. No, she replied, I was as cool as I now am; and would much rather kill them at once, and thus end their sufferings, than have them taken back to slavery, and be murdered by piece-meal. She then told the story of her wrongs. She spoke of her days of suffering, of her nights of unmitigated toil, while the bitter tears coursed their way down her cheeks, and fell in the face of the innocent child as it looked smiling up, little conscious of the danger and probable suffering that awaited it.

As I listened to the facts, and witnessed the agony depicted in her countenance, I could not but exclaim, Oh how terrible is irresponsible power, when exercised over intelligent beings! She alludes to the child that she killed as being free from all trouble and sorrow, with a degree of satisfaction that almost chills the blood in one's veins; yet she evidently possesses all the passionate tenderness of a mother's love. She is about twenty-five years of age, and apparently possesses an average amount of kindness, with a vigorous intellect, and much energy of character.

The two men and the two other children were in another apartment, but her mother-in-law was in the same room. She says she is the mother of eight children, most of whom have been separated from her; that her husband was once separated from her twenty-five years, during which time she did not see him; that could she have prevented it, she would never have permitted him to return, as she did not wish him to witness her sufferings, or be exposed to the brutal treatment that he would receive.

She states that she has been a faithful servant, and in her old age she would not have attempted to obtain her liberty; but as she became feeble, and less capable of performing labor, her master became more and more exacting and brutal in his treatment, until she could stand it no longer; that the effort could result only in death, at most – she therefore made the attempt.

She witnessed the killing of the child, but said she neither encouraged nor discouraged her daughter-in-law – for under similar circumstances she would probably have done the same. The old woman is from sixty to seventy years of age, has been a professor of religion about twenty years, and speaks with much feeling of the time when she shall be delivered from the power of the oppressor, and dwell with the Savior, 'where the wicked cease from troubling, and the weary are at rest'.

These slaves (as far as I am informed) have resided all their lives within sixteen miles of Cincinnati. We are frequently told that Kentucky slavery is very innocent. If these are its fruits, where it exists in a mild form, will some one tell us what we may expect from its more objectionable features? But comments are unnecessary. □

The meeting that this account stages between Bassett and Garner – white Christian abolitionist and black slave mother – raises some complex questions about *Beloved*'s relation to history, a category that has been the subject of much recent theoretical debate. As the work of New Historicist critics and post-modern theorists has shown, the events of the past do not allow themselves to be taken in a pure or unmediated form; rather, as Dominick LaCapra puts it, past events are always encountered through 'texts and textualized remainders – memories, reports, published writings',[4] of which 'A Visit to the Slave Mother Who Killed Her Child' is an example. In this sense, *Beloved*'s relation to Garner – like that of fiction to history in general – is as much as an intertextual one as its relation to the tradition of the African-American slave narrative.

It is crucial, however, to distinguish such a New Historicist/postmodern emphasis on the textuality of history from the kind of position that empties the past of ontological status altogether. This is a point made by Linda Hutcheon in *The Politics of Postmodernism*:

■ To say that the past is only *known* to us through textual traces is not [. . .] the same as saying that the past is only textual, as the semiotic idealism of some forms of poststructuralism seems to assert. This ontological reduction is not the point of postmodernism: past events existed empirically, but in epistemological terms we can only know them today through texts. Past events are given *meaning*, not *existence*, by their representation in history.[5] □

Hutcheon's warning against the 'ontological reduction' of history to text is made with good reason. As Nancy J. Peterson notes, commenting on this passage in a discussion of *Tracks* (1988), by the part-Ojibwa novelist Louise Erdrich, to make such a reduction

■ is to question or even to deny that the Holocaust occurred – or the massacre at Wounded Knee or slavery or the internment of Japanese Americans during World War II and so on. To use poststructuralism to question the occurrence of these horrific events is to inflict further violence on the victims and survivors.[6] □

Nonetheless, Peterson continues, 'a historical position in postmodern culture necessitates the recognition that history is a text composed of competing and conflicting representations and meanings – a recognition that precludes any return to a naive belief in transparent historical representation or even realism'.[7] Like *Tracks*, *Beloved* is informed by just such a 'historical position'. Both Morrison and Erdrich might be said to be engaged in the project of writing history from the standpoint of those who, in their respective contexts, have indeed been its victims – African-Americans and Native Americans: yet they do so with an awareness that the possibility of 'authentic' historical representation itself would seem to have become a thing of the past.

This brings us to Morrison's 'The Site of Memory', originally delivered as a lecture and subsequently published in *Inventing the Truth: The Art and Craft of Memoir* (1987), edited by William Zinsser. In the extract reprinted here, Morrison examines her own complex stance towards that large body of writings – the slave narratives – that constitutes the inaugural moment of the African-American literary tradition. What is perhaps most salient about Morrison's discussion is the conflict that it identifies within the slave narratives between what is said and what is unsaid, as it operates in political and psychic terms alike.

At one level, the slave narrative is autobiographical in form and theme, a linear charting of the journey of its author from bondage to freedom. Such a journey is also a movement from silence to language, 'other' to self, ownership to self-possession and encapsulated in Frederick Douglass's famous liberatory chiasmus in *Narrative of the Life of Frederick Douglass* (1845): 'You have seen how a man was made a slave; now you shall see how a slave was made a man.'[8] At the same time, however, the slave narrative is a political text, designed to further the goals of an abolitionist campaign becoming increasingly powerful in the period leading up to the American Civil War of 1861–65. Yet if this is what Morrison refers to as the 'milieu' of the slave narrative, it is one that is vexed with difficulties. For as Betty J. Ring puts it, the abolitionist movement 'enabled the liberation of many slaves, along with their stories, while simultaneously imposing constraints upon the speaking/writing self'.[9] To bring slavery to an end entailed disclosing the suffering that it inflicted upon its victims; but the extremity of such suffering meant, ironically, that any attempt at representing it fully ran the risk of being deemed a fiction, a fraud, a lie. It is for this reason, as

Morrison notes, that the 'narratives [. . .] include introductions and prefaces by white sympathizers to authenticate them'.

Even when the credentials of the narrating ex-slave are authenticated in this way, other problems remain: to tell the 'truth' of slavery is also to court the possibility of alienating and offending the very constituency – in the shape of a white middle-class Northern readership – that had the power to effect political change in America. Nowhere is this danger more acute than in terms of the kind of sexual violence performed by the white master upon his female slave, to which Morrison alludes in discussing Harriet Jacobs's *Incidents in the Life of a Slave Girl* (1861). Even as they are the written signs of freedom, the slave narratives are thus produced and disseminated in a historical context marked by the operation of certain kinds of constraint that set the limits of representation and divide what can be said from what cannot.

Yet Morrison is not just concerned here with the ways in which the most horrifying aspects of slaves' physical or bodily oppression must be excluded from the narrative of slavery. There is a still more telling silence, which has to do with the 'excising from the records the slaves themselves told' of what she calls the 'interior life'. It is this interior life, perhaps more than anything else, which *Beloved* strives to recuperate, mobilising the resources of fiction to effect a historical return to a 'site of memory' that is also invariably a site of terror and trauma. From this perspective, the intertextual relation between *Beloved* and the slave narratives might be said to function according to the kind of doubled and contradictory logic of the supplement, as formulated in the work of Jacques Derrida.[10] For Derrida, the supplement defines that which is added to something apparently complete in itself while at the same time being essential to or constitutive of it. On the one hand, *Beloved* makes a radically innovative contribution to the genre of the African-American slave narrative. Not only is it able to dwell much more graphically and at greater length on details of physical and sexual violence, particularly rape, but also focuses precisely on the ways in which slavery violates, structures and determines the psychic life of the black subject. On the other hand, however, the 'literary archeology' in which *Beloved* engages is linked to the retrieval of aspects of slavery that already inhabit the slave narrative but remain hidden or encrypted within it. If *Beloved* is a story about a ghost, it is a story which itself has a ghostly status or existence, haunting, as it does, the gaps and silences of the tradition on which it draws, seeking release. Difference between is difference within.

■ In this country the print origins of black literature (as distinguished from the oral origins) were slave narratives. These book-length narratives (autobiographies, recollections, memoirs), of which well over a hundred were published, are familiar texts to historians and students of black history. They range from the adventure-packed life of Olaudah Equiano's *The Interesting Narrative of the Life of Olaudah Equiano, or Gustavus Vassa, the African, Written by Himself* (1789) to the quiet desperation of *Incidents in the Life of a Slave Girl: Written by Herself* (1861), in which Harriet Jacobs ('Linda Brent') records hiding for seven years in a room too small to stand up in; from the political savvy of Frederick Douglass's *Narrative of the Life of Frederick Douglass, an American Slave, Written by Himself* (1845) to the subtlety and modesty of Henry Bibb, whose voice, in *Life and Adventures of Henry Bibb, an American Slave, Written by Himself* (1849), is surrounded by ('loaded with' is a better phrase) documents attesting to its authenticity. [. . .]

Whatever the style and circumstances of these narratives, they were written to say principally two things. One: 'This is my historical life – my singular, special example that is personal, but that also represents the race.' Two: 'I write this text to persuade other people – you, the reader, who is probably not black – that we are human beings worthy of God's grace and the immediate abandonment of slavery.' With these two missions in mind, the narratives were clearly pointed.

In Equiano's account, the purpose is quite up-front. [. . .] With typically eighteenth-century reticence he records his singular and representative life for one purpose: to change things. In fact, he and his co-authors did change things. Their works gave fuel to the fires that abolitionists were setting everywhere. [. . .]

As determined as these black writers were to persuade the reader of the evil of slavery, they also complimented him by assuming his nobility of heart and his high-mindedness. They tried to summon up his finer nature in order to encourage him to employ it. They knew that their readers were the people who could make a difference in terminating slavery. Their stories – of brutality, adversity and deliverance – had great popularity in spite of critical hostility in many quarters and patronizing sympathy in others. There was a time when the hunger for 'slave stories' was difficult to quiet, as sales figures show. [. . .]

In addition to using their own lives to expose the horrors of slavery, they had a companion motive for their efforts. The prohibition against teaching a slave to read and write (which in many Southern states carried severe punishment) and against a slave's learning to read and write had to be scuttled at all costs. These writers knew that literacy was power. Voting, after all, was inextricably connected to the ability to read; literacy was a way of assuming and proving the 'humanity' that the Constitution denied them. That is why the narratives carry the subtitle 'written by himself', or 'herself', and include introductions and prefaces by white sympathizers to authenticate them. Other narratives, 'edited by' such well-known anti-slavery figures as Lydia Maria Child and John Greenleaf Whittier, contain prefaces to assure the reader how little editing was needed. A literate slave was supposed to be a contradiction in terms.

One has to remember that the climate in which they wrote reflected not only the Age of Enlightenment but its twin, born at the same time, the Age of Scientific Racism. David Hume, Immanuel Kant and Thomas Jefferson, to mention only a few, had documented their conclusions that blacks were incapable of intelligence. Frederick Douglass knew otherwise, and he wrote refutations of what Jefferson said in 'Notes on the State of Virginia': 'Never yet could I find that a black had uttered a thought above the level of plain narration, never see even an elementary trait of painting or sculpture.' A sentence that I have always thought ought to be engraved at the door to the Rockefeller Collection of African Art. Hegel, in 1813, had said that Africans had no 'history' and couldn't write in modern languages. Kant disregarded a perceptive observation by a black man by saying, 'This fellow was quite black from head to foot, a clear proof that what he said was stupid.'

Yet no slave society in the history of the world wrote more – or more thoughtfully – about its own enslavement. The milieu, however, dictated the purpose and the style. The narratives are instructive, moral and obviously representative. Some of them are patterned after the sentimental novel that was in vogue at the time. But whatever the level of eloquence or the form, popular taste discouraged the writers from dwelling too long or too carefully on the more sordid details of their experience. Whenever there was an unusually violent incident, or a scatological one, or something 'excessive', one finds the writer taking refuge in the literary conventions of the day. 'I was left in a state of distraction not to be described' (Equiano). 'But let us now leave the rough usage of the field . . . and turn our attention to the less repulsive slave life as it existed in the house of my childhood' (Douglass). 'I am not about to harrow the feelings of my readers by a terrific representation of the untold horrors of that fearful system of oppression. . . . It is not my purpose to descend deeply into the dark and noisome caverns of the hell of slavery' (Henry Box Brown).

Over and over, the writers pull the narrative up short with a phrase such as, 'But let us drop a veil over these proceedings too terrible to relate'. In shaping the experience to make it palatable to those who were in a position to alleviate it, they were silent about many things, and they 'forgot' many other things. There was a careful selection of the instances that they would record and a careful rendering of those that they chose to describe. Lydia Maria Child identified the problem in her introduction to 'Linda Brent's' tale of sexual abuse: 'I am well aware that many will accuse me of indecorum for presenting these pages to the public; for the experiences of this intelligent and much-injured woman belong to a class which some call delicate subjects, and others indelicate. This peculiar phase of Slavery has generally been kept veiled; but the public ought to be made acquainted with its monstrous features, and I am willing to take the responsibility of presenting them with the veil drawn [aside].'

But most importantly – at least for me – there was no mention of their interior life.

For me – a writer in the last quarter of the twentieth century, not much more than a hundred years after Emancipation, a writer who is black and a woman – the exercise is very different. My job becomes how to rip that veil drawn over 'proceedings too terrible to relate'. The exercise is also critical for any person who is black, or who belongs to any marginalized category, for, historically, we were seldom invited to participate in the discourse even when we were its topic.

Moving that veil aside requires, therefore, certain things. First of all, I must trust my own recollections. I must also depend on the recollections of others. Thus memory weighs heavily in what I write, in how I begin and in what I find to be significant. Zora Neale Hurston said, 'Like the dead-seeming cold rocks, I have memories within that came out of the material that went to make me.' These 'memories within' are the subsoil of my work. But memories and recollections won't give me total access to the unwritten interior life of these people. Only the act of the imagination can help me.

If writing is thinking and discovery and selection and order and meaning, it is also awe and reverence and mystery and magic. I suppose I could dispense with the last four if I were not so deadly serious about fidelity to the milieu out of which I write and in which my ancestors actually lived. Infidelity to that milieu – the absence of the interior life, the deliberate excising of it from the records that the slaves themselves told – is precisely the problem in the discourse that proceeded without us. How I gain access to that interior life is what drives me [. . .]. It's a kind of literary archeology: on the basis of some information and a little bit of guesswork you journey to a site to see what remains were left behind and to reconstruct the world that these remains imply. What makes it fiction is the nature of the imaginative act: my reliance on the image – on the remains – in addition to recollection, to yield up a kind of a truth. By 'image', of course, I don't mean 'symbol'; I simply mean 'picture' and the feelings that accompany the picture.

Fiction, by definition, is distinct from fact. Presumably it's the product of imagination – invention – and it claims the freedom to dispense with 'what really happened', or where it really happened, or when it really happened, and nothing in it needs to be publicly verifiable, although much in it can be verified. By contrast, the scholarship of the biographer and the literary critic seems to us only trustworthy when the events of fiction can be traced to some publicly verifiable fact. It's the research of the 'Oh, yes, this is where he or she got it from' school, which gets its own credibility from excavating the credibility of the sources of the imagination, not the nature of the imagination.

The work that I do frequently falls, in the minds of most people, into that realm of fiction called fantastic, or mythic, or magical, or unbelievable. I'm not comfortable with these labels. I consider that my single gravest responsibility (in spite of that magic) is not to lie. When I hear someone say, 'Truth is stranger than fiction', I think that old chestnut is truer than we know, because it doesn't say that truth is truer than fiction; just that it's stranger, meaning that it's odd. It may be excessive, it may be more interesting, but the important thing is that it's random – and fiction is not random.

Therefore the crucial distinction for me is not the difference between fact and fiction, but the distinction between fact and truth. Because facts can exist without human intelligence, but truth cannot. So if I'm looking to find and expose a truth about the interior life of people who didn't write it (which doesn't mean that they didn't have it); if I'm trying to fill in the blanks that the slave narratives left – to part the veil that was so frequently drawn, to implement the stories that I heard – then the approach that's most productive and most trustworthy for me is the recollection that moves from the image to the text. Not from the text to the image. [. . .] □

Reprinted with no major cuts, the third and final piece in this chapter is Mobley's 'A Different Remembering: Memory, History and Meaning in Toni Morrison's *Beloved*', which first appeared in a collection on Morrison's work edited by Harold Bloom in 1990. While Mobley nowhere explicitly refers to 'The Site of Memory', her essay clearly echoes many of its insights and works to explore the possibilities which they contain for a critical analysis of *Beloved* as a 'revisionary rereading' of the slave narratives.

The essay begins by historicising the project of *The Black Book* as an 'intervention' designed to counter what, it is argued, Morrison saw as a dangerously romanticised construction of black history emergent in the 1960s and early 1970s. The notion of texts as historically specific interventions in turn provides, for Mobley, a way of thinking not only about the slave narratives but *Beloved* also: while the slave narrative sought to 'disrupt the system of slavery', Mobley writes, *Beloved* challenges the cultural assumption that 'the untold story of the black slave mother is [. . .] "something to leave behind"'.

In establishing such parallels between the slave narrative and Morrison's novel, Mobley at the same time highlights an important difference between the audiences each text addresses. Unlike the slave narrative, *Beloved* is not intended 'to convince white readers of the slave's humanity' (though it does of course have this retrospective effect) but directed, principally, toward black readers, whom it confronts with those elements of the past which they have 'repressed, forgotten or ignored'.

In considering such confrontations Mobley's essay also draws attention to some significant differences of form. As autobiographies, the slave narratives necessarily make use of a first person perspective which remains fixed and stable throughout, just as the sequence in which events are recounted largely corresponds to the experiential order in which they occur. *Beloved*, by contrast, is framed by a third person narrative which enables the development of a multiplicity of fractured perspectives: the major figures in the text – Sethe, Paul D, Denver, Baby Suggs and Beloved herself – shuttle constantly between present and past, as memories of slavery cut in and out of one another. Together with the disordering of linear narrative, the dislocations and displacements of memory make the experience of reading *Beloved* very different from that of reading a slave narrative. Morrison's formal strategies, and their effects, are described by Judith Thurman:

■ She treats the past as if it were one of those luminous old scenes painted on dark glass [. . .] and she breaks the glass, and recomposes it in disjointed and puzzling modern form. As the reader struggles with its fragments and mysteries, he [or she] keeps being startled by flashes of his [or her] own reflection in them.[11]

The slave woman ought not to be judged by the same standards as others.

Harriet Jacobs, *Incidents in the Life of a Slave Girl*

. . . when we get a little farther away from the conflict, some brave and truth-loving man, with all the facts before him . . . will gather . . . the scattered fragments . . . and give to those who shall come after us an impartial history of this the grandest moral conflict of the century. [For] Truth is patient and time is just.

Frederick Douglass[12]

Every age re-accentuates in its own way the works of its most immediate past.

Mikhail Bakhtin, 'Discourse in the Novel'

In 1974 Toni Morrison edited an often overlooked publication called *The Black Book*.[13] This collection of memorabilia represents 300 years of black history, and not only records the material conditions of black life from slavery to freedom, but also exhibits the black cultural production that grew out of and in spite of these conditions. Compiled in scrapbook fashion, it contains everything from bills of sale for slaves to jazz and poetry. Through diverse images of black life presented in such items as photos of lynchings, sharecropping families and slave-made quilts, and encoded in excerpts from such sources as slave narratives, folk sayings and black newspapers, *The Black Book* tells a complex story of oppression, resistance and survival. More importantly, it was published at a moment in American history when many feared that the Black Power movement of the 1960s and early 1970s would be reduced to faddish rhetoric and mere image rather than understood for its cultural and political implications. Morrison herself feared the movement propounded a kind of historical erasure or denial of those aspects of the past which could not be easily assimilated into its rhetorical discourse or into the collective consciousness of black people as a group. She feared, for example, that the rhetoric of the movement, in its desire to create a new version of history that would affirm the African past and the heroic deeds of a few great men, had inadvertently bypassed the equally heroic deeds of ordinary African-Americans who had resisted and survived the painful traumas of slavery. In other words, she questioned what she perceived to be a romanticization of both the African past and the American past that threatened to devalue 300 years of black life on American soil before it was fully recorded, examined or understood for its complexity and significance. Thus, *The Black Book* was a literary intervention in the historical dialogue of the period to attest to 'Black life as lived' experience.[14]

What is particularly pertinent, however, is that in the process of editing *The Black Book*, Morrison discovered the story that would become the basis of her fifth novel, *Beloved*.[15] Indeed, on the tenth page of *The Black Book* is a copy of a news article, 'A Visit to the Slave Mother Who Killed Her Child', that documents the historical basis for what would later become Morrison's most challenging fictional project.[16] [. . .]

Yet the intertextual relationship between *The Black Book* and *Beloved* is not the only one that can illuminate the compelling intricacies of this novel. Several reviewers place it in the American literary tradition with intertextual connections to Harriet Beecher Stowe's *Uncle Tom's Cabin* (1852). Others compare Morrison's narrative strategies to those of William Faulkner, who incidentally, along with Virginia Woolf, was the subject of her master's thesis. Certainly, the thematics of guilt and the complex fragmentation of time that shape Morrison's fiction are inherent in Faulkner's writing, as well as in the work of many other white authors of the American literary tradition. Yet Morrison's own expressed suspicions of critical efforts to place her in a white literary tradition are instructive. She explains:

> Most criticism . . . justifies itself by identifying black writers with some already accepted white writer . . . I find such criticism dishonest because it never goes into the work on its own terms. It comes from some other place and finds content outside of the work and wholly irrelevant to it to support the work. . . . It's merely trying to place the book into an already established literary tradition.[17]

With Morrison's own comments in mind, I would like to suggest that the intertextual relationship between *Beloved* and the slave narratives – the genre that began the African-American literary tradition in prose – offers significant interpretative possibilities for entering the hermeneutic circle of this novel. More specifically, I would like to argue that Morrison uses the trope of memory to revise the genre of the slave narrative and thereby to make the slave experience it inscribes more accessible to contemporary readers. In other words, she uses memory as the metaphorical sign of the interior life to explore and represent dimensions of slave life that the classic slave narrative omitted. By so doing, she seeks to make slavery accessible to readers for whom slavery is not a memory, but a remote historical fact to be ignored, repressed or forgotten. Thus, just as the slave narratives were a form of narrative intervention[18] designed to disrupt the system of slavery, *Beloved* can be read as a narrative intervention that disrupts the cultural notion that the untold story of the black slave mother is, in the words of the novel, '[. . .] something to leave behind' (p. 256).

One of the first observations often made about the slave narratives is the striking similarities that exist among the hundreds of them that were written. In the 'Introduction' to *The Classic Slave Narratives*, Henry Louis Gates, Jr., accounts for this phenomenon by reminding us that

> when the ex-slave author decided to write his or her story, he or she did so only after reading and rereading the telling stories of other slave authors who preceded them.[19]

While we cannot know exactly which narratives Morrison read, it is certain that she read widely in the genre and that she is familiar with the two most popular classics – Frederick Douglass's *Narrative* (1845) and Harriet Jacobs's *Incidents in the Life of a Slave Girl* (1861).[20] As prototypical examples of the genre, they adhere to the narrative conventions carefully delineated and described by James Olney. According to him, the vast majority of narratives begin with the three words 'I was born' and proceed to provide information about parents, siblings, the cruelty of masters, mistresses and overseers, barriers to literacy, slave auctions, attempts, failures and successes at escaping, name changes, and general reflections on the peculiar institution of slavery.[21] As Valerie Smith points out, however, the important distinction between the narratives of Douglass and Jacobs is that while his narrative not only concerns 'the journey from slavery to freedom but also the journey from slavery to manhood', her narrative describes the sexual exploitation that challenged the womanhood of slave women and tells the story of their resistance to that exploitation.[22] *Beloved* contains all these characteristics with several signifying differences. While the classic slave narrative draws on memory as though it is a monologic, mechanical conduit for facts and incidents, Morrison's text foregrounds the dialogic characteristics of memory along with its imaginative capacity to construct and reconstruct the significance of the past. Thus, while the slave narrative characteristically moves in a chronological, linear narrative fashion, *Beloved* meanders through time, sometimes circling back, other times moving vertically, spirally out of time and down into space. Indeed, Morrison's text challenges the Western notion of linear time that informs American history and the slave narratives. It engages the reader not just with the physical, material consequences of slavery, but with the psychological consequences as well. Through the trope of memory, Morrison moves into the psychic consequences of slavery for women, who, by their very existence, were both the means and the source of production. In the words of the text, the slave woman was 'property that reproduced itself without cost' (p. 228). Moreover, by exploring this dimension of slavery, Morrison produces a text that is at once very different from and similar to its literary antecedent with its intervention in the cultural, political and social order of black people in general and of black women in particular. What the reader encounters in this text is Morrison as both writer and reader, for inscribed in her writing of the novel is her own 'reading' – a revisionary rereading – of the slave's narrative plot of the journey from bondage to freedom. In the process of entering the old text of slavery from 'a new critical direction', Morrison discovers what Adrienne Rich refers to as a 'whole new psychic geography to be explored', and what Morrison herself identifies as the 'interior life of black people under those circumstances'.[23] Ultimately, *Beloved* responds to Fredric Jameson's dictum to 'always historicize' by illustrating the dynamics of the act of interpretation that memory performs on a regular basis at any given historical moment.[24]

Unlike the slave narratives which sought to be all-inclusive eye-witness accounts of the material conditions of slavery, Morrison's novel exposes the unsaid of the narratives, the psychic subtexts that lie within and beneath the historical facts. In the author's words, she attempts to leave 'spaces so the reader can come into it'.[25] Critic Steven Mallioux refers to such hermeneutic gaps as places where the text must be 'supplemented by its readers before its meaning can be discovered'.[26] By examining the use of memory in *Beloved*, we can not only discover to what extent she revises the slave narrative, but also explore how her narrative poetics operate through memory and history to create meaning.

The actual story upon which the novel is based is an 1856 newspaper account of a runaway slave from Kentucky named Margaret Garner. When she realizes she is about to be recaptured in accordance with the Fugitive Slave Law, she kills her child rather than allow it to return to a 'future of servitude'.[27] Indeed, the story itself involves a conflation of past, present and future in a single act. In the novel, Margaret Garner becomes Sethe, a fugitive slave whose killing of her two-year-old daughter, Beloved, haunts her first as a ghost and later as a physical reincarnation. But time is not so much conflated as fragmented in the fictional rendering of the tale. Moreover, the text contains not only Sethe's story or version of the past, but those of her friend and eventual lover, Paul D, her mother-in-law, Baby Suggs, her remaining child, a daughter named Denver, and later, Beloved herself. Each of their fragments amplifies or modifies Sethe's narrative for the reader. In that the fragments constitute voices which speak to and comment on one another, the text illustrates the call and response pattern of the African-American oral tradition.[28]

The setting of the novel is 1873 in Cincinnati, Ohio, where Sethe resides in a small house with her daughter, Denver. Her mother-in-law, Baby Suggs, has recently died and her two sons, Howard and Buglar, have left home, unable to live any longer in a ghost-haunted house with a mother who seems oblivious or indifferent to the disturbing, disruptive presence. Sethe seems locked in memories of her escape from slavery, the failure of her husband, Halle, to show up at the planned time of escape, her murder of her child, and the Kentucky plantation referred to by its benevolent white slave owner as Sweet Home. One of the Sweet Home men, Paul D, inadvertently arrives on her porch after years of wandering, locked in his own guilt, alienation and shame from the psychic scars of slavery. They become lovers, but more importantly, his arrival initiates the painful plunge into the past through the sharing of their individual stories, memories and experiences. Unable to tolerate the presence of the ghost, however, he drives it away, only to be driven away himself by his inability to cope with

Sethe's obsession with Beloved, whom he calls a 'room-and-board witch' (p.164). A bond of affection unites Sethe, Denver and Beloved until Denver realizes that her mother has become oblivious to her and has begun to devote her attention exclusively to Beloved. As she watches her mother deteriorate physically and mentally in the grips of overwhelming guilt and consuming love, Denver realizes she must abandon the security of home to get help for her mother and to rid their lives of Beloved once and for all. With the help of the black community, she eventually rescues her mother and Beloved vanishes.

What this cursory synopsis of the plot cannot account for is the ways in which Sethe modifies, amplifies and subverts her own memory of the murder that serves as the locus of the narrative. In fact, even in freedom she lives in a kind of psychic bondage to the task of 'keeping the past at bay' (p. 43). While she had murdered Beloved to save her from the future, she raises Denver by 'keeping her from the past' (p. 43). The two different manifestations of maternal love are just one source of the novel's narrative tension that evolves from Sethe's response to slavery. The more compelling source of tension lies in the complexity Morrison brings to the normal property of literature Frank Kermode refers to as the 'secrecy of narrative'.[29] While all texts develop to a certain extent by secrecy or by what information they withhold and gradually release to the reader, the text of *Beloved* moves through a series of narrative starts and stops that are complicated by Sethe's desire to forget or 'disremember' the past (p. 118). Thus, at the same time that the reader seeks to know 'the how and why' (p. 120) of Sethe's infanticide, Sethe seeks to withhold that information not only from everyone else, but even from herself. Thus, the early sections of the novel reveal the complex ways in which memories of the past disrupt Sethe's concerted attempt to forget.

The first sign of this tension between remembering and forgetting occurs on the second page of the text in a scene where Denver and Sethe attempt to call the ghost forth. When Denver grows impatient with the seeming reluctance of the ghost to make its presence felt, Sethe cautions her by saying: 'You forgetting how little it is. . . . She wasn't even two years old when she died' (p. 4). Denver's expression of surprise that a baby can throw such a 'powerful spell' is countered in the following passage:

> "No more powerful than the way I loved her," Sethe answered and there it was again. The welcoming cool of unchiseled headstones; the one she selected to lean against on tiptoe, her knees wide open as any grave. Pink as a fingernail it was, and sprinkled with glittering chips. . . . Counting on the stillness of her own soul, she had forgotten the other one: the soul of her baby girl. (pp. 4–5)

In this passage we have several things occurring at once. First, Sethe's verbalization of love triggers her memory of selecting a tombstone for the baby she murdered. The phrase 'there it was again' signals that this is a memory that recurs and that brings the ambivalent emotions of consolation and anguish. Second, the memory of the tombstone triggers her memory of the shameful circumstances of getting it engraved. In this memory, the reality of gender and oppression converge, for the engraver offers to place seven letters – the name 'Beloved' – on the headstone in exchange for sex. She also remembers that for ten more minutes, she could have gotten the word 'dearly' added. Thirdly, this memory raises the issue around which the entire novel is constructed and which is the consequence and/or responsibility that she must carry for her actions.

Throughout the novel there are similar passages that signal the narrative tension between remembering and forgetting. At various points in the text, a single phrase, a look or the most trivial incident rivets Sethe's attention to the very details of the past she is least ready to confront. In the words of the text, 'she worked hard to remember as close to nothing as was safe' (p.6). In another place the text refers to the 'serious work of beating back the past' (p.73). Moreover, a mindless task such as folding clothes takes on grave significance, as the following passage suggests: 'She had to do something with her hands because she was remembering something she had forgotten she knew. Something privately shameful that had seeped into a slit in her mind' (p.61). Morrison even includes vernacular versions of words to suggest the slaves' own preoccupation with mnemonic processes. For example, at one point 'rememory' is used as a noun, when Sethe refers to what Paul D stirs up with his romantic attention to her. Later, the same word is used as a verb, when Sethe begins to come to terms with the past through her relationship with Beloved. She allows her mind to be 'busy with the things she could forget' and thinks to herself: 'Thank God I don't have to rememory or say a thing' (p.191). Even the vernacular word for forgetting, 'disremember' (p.118), calls our attention to its binary opposite of remembering.

When Paul D arrives at Sethe's home on 124 Bluestone, Denver seeks to frighten this unwanted guest away by telling him they have a 'Lonely and rebuked' ghost on the premises (p.13). The obsolete meaning of rebuked – repressed – not only suggests that the ghost represents repressed memory, but that, as with anything that is repressed, it eventually resurfaces or returns in one form or another. Paul D's arrival is a return of sorts in that he is reunited with Sethe, his friend from Mr. Garner's Sweet Home plantation. His presence signals an opportunity to share both the positive and negative memories of life there. On the one hand, he and Sethe talk fondly of the 'headless bride back behind Sweet Home' (p. 13) and thus share a harmless ghost story of a haunted house. On the other hand, when they remember Sweet Home as a place, they regard it with ambivalence and admit that 'It wasn't sweet and it sure wasn't home' (p. 14). Sethe warns against a total dismissal of it, however, by saying: 'But it's where we were [. . .]. Comes back whether we want it to or not' (p. 14).

What also comes back through the stories Paul D shares are fragments of history Sethe is unprepared for such as the fact that years ago her husband had witnessed the white boys forcibly take milk from her breasts, but had been powerless to come to her rescue or stop them. Furthermore, his personal stories of enduring a 'bit' (p. 69) in his mouth – the barbaric symbol of silence and oppression that Morrison says created a perfect 'labor force' – along with numerous other atrocities, such as working on the chain gang, introduce elements of the classic slave narrative into the text. Perhaps more importantly, these elements comprise the signs of history that punctuate the text and that disrupt the text of the mind which is both historical and ahistorical at the same time.

I believe the meaning of Morrison's complex use of the trope of memory becomes most clear in what many readers regard as the most poetic passages in the text. These passages appear in sections two through five of Part Two, where we have a series of interior monologues that become a dialogue among the three central female characters. The first is Sethe's, the second is Denver's, the third is Beloved's and the last one is a merging of all three. Beloved's is the most intriguing, for the text of her monologue contains no punctuation. Instead, there are literal spaces between groups of words that signal the timelessness of her presence as well as the unlived spaces of her life. Earlier in the novel, Sethe even refers to Beloved as 'her daughter [who had] . . . come back home from the timeless place' (p. 182). Samples of phrases from Beloved's monologue reveal the meaning of her presence: '[H]ow can I say things that are pictures   I am not separate from her   there is no place where I stop   her face is my own . . . All of it is now   it is always now' (p. 210). These words suggest not only the seamlessness of time, but the inextricability of the past and present, of ancestors and their progeny. In the last interior 'dialogue', the voices of Sethe, Denver and Beloved blend to suggest not only that it is always now, but to suggest that the past, present and future are all one and the same.

In an article entitled 'Rediscovering Black History', written on the occasion of the publication of *The Black Book*, Toni Morrison speaks of the 'complicated psychic power one had to exercise to resist devastation'.[30] She was speaking, of course, not just of slavery, but of the black existence in America after slavery as well. *Beloved* and all her novels, to a certain extent, bear witness to this psychic power. It must be stated as I conclude, however, that my intertextual reading of this novel as a revision of the slave narrative should not be construed as an attempt to diminish the form and content of the slave narratives themselves in any way. It is, instead, a recognition of the truth that Gates offers in the introduction to *The Slave's Narrative*:

> Once slavery was abolished, no need existed for the slave to write himself [or herself] into the human community through the action of first-person narration. As Frederick Douglass in 1855 succinctly put the matter, the free human being "cannot see things in the same light with the slave, because he does not and cannot look from the same point from which the slave does". . . . The nature of the narratives, and their rhetorical strategies and import, changed once slavery no longer existed.[31]

Beloved is a complex, contemporary manifestation of this shift. In a larger sense, however, it is what Mikhail Bakhtin calls a 're-accentuation' of the past (in this case, the past of slavery) to discover newer aspects of meaning embedded in the classic slave narrative.[32] Morrison's purpose is not to convince white readers of the slave's humanity, but to address black readers by inviting us to return to the very part of our past that many have repressed, forgotten or ignored. At the end of the novel, after the community has helped Denver rescue her mother from Beloved's ferocious spell by driving her out of town, Paul D returns to Sethe 'to put his story next to hers' (p. 273). Despite the psychic healing that Sethe undergoes, however, the community's response to her healing is encoded in the choruslike declaration on the last two pages of the text, that this was 'not a story to pass on' (p. 274). Yet, as readers, if we understand Toni Morrison's ironic and subversive vision at all, we know that our response to the text's apparent final call for silence and forgetting is not that at all. Instead, it is an ironic reminder that the process of consciously remembering not only empowers us to tell the difficult stories that must be passed on, but it also empowers us to make meaning of our individual and collective lives as well. □

CHAPTER THREE

'My Girl Come Home':
Reading Beloved

■ I [. . .] blend the acceptance of the supernatural and a profound rootedness in the real world at the same time with neither taking precedence
over the other. It is indicative of the cosmology, the way in which
Black people looked at the world. We are a very practical people, very
down-to-earth, even shrewd people. But within that practicality we
also accepted what I suppose could be called superstition and magic,
which is another way of knowing things. [. . .] And some of those
things were "discredited knowledge" that Black people had;
discredited only because Black people were discredited. [. . .] That
kind of knowledge has a very strong place in my work. □

Toni Morrison[1]

A T THE end of *Beloved* the narrator offers a vision of the (not quite final)
fate that befalls the figure who gives Morrison's novel its title: 'In the
place where long grass opens, the girl who waited to be loved and cry
shame erupts into her separate parts, to make it easy for the chewing
laughter to swallow her all away' (p.274). This peculiar vision would
appear to confirm Beloved's own anxious premonition, articulated earlier
in the text after the loss of a tooth, that 'she could wake up any day and
find herself in pieces' (p.133). Yet the spectacle of Beloved's explosion
into 'separate parts' is to be witnessed not only within the text itself but
also the criticism that she has generated. Something of the variety of the
interpretations Beloved has prompted is suggested in a recent essay by
Shlomith Rimmon-Kenan. First noting how the novel's 'enigmatic title-
character' is characteristically viewed by readers 'as a double symbol,
operating simultaneously on a personal (or psychological) and a collective level',[2] Rimmon-Kenan goes on to catalogue the major trends and
emphases that mark Beloved's critical construction. On the personal/
psychological level, Beloved assumes a number of symbolic identities,

from being the 'condensation of Sethe's daughter and her African mother' to a 'preoedipal child who desires a merger with her mother'.[3] On the collective level, Rimmon-Kenan writes, 'most critics – with differences in nuances – interpret her as symbolic of "a whole lineage of people obliterated by slavery, beginning with the Africans who died on the Middle Passage"'.[4] Under the gaze of criticism, as in the novel, Beloved thus 'dissolves', in James Phelan's phrase, 'into multiple fragments'.[5]

While Rimmon-Kenan acknowledges the importance and viability of each of these interpretations, her own concern, as she puts it, is 'much more elementary',[6] directed, as it is, towards issues of narrative rather than symbolic identity. Such issues are ontological and relate to the puzzle of 'who Beloved is at the level of the events'.[7] Is the 'fully dressed woman' who climbs 'out of the water' on page fifty of Morrison's text a supernatural being, the fleshed-out version of the ghost of the child whose throat Sethe slit some eighteen years earlier? Or is she simply a natural being, a fugitive who traces her way to 124 Bluestone Road 'after horrendous tribulations, mistaking Sethe for her lost mother'?[8] These questions function as a kind of framing context for the critical material selected for this chapter, even as the terms of the opposition under-pinning them – 'supernatural' versus 'natural' – need to be seen as symptomatic of a Western epistemological schema, culturally deter-mined rather than absolute and pregiven. As this chapter's epigraph puts it, neither term should be viewed as 'taking precedence over the other'. Indeed what is 'supernatural' from one perspective can equally be seen as 'natural' from another: what might 'be called superstition and magic' in the West is for Morrison and the African-American tradition out of which she writes just 'another way of knowing things', an alternative epistemology 'discredited' only because those who subscribe to it have themselves been similarly negated historically.

The first extract is from Deborah Horvitz's 'Nameless Ghosts: Possession and Dispossession in *Beloved*', originally published in *Studies in American Fiction* in 1989. Excluding reviews, Horvitz's essay is one of the earliest critical responses to Morrison's novel and adopts the position that Beloved is without question a 'supernatural' figure, or revenant. Yet Beloved is not only the adult reincarnation of Sethe's ubiquitously 'crawling-already?' daughter; she is equally identified by the text, Horvitz argues, with Sethe's mother and, by implication, with 'all the women dragged onto slave ships in Africa and also all black women in America trying to trace their ancestry back to the mother on the ship attached to them'.[9] Personal and collective in significance indeed, Beloved thus emerges, in Horvitz's reading, as a powerful link in the matrilineal chain that slavery did its best to break.

■ In Beloved the ghost-child who comes back to life is not only Sethe's two-year-old daughter, whom she murdered eighteen years ago; she is also Sethe's African mother. This inter-generational, inter-continental, female ghost-child teaches Sethe that memories and stories about her matrilineal ancestry are life-giving. Moreover, Beloved stimulates Sethe to remember her own mother because, in fact, the murdered daughter and the slave mother are a conflated or combined identity represented by the ghost-child Beloved.

Mother-daughter bonding and bondage suffuses Morrison's text. Sethe's nameless mother is among the African slaves who experienced the Middle Passage and, late in the text, she relates that ordeal through a coded message from the ship revealing that she too is a Beloved who, like Sethe, has been cruelly separated from her own mother. This cycle of mother-daughter loss, perceived abandonment, betrayal, and recovery is inherent in and characterizes each mother-daughter relationship in the novel. But in the present tense of the novel – Ohio in 1873 – Sethe barely remembers, from so long ago,

> her own mother, who was pointed out to her by the eight-year-old child who watched over the young ones – pointed out as the one among many backs turned away from her, stooping in a watery field. Patiently Sethe waited for this particular back to gain the row's end and stand. What she saw was a cloth hat as opposed to a straw one, singularity enough in that world of cooing women each of whom was called Ma'am (p. 30).

This is mainly how she remembers her mother, simply as an image, a woman in a field with a stooped back in a cloth hat.

Sethe does, however, have one other quite specific memory of this obscure mother, of what may have been their only interaction following the two weeks the nameless Ma'am was allowed to nurse her. She remembers that Ma'am

> 'picked me up and carried me behind the smokehouse. Back there she opened up her dress front and lifted her breast and pointed under it. Right on her rib was a circle and a cross burnt right in the skin. She said, "This is your ma'am. This," and she pointed. "I am the only one got this mark now. The rest dead. If something happens to me and you can't tell me by my face, you can know me by this mark." Scared me so. All I could think of was how important this was and how I needed to have something important to say back, but I couldn't think of anything so I just said what I thought. "Yes, Ma'am," I said. "But how will you know me? How will you know me? Mark me, too," I said. "Mark the mark on me too."' (p. 61)

[. . .] before Beloved helps Sethe's memory unfold, Sethe firmly believes that because Ma'am is physically dead, they are not emotionally tied. When her mother was hanged, Sethe did not know why. Probably Ma'am was caught trying to escape from the plantation, but the daughter born in bondage refuses to believe her mother could have run. It would mean that she left Sethe behind, emphasizing in this generation the continuous pattern of severed mother-daughter relationships. In other words, her memories of Ma'am are buried not only because their relationship was vague and their contact prohibited but also because those recollections are inextricably woven with feelings of painful abandonment. If Sethe remembers her mother, she must also remember that she believes her mother deserted her.

As Sethe tells this story [. . .] she becomes frightened: 'she was remembering something [Ma'am's language] she had forgotten she knew' (p. 61). Murky pictures and vague words begin to creep into her mind and she knows that they come from that place inside her – the place Paul D refers to as the locked and rusted tobacco tin – that stores, but can never lose, forgotten memories. Ma'am's language erupts into her conscious mind signaling the beginning of Sethe's slow metamorphosis. 'Something privately shameful . . . had seeped into a slit in her mind right behind the . . . circled cross' (p. 61), and she remembers that she does or did have a link with her mother that transcends the cross in the circle. She is afraid to remember but ashamed not to. Recollections of 'the language her ma'am spoke . . . which would never come back' creep into her consciousness (p. 62). She remembers one-armed Nan, the slave who was in charge of Sethe and the other children on the plantation where Sethe grew up. Nan 'used different words' (p. 62), words that expressed her mother's native African, and these words link Sethe back both to her mother and to her mother's land, the place where women gathered flowers in freedom and played in the long grass before the white men came:

> Words Sethe understood then but could neither recall nor repeat now. She believed that must be why she remembered so little before Sweet Home except singing and dancing and how crowded it was. What Nan told her she had forgotten, along with the language she told it in. [. . .] But the message – that was and had been there all along. Holding the damp white sheets against her chest, she was picking meaning out of a code she no longer understood. Nighttime. (p. 62)

Although Sethe has forgotten the words of her mother's language, they continue to exist inside her as feelings and images that repeatedly emerge as a code that she relies on without realizing it. This code holds animated, vital memories, such as the one of her mother dancing juba, as well as the most painful fact of Sethe's life: her mother's absence.

Sethe is shocked as she continues to find meaning in a code she thought she no longer understood. She remembers that she felt the dancing feet of her dead mother as she was about to give birth to Denver. Pregnant and thinking she is going to die because her swollen feet cannot take another step, she wants to stop walking; every time she does so, the movement of her unborn child causes her such pain that she feels she is being rammed by an antelope. Although Sethe wonders why an antelope, since she cannot remember having ever seen one, it is because the image of the antelope is really an image of Ma'am dancing. Sethe's antelope kicking baby and her antelope dancing mother are one and the same:

> Oh but when they sang. And oh but when they danced and some-times they danced the antelope. The men as well as the ma'ams, one of whom was certainly her own. They shifted shapes and became something other. Some unchained, demanding other whose feet knew her pulse better than she did. Just like this one in her stomach. (p. 31)

Stored in childhood but only now unlocked, the link between the unborn Denver's kicks and the dead ma'am's kicks as she danced the antelope erupts in Sethe's memory. As she bears the next generation in her matrilineal line, Sethe keeps her mother's African antelope dancing alive: she links the pulses of her unchained, vigorously moving mother and her energetic, womb-kicking daughter forever.

A second and perhaps the most critical part of this story from her past is that Sethe, as Nan tells her, is the only child her mother did not kill:

> She told Sethe that her mother and Nan were together from the sea. Both were taken up many times by the crew. 'She threw them all away but you. The one from the crew she threw away on the island. The others from more whites she also threw away. Without names, she threw them. You she gave the name of the black man. She put her arms around him. The others she did not put her arms around. Never. Never. Telling you. I am telling you, small girl Sethe.' (p. 62)

Conceived with a black man in love, rather than with a white master through rape, Sethe, named after her father, is the only child her mother allowed to survive.

Significantly, she is flooded with these memories in response to questions from her own daughter, Beloved, who wants to know everything in Sethe's memory and actually feeds and fattens on these stories. What Beloved demands is that Sethe reveal memory and story about her life before Sweet Home, memory about her African speaking, branded mother and her life right after Sweet Home when she cut Beloved's throat. In other words, because they share identities, the ghost-child's fascination lies in the 'joined' union between Sethe's mother and herself. Sethe's memory is being pried wide open by Beloved's presence. She forces Sethe to listen to her own voice and to remember her own mother, her ma'am with the special mark on her body, along with her mother's native language, songs, and dances.

This cycle of mother-daughter fusion, loss, betrayal, and recovery between Sethe and her mother plays itself out again in the present relationship between Sethe and Beloved. Beloved transforms from a lonely, affectionate girl into a possessive, demanding tyrant, and her ruthlessness almost kills Sethe. There is even a connection between this ruling Beloved and the slave-driver. Because any attempt to possess another human being is reminiscent of the slave-master relationship, Denver links Sethe and the slave-drivers when she warns Beloved that Sethe, like 'the men without skin' from the ship, 'chews and swallows' (p. 216). Beloved is furious and ferocious. When she first comes to the farmhouse where Sethe and Denver live, she appears because the other side is lonely – devoid of love and memory. She yearns for Sethe and cannot take her eyes off her. 'Sethe was licked, tasted, eaten by Beloved's eyes' (p. 57). But what starts out as a child's love and hunger for a mother from whom she has long been separated turns into a wish to own Sethe, to possess her, to merge with her and be her. Beloved gets rid of Paul D and eventually excludes Denver from their play. Just as the disembodied baby ghost Beloved hauntingly possessed Sethe, so the flesh-and-blood adolescent Beloved tries to own and dominate her. Sethe is as haunted by the girl's presence as she was by her absence because possession of any kind involving human beings is destructive.

These 'possessive' attachments raise the important moral dilemma underlying Sethe's act; either Sethe must be held accountable for Beloved's death or the institution of slavery alone killed the child. If Morrison wants to humanize and individualize the 'great lump called slaves',[10] then perhaps she is suggesting that Sethe, like any individual, is answerable and responsible for her own actions. The namesake for Beloved's Sethe is the biblical Seth, born to replace his brother, the murdered Abel. Perhaps Morrison's Sethe, too, is a 'replacement' for her brothers and sisters murdered by the system of slavery and lost to her nameless ma'am. If so, then the inevitable confrontation between

Sethe, the replacement child saved by her ma'am, and Beloved, the protected child murdered by hers, represents the impossible choice available to the enslaved mother.

Certainly one reason Beloved comes back is to pass judgment on Sethe. When Sethe first realizes that Beloved is the ghost of her third child, she wants desperately for the girl to understand that she tried to kill her babies so that they would be protected from captivity forever. Sethe assumes Beloved will forgive her. She does not. For Beloved, her mother's protection became the act of possession that led to her own death, which was murder. Beloved becomes mean-spirited and exploits her mother's pain. Sethe gives Beloved story after story of her love and devotion to her. She tells her how nothing was more important than getting her milk to her, how she waved flies away from her in the grape arbor, how it pained her to see her baby bitten by a mosquito, and how she would trade her own life for Beloved's. Sethe tries to impress upon her how slavery made it impossible for her to be the mother she wanted to be.

For Sethe her children are her 'best thing' (p. 272), yet they have all been ruined. The murdered Beloved torments Sethe, Howard and Buglar have left home, and Denver is so afraid of the world that it is only starvation that forces her off the front porch. Sethe begs the ruling Beloved not only for forgiveness for the obvious but also for the return of her 'self'. But Beloved does not care:

> She said when she cried there was no one. That dead men lay on top of her. That she had nothing to eat. Ghosts without skin stuck their fingers in her and said beloved in the dark and bitch in the light. . . . Sethe never came to her, never said a word to her, never smiled and worst of all never waved goodbye or even looked her way before running away from her. (pp. 241–42)

What is most striking here is that Beloved responds to Sethe's entreaties not only in the language of the murdered daughter but also in the tortured language of the woman 'from the sea' (p. 62). Death and the Middle Passage evoke the same language. They are the same existence; both were experienced by the multiple-identified Beloved. [. . .]

The American and African Beloveds join forever in the last two pages of the novel as symbols of the past – exploding, swallowing, and chewing – and fuse with these same images in the present. The sickening fear of her body exploding, dissolving, or being chewed up and spit out links each enslaved Beloved with her sister in captivity. Africa is 'the place where long grass opens' (p. 274), the slave ship is the crouching place, and the ghost-child is the girl seen 'that day on the porch' (p. 274). The Beloved from each place is another's matrilineal heritage and future; and each Beloved merges with her other 'selves' in the shared and horrific fear of losing her body. The gap is bridged between America and Africa, the past and the present, the dead and the living, the flesh and the spirit. But they are joined in a specific shared, secret horror, perhaps the most devastating effect of the violence heaped upon them by 'the men without skin'. Each lives in terror that her body will disintegrate or, quite literally, explode. Earlier in the text the ghost-child loses a tooth and

> Beloved looked at the tooth and thought, This is it. Next would be her arm, her hand, a toe. Pieces of her would drop maybe one at a time, maybe all at once. Or on one of those mornings before Denver woke and after Sethe left she would fly apart. It is difficult keeping her head on her neck, her legs attached to her hips when she is by herself. Among the things she could not remember was when she first knew that she could wake up any day and find herself in pieces. She had two dreams: exploding, and being swallowed. When her tooth came out – an odd fragment, last in the row – she thought it was starting. (p. 133)

She cannot remember when she first knew 'she could wake up any day and find herself in pieces', not simply because she was only two when her mother cut her throat, but because the fear predates her birth; it comes from the Beloveds in Africa and the ship: 'In the place where long grass opens, the girl who waited to be loved and cry shame erupts into her separate parts, to make it easy for the chewing laughter to swallow her all away' (p. 274). The voice on the ship repeatedly hears 'chewing and swallowing and laughter' (p. 212). The point is that enslaved women, not in possession of their own bodies, survived barbaric beatings, rapes, and being 'swallowed' [. . .] by emotionally dissociating themselves from their bodies. The price they paid was, of course, an enormous one; those that survived often did so with no shred of basic integrity or dignity regarding their bodies. The imagery emphasizes, too, those African women who did not survive the Middle Passage – those who were chewed up, spit out, and swallowed by the sea – those whose bodies and stories were never recovered. Morrison, speaking of the women whose stories are lost, says they are 'disremembered' (p. 275), meaning not only that they are forgotten, but also that they are dismembered, cut up and off, and not re-membered.

The very end of the novel paradoxically appears to belie the crucial theme of the book, that it is imperative to preserve continuity through story, language, and culture between generations of Black women. The authorial voice says repeatedly 'This is not a story to pass on'

(p. 275), although it seems in this text that not to repeat is to lose stories crucial to Black heritage and American history and to the personal lives of Black women.

The paradox is the one posed by memory and history themselves when past memories hurt so much they feel as though they must be forgotten. Sethe could not pass on her mother's story for the same reason that, before Beloved came, she could not talk about the murder: 'every mention of her past life hurt. . . . the hurt was always there – like a tender place in the corner of her mouth that the bit left' (p.58). Remembering horrors of such enormous magnitude can cause a despair so profound that the memories cancel out the possibility of resolution or pleasure in the present and future. For example, the happiness that seemed possible between Sethe and Paul D at the carnival was obliterated by the past, in the form of Beloved's arrival that very day. However, Morrison implies, even though memory of the past can prevent living in the present, to pursue a future without remembering the past has its own and even deeper despair for it denies the reality and sacrifice of those who died. Assuming individual and collective responsibility is a crucial concern of *Beloved*, and it is a responsibility to remember.[11]

Like Sethe, Beloved herself is trapped by painful memories of the past at the end of her narrative. When white Mr Bodwin comes to pick up Denver, Sethe becomes terrified because she associates Bodwin's hat with schoolteacher's. She temporarily forgets where she is and who he is, and she tries to kill him. Sethe runs from Beloved into the crowd of women outside her house. The ghost-child, left 'Alone. Again.' (p.262), watches Sethe run 'Away from her to the pile of people out there. They make a hill. A hill of black people, falling' (p.262). What Beloved sees is the 'little hill of dead people' from the slave ship; she sees 'those able to die . . . in a pile' (p.211). She sees 'rising from his place with a whip in his hand, the man without skin, looking. He is looking at her' (p.262). While Sethe sees Bodwin as schoolteacher, Beloved sees him as a slave-driver from the slave ship looking at her, suggesting again that Beloved, the daughter, is also the woman 'from the sea', Sethe's mother. She runs away, naked and pregnant with stories from the past, back to the water from which she emerged, where the narrator says she will be forgotten.

The paradox of how to live in the present without cancelling out an excruciatingly painful past remains unresolved at the end of the novel. At the same time, something healing has happened. Sethe's narrative ends with her considering the possibility that she could be her own 'best thing'. Denver has left the front porch feeling less afraid and more sure of herself. Now that Beloved is gone there is the feeling that perhaps Sethe can find some happiness with Paul D, who 'wants to put his story next to hers' (p. 273). As the embodiment of Sethe's memories, the ghost Beloved enabled her to remember and tell the story of her past, and in so doing shows that between women words used to make and share a story have the power to heal. Although Toni Morrison states that 'It was not a story to pass on' (p. 274), she herself has put words to Beloved's tale. Though the ghost-child-mother-sister returns, unnamed, to the water, her story is passed on. □

Horvitz's essay and the assumptions it makes about Beloved's status as a 'powerful corporeal ghost'[12] have been influential in shaping the approaches of many subsequent critics to Morrison's novel. Yet the 'supernaturalist' reading of Morrison's novel has not gone unchallenged. The sharpest scrutiny it has received is provided by Elizabeth B. House in 'Toni Morrison's Ghost: The Beloved Who is Not Beloved'. In this essay (also published in *Studies in American Fiction*, one year after Horvitz's), House argues that Beloved is not in fact ghostly but human. Drawing on textual evidence, particularly from sections four and five of the novel's second part, House suggests that Beloved is nothing more nor less than a 'young woman who has herself suffered the horrors of slavery' and has no blood relation to the family she enters and comes to control. The reclamation of Beloved's humanity results in an exploration of Morrison's text precisely in terms of the 'psychic consequences of slavery for women' that are examined by Mobley in chapter two above. Reality comes to be shaped by the pressures of desire and fantasy: mourning the absence of her African parents, Beloved is more than prepared to accept Sethe as a mother found once more, while Sethe, yearning for the child she has slain, receives Beloved as a daughter returned, coming 'right on back like a good girl' (p. 203). Each figure compensates for the loss that the other has sustained, in an emotional economy based as much on misrecognition as mutual need, a kind of collaborative family romance.[13]

The extract that follows is taken from the first half of House's essay:

■ Most reviewers of [. . .] *Beloved* have assumed that the mysterious title character is the ghostly reincarnation of Sethe's murdered baby, a flesh and blood version of the spirit Paul D drives from the house. [. . .] Such uniform acceptance of this notion is surprising, for evidence throughout the book suggests that the girl is not a supernatural being of any kind but simply a young woman who has herself suffered the horrors of slavery.

In large part, Morrison's Pulitzer Prize-winning fifth novel is about the atrocities slavery wrought both upon a mother's need to love and care for her children as well as a child's deep need for a family: Sethe murders her baby girl rather than have her taken back into slavery;[14] Baby Suggs grieves inconsolably when her children are sold; Sethe sees her own mother, a woman who was brought from Africa on a slave ship, only a few times before the woman is killed;[15] Denver loves her mother, Sethe, but also fears the woman because she is a murderer. These and other incidents illustrate the destruction of family ties brought by slavery, and Beloved, seen as a human being, emphasizes and illuminates these themes.

Unraveling the mystery of the young woman's identity depends to a great extent upon first deciphering chapters four and five of Part II, a section that reveals the points of view of individual characters. Both of these chapters begin with the line 'I am Beloved and she is mine', and in these narratives Morrison enters Beloved's consciousness. From Beloved's disjointed thoughts, her stream-of-conscious rememberings set down in these chapters, a story can be pieced together that describes how white slave traders, 'men without skin', captured the girl and her mother as the older woman picked flowers in Africa. In her narrative, Beloved explains that she and her mother, along with many other Africans, were then put aboard an abysmally crowded slave ship, given little food and water, and in these inhuman conditions, many blacks died. To escape this living hell, Beloved's mother leaped into the ocean, and, thus, in the girl's eyes, her mother willingly deserted her.

In order to grasp the details of this story chapters four and five of Part II must be read as a poem: thus, examining the text line by line is often necessary. As Beloved begins her narrative, she is recalling a time when she was a young girl, for she says 'I am not big' (p.210) and later remarks again 'I am small' (p.211). However, the memory of these experiences is so vivid that, to her, 'All of it is now' (p.210). One of the first traumas Beloved describes is being in the lower hold of a slave ship. The captured Africans have been crouching, crammed in the overcrowded space for so long that the girl thinks 'there will never be a time when I am not crouching and watching others who are crouching' and then she notes that 'someone is thrashing but there is no room to do it in' (p.210). At first the men and women on the ship are separated, but then Beloved says that 'storms rock us and mix the men into the women and the women into the men that is when I begin to be on the back of the man' (p.211). This person seems to be her father or at least a father figure, for he carries the young girl on his back. Beloved says 'I love him because he has a song' and, until he dies on the ship, this man sings of his African home, of the 'place where a woman takes flowers away from their leaves and puts them in a round basket before the clouds' (p.211).

These lyrics bring to mind the first scene in Part II, chapter four. Beloved's tale begins with the girl watching her mother as the woman takes 'flowers away from leaves she puts them in a round basket . . .

she fills the basket   she opens the grass' (p.210). This opening of the grass is probably caused by the mother's falling down, for Beloved next says, 'I would help her but the clouds are in the way'. In the following chapter, the girl clarifies this thought when she explains, 'I wanted to help her when she was picking the flowers, but the clouds of gunsmoke blinded me and I lost her' (p.214). Thus, what the girl is remembering is the capture of her mother by the men without skin, the armed white slave traders. Later, Beloved sums up her story by explaining that the three crucial points in her life have been times when her mother left her: 'Three times I lost her: once with the flowers because of the noisy clouds of smoke; once when she went into the sea instead of smiling at me; once under the bridge when I went in to join her and she came toward me but did not smile' (p.214). Thus, the slave traders' capture of her mother is the first of three incidents that frame the rest of Beloved's memories.

Once incarcerated on the ship, Beloved notices changes in her mother. She remembers seeing the diamond earrings, 'the shining in her ears' (p.211), as they were picking flowers. Now on the ship, her mother 'has nothing in her ears', but she does have an iron collar around her neck. The child knows that she 'does not like the circle around her neck' and says 'if I had the teeth of the man who died on my face I would bite the circle around her neck bite it away I know she does not like it'. Sensing her mother's unhappiness, her longing for Africa, Beloved symbolizes the woman's emotions by ascribing to her a wish for physical items: 'she wants her earrings she wants her round basket' (p.211).

As Beloved continues her tale, she explains that in the inhuman conditions of the ship, many blacks die. She says 'those able to die are in a pile' and the 'men without skin push them through with poles', evidently 'through' the ship's portholes, for the hills of dead people 'fall into the sea which is the color of the bread' (p.211). The man who has carried her on his back is one of those who succumbs, and as he takes his last breath, he turns his head and then Beloved can 'see the teeth he sang through' (p.211). She knows that 'his song is gone', so now she loves 'his pretty little teeth instead' (p.212). Only after the man's head drops in death is the girl able to see her mother; Beloved remembers, 'when he dies on my face I can see hers   she is going to smile at me'. However, the girl never receives this gesture of affection, for her mother escapes her own pain by jumping into the ocean, thus committing suicide. The scene is etched in Beloved's memory: 'they push my own man through   they do not push the woman with my face through   she goes in   they do not push her   she goes in the little hill is gone   she was going to smile at me' (p.212). Beloved is haunted by this second loss of her mother for, unlike the separation caused by the slave traders' attack, this time the mother chooses to leave her. The girl agonizes as she tries to understand her mother's action and later thinks that 'all I want to know is why did she go in the water in the place where we crouched? Why did she do that when she was just about to smile at me? I wanted to join her in the sea but I could not move' (p. 214).[16]

Time passes and Beloved notes that 'the others are taken   I am not taken' (p. 212). These lines suggest that when the other slaves are removed from the ship, Beloved, whose beauty is noted by several characters, is perhaps kept by one of the ship's officers.[17] At any rate, she is now controlled by a man who uses her sexually, for 'he hurts where I sleep' (p. 212), thus in bed, and 'he puts his finger there'. In this situation Beloved longs for her mother and explains, 'I wait on the bridge because she is under it' (p. 212). Although at this point she may be on an inland bridge, Beloved is most likely waiting for her mother on the ship's bridge; if she is being kept by one of the vessel's officers, the girl would logically be there. But, wherever she is at this time, Beloved last saw her mother as the woman went into the sea; thus, the girl associates water with her parent and believes she can be found in this element.

Beloved's stream-of-consciousness narrative then jumps to the time, apparently several years later, when she arrives at the creek behind Sethe's house. Morrison does not specify exactly how Beloved comes to be there, but various characters give possible explanations. The most plausible theory is that offered by Stamp Paid who says, 'Was a girl locked up in the house with a whiteman over by Deer Creek. Found him dead last summer and the girl gone. Maybe that's her. Folks say he had her in there since she was a pup' (p. 235). This possibility would explain Beloved's 'new' skin, her unlined feet and hands, for if the girl were constantly kept indoors, her skin would not be weathered or worn. Also, the scar under Beloved's chin could be explained by such an owner's ill-treatment of her. Morrison gives credence to Stamp Paid's guess by having Sethe voice a similar hypothesis and then note that her neighbor, Ella, had suffered the same fate. When Beloved first comes to live with the family, Sethe tells Denver 'that she believed Beloved had been locked up by some whiteman for his own purposes, and never let out the door. That she must have escaped to a bridge or someplace and rinsed the rest out of her mind. Something like that had happened to Ella . . .' (p.119). In addition, Beloved's own words suggest that she has been confined and used sexually. The girl explains to Denver that she 'knew one whiteman' (p.119), and she tells Sethe that a white man 'was in the house I was in. He hurt me' (p. 215). In a statement that reveals the source of her name, Beloved says that men call her 'beloved in the dark and bitch in the light' (p.241), and in response to another question about her name, she says, 'in the dark my name is Beloved' (p.75).

Whatever situation Beloved has come from, when she reaches the creek behind Sethe's house, she is still haunted by her mother's absence. The lonely girl sees the creek, remembers the water under the ship's bridge where she last glimpsed her mother, and concludes that her lost loved ones are beneath the creek's surface. In her soliloquy, Beloved links the scene to her mother and father figure by evoking images of the African mother's diamond earrings and the father's teeth. She says that she knows the man who carried her on his back is not floating on this water, but his 'teeth are down there where the blue is . . . so is the face I want the face that is going to smile at me' (p.212). And, in describing the creek she says, 'in the day diamonds are in the water where she is and turtles[18] in the night I hear chewing and swallowing and laughter it belongs to me' (p.212). The diamonds Beloved thinks she sees in the water are most likely reflected bits of sunlight that make the water sparkle. Similarly, the noises the girl interprets as 'chewing and swallowing and laughter' are probably made by the turtles. Alone in the world, Beloved's intense need to be with those she loves undoubtedly affects her interpretation of what her senses perceive.[19]

If Stamp Paid is right and the girl has been locked up for years, then she has not had normal experiences with people or places. She lacks both formal learning and the practical education she would have gained from a family life. These deficiencies also undoubtedly affect her perceptions, and, thus, it is not especially surprising that she does not distinguish between the water under the ship's bridge and that in the creek behind Sethe's house. To the untutored girl, all bodies of water are connected as one.

Apparently, Beloved looks into the creek water, sees her own reflection, and concludes that the image is her mother's face. She then dives into the water, believing that in this element her mother will at last give her the smile that was cut short on the slave ship. Beloved says,

> I see her face which is mine   it is the face that was going to smile
> at me in the place where we crouched   now she is going to
> her face comes through the water . . . her face is mine   she is not
> smiling . . . I have to have my face   I go in . . . I am in the water
> and she is coming   there is no round basket   no iron circle
> around her neck. (pp.212–13)

In the water, Beloved cannot 'join' with the reflection, and thus she thinks her mother leaves her for a third time; distraught, she says, 'my own face has left me   I see me swim away . . . I see the bottoms of my feet   I am alone' (p.213).

Beloved surfaces, sees Sethe's house, and by the next day she has made her way to the structure. Exhausted by her ordeal, the girl is sleeping near the house when Sethe returns from the carnival.[20] Beloved says,

I come out of blue water . . . I need to find a place to be . . . there is a house . . . I sit the sun closes my eyes   when I open them I see the face I lost   Sethe's is the face that left me . . . I see the smile . . . it is the face I lost   she is my face smiling at me   doing it at last. (p.213)

Thus, when Beloved awakens and sees Sethe smiling at her, the girl mistakenly thinks that the woman is her long lost mother. In the second half of her narrative, Beloved even more clearly states her erroneous conclusions when she asserts, 'Sethe is the one that picked flowers . . . in the place before the crouching. . . . She was about to smile at me when the men without skin came and took us up into the sunlight with the dead and shoved them into the sea. Sethe went into the sea. . . . They did not push her . . .' (p.214).

What finally emerges from combining Beloved's thoughts and the rest of the novel is a story of two probable instances of mistaken identity. Beloved is haunted by the loss of her African parents and thus comes to believe that Sethe is her mother. Sethe longs for her dead daughter and is rather easily convinced that Beloved is the child she has lost. [. . .] □

The positions on Beloved adopted by Horvitz and House are clearly opposed to one another, while at the same time being equally valuable for the complex light they cast on Morrison's text. To decide between them – adjudicating one to be 'right' and the other 'wrong' – would, however, itself be a mistake. Instead, the point – to return to Rimmon-Kenan – is to recognise the way in which both readings are simultaneously accommodated by Morrison's novel, as it 'oscillates between [the] two alternatives in an insoluble ambiguity'.[21]

Such ambiguity is sensed, though not elaborated, in three of the earliest reviews of Beloved – by Margaret Atwood, Walter Clemons and Paul Gray – all of which appeared within the space of two weeks in September 1987.[22] In Clemons's representative formulation: 'Beloved . . . has an anterior life deeper than the ghostly role she fulfills . . . in the household she visits.'[23] Nor should it be entirely surprising when Morrison's own remarks on Beloved's possible origins are recalled from the interview with Darling cited above in chapter one. Whether Beloved comes from the other side of life or the other side of the world, there is,

Morrison states, 'evidence in the text so that both things could be approached, because the language of both experiences – death and the Middle Passage – is the same'.

Beloved's deliberately ambiguous representation of the identity of its title-figure is one of the ways in which the text thwarts the reader's desire for interpretative mastery, constituting, for Phelan, a 'paradigm case' of the textually 'stubborn' (as distinct from the merely 'difficult') – a 'recalcitrance that will not yield' to 'explanatory efforts'.[24] As such, it is also a sign of the larger fact that slavery's horrors are necessarily incomprehensible to the kind of 'privileged, white, male reader'[25] whom Phelan openly describes himself to be. Yet there is a sense in which Phelan's very refusal to master either Beloved or the text in which she appears on the grounds of his own particular subject position is an assertion of privilege despite itself. As Rimmon-Kenan points out, responding to Phelan's readerly misgivings:

■ the impossibility of grasping such an emotionally wrenching experience [as slavery] is not confined to white male readers. For similar or different reasons, African-American readers probably find Beloved just as stubborn as white readers do, and the horrors of slavery just as ungraspable or unmasterable.[26] □

Beloved's status as a spectral presence in the text is also the assumption informing Pamela Barnett's 'Figurations of Rape and the Supernatural in *Beloved*', one of the most powerful essays to have appeared on Morrison's novel, recently published in the May 1997 issue of *PMLA* and given in full below. Yet for Barnett, Beloved is something more and other than merely 'the ghost of Sethe's dead child': she is a succubus figure, a 'demon in female form supposed to have carnal intercourse with men in their sleep' (*OED*). The succubus, Barnett suggests, is *Beloved*'s 'dominant trope', and is combined in the novel with the figure of the shape-shifting witch, derived from African-American folkloric traditions, whose attributes Beloved also shares.

The specificity of Barnett's treatment of Beloved as succubus/witch – a menacing hybrid of Euro-American and African-American cultural traditions – is mirrored by the way in which she addresses questions of memory and history in the novel. The memories that haunt Morrison's text and its central characters are not just memories of slavery 'in general' but of rape in particular. Beloved is not only the uncanny and embodied sign of such memories – strange and familiar at once; she also re-enacts them through the sexual assaults she carries out on Paul D and Sethe, draining the one of semen and the other of vitality. These assaults have a double significance. On the one hand, they gesture back towards the institutionalised effects of sexual violence under slavery, as the black male subject is emasculated and the black female commodified into a source for the reproduction of labour. On the other hand, they are the index of *Beloved*'s status as a novel of trauma, as the concept is first formulated in Freudian psychoanalysis. In reading Morrison's text in terms of trauma, Barnett draws both on the Freud of *Beyond the Pleasure Principle* and the development of his thinking in Cathy Caruth's *Unclaimed Experience: Trauma, Narrative, and History* (1996). The paradox of traumatic experience is that it is in fact not properly experience at all, initially occurring 'too soon, too unexpectedly, to be fully known and [. . .] therefore not available to consciousness until it imposes itself again, repeatedly, in the nightmares and repetitive actions' of the subject who is both its victim and its survivor:[27] indeed, as Barnett notes and *Beloved* demonstrates, it is precisely the 'apparent forgetting' or repression of the traumatic event that forms the condition of its terrifying return at a later point.

The most original and challenging part of Barnett's argument relates less to her analysis of rape as trauma, however, than to the way in which she reads *Beloved* as a reconfiguring of the discourse of rape itself. The respective positions of rapist and victim are not necessarily occupied by male and female subjects in this novel – a point illustrated most graphically, Barnett shows, in Paul D's traumatic experiences on the chain gang in Alfred, Georgia and their repetition in the assault that he suffers at the hands of Beloved. Rather it is race – the categories of white and black – that determines the distribution of sexual violence. In this way *Beloved* emerges as a text that provides a narrative for the white male oppression of black women and men, which, in Barnett's phrase, has been 'largely absent in twentieth-century America'.

■ Toni Morrison's *Beloved* is haunted by history, memory, and a specter that embodies both; yet it would be accurate to say that *Beloved* is haunted by the history and memory of rape specifically. While Morrison depicts myriad abuses of slavery like brutal beatings and lynchings, the depictions of and allusions to rape are of primary importance; each in some way helps explain the infanticide that marks the beginnings of Sethe's story as a free woman.[28] Sethe kills her child so that no white man will ever 'dirty' her, so that no young man with 'mossy teeth' will ever hold the child down and suck her breasts (pp. 251, 70). Of all the memories that haunt Morrison's characters, those that involve sexual abuse and exploitation hold particular power: rape is the trauma that forces Paul D to lock his many painful memories in a 'tobacco tin' heart (p. 113), that Sethe remembers more vividly than the beating that leaves a tree of scars on her back, that destroys Halle's mind, and against which Ella measures all evil.

I say that the book is haunted by rape not to pun idly on the ghostly presence that names the book but to establish the link between haunting and rape that invigorates the novel's dominant trope: the succubus figure.[29] The character Beloved is not just the ghost of Sethe's dead child; she is a succubus, a female demon and nightmare figure that sexually assaults male sleepers and drains them of semen.[30] The succubus figure, which is related to the vampire, another sexualized figure that drains a vital fluid, was incorporated into African American folklore in the form of shape-shifting witches who 'ride' their terrified victims in the night and Beloved embodies the qualities of that figure as well.[31] In separate assaults, Beloved drains Paul D of semen and Sethe of vitality; symptomatically, Beloved's body swells as she also feeds off her victims' horrible memories of and recurring nightmares about sexual violations that occurred in their enslaved past. But Beloved functions as more than the receptacle of remembered stories; she reenacts sexual violation and thus figures the persistent nightmares common to survivors of trauma.[32] Her insistent manifestation constitutes a challenge for the characters who have survived rapes inflicted while they were enslaved: directly, and finally communally, to confront a past they cannot forget. Indeed, it is apparent forgetting that subjects them to traumatic return; confrontation requires a direct attempt at remembering.

Morrison uses the succubus figure to represent the effects of institutionalized rape under slavery. When the enslaved persons' bodies were violated, their reproductive potential was commodified. The succubus, who rapes and steals semen, is metaphorically linked to such rapes and to the exploitation of African Americans' reproduction. Just as rape was used to dehumanize enslaved persons, the succubus or vampire's assault robs victims of vitality, both physical and psychological. By representing a female rapist figure and a male rape victim, Morrison foregrounds race, rather than gender, as the category determining domination or subjection to rape.

History and Collective Memory: 'The Serious Work of Beating Back the Past'

Two memories of rape that figure prominently in the novel echo the succubus's particular form of sexual assault. The narrator refers several times to the incident in which two 'mossy-toothed' boys (p. 70) hold Sethe down and suck her breast milk (pp. 6, 16–17, 31, 68–70, 200, 228). No less important, Paul D works on a chain gang in Alfred, Georgia, where prisoners are forced to fellate white guards every morning (pp. 107–09, 229). In addition, Ella is locked up and repeatedly raped by a father and son she calls 'the lowest yet' (pp. 119, 256), and Stamp Paid's wife, Vashti, is forced into sex by her enslaver (pp. 184, 232). Baby Suggs is compelled to have sex with a straw boss who later breaks his coercive promise not to sell her child (p. 23) and again with an overseer (p. 144). Sethe's mother is 'taken up many times by the crew' during the Middle Passage (p. 62), as are many other enslaved women (p. 180). And three women in the novel – Sethe's mother, Baby Suggs, and Ella – refuse to nurse babies conceived through rape. Other allusions to sexual violation include the Sweet Home men's dreams of rape (pp. 10, 11), Sethe's explanation for adopting the mysterious Beloved – her fears that white men will 'jump on' a homeless, wandering black girl (p. 68) – and the neighborhood suspicion that Beloved is the black girl rumored to have been imprisoned and sexually enslaved by a local white man who has recently died (pp. 119, 235). There are also acts of desperate prostitution that are akin to rape: Sethe's exchange of sex for the engraving on her baby's tombstone (pp. 4–5, 184) and the Saturday girls' work at the slaughterhouse (p. 203).

These incidents of rape frame Sethe's explanation for killing her baby daughter. Sethe tries to tell the furious Beloved that death actually protected the baby from the deep despair that killed Baby Suggs, from 'what Ella knew, what Stamp saw and what made Paul D tremble' (p. 251): horrific experiences and memories of rape. Whites do 'Not just work, kill, or maim you, but dirty you', Sethe tells Beloved, 'Dirty you so bad you [can't] like yourself anymore.' Sethe passionately insists that she protected her beloved daughter and also herself from 'undreamable dreams' in which 'a gang of whites invaded her daughter's private parts, soiled her daughter's thighs and threw her daughter out of the wagon' (p. 251). For Sethe, being brutally overworked, maimed, or killed is subordinate to the overarching horror of being raped and 'dirtied' by whites; even dying at the hands of one's mother is subordinate to rape.

Sethe is haunted by the ghost of the child she has killed; Beloved's return to life corresponds to the return of many of Sethe's painful repressed memories of her enslaved past. Memory is figured as a menacing force in Sethe's life – it seems to stalk her – and she works hard to avoid it. She sees her future as 'a matter of keeping the past at bay' and begins each day with the 'serious work of beating back the past' (pp. 42, 73). As Freud observes in *Beyond the Pleasure Principle*, 'patients suffering from traumatic neurosis' are not 'much occupied in their waking lives with memories. . . . Perhaps they are more concerned with *not* thinking of it [the traumatic event].'[33] Cathy Caruth, in a reading of Freud, argues that such unsuccessful effort is at the center of traumatic experience. Trauma is the event survived, but it is also defined by 'the literal return of the event against the will of the one it inhabits', often in the form of hallucinations and nightmares.[34] Traumatic nightmares make the painful event available to a consciousness that could not initially assimilate or 'know' it.[35] Sethe is traumatized both by the past and by the present task of surviving it. For Caruth, the core of trauma stories is the 'oscillation between a *crisis of death* and the correlative *crisis of life*: between the story of the unbearable nature of an event and the story of the unbearable nature of its survival'.[36] Sethe's infanticide manifests that correlative crisis as certainly as any story of trauma can: she has survived what she prevents her daughter from surviving.

Beloved, like the repressed, returns against Sethe's will, and when she arrives, she is hungry for more than her mother's love and attention. She has an insatiable appetite, a 'thirst for hearing' the 'rememoried' stories that animate her ghostly frame, a hunger for the voicing of the unspeakable. As Sethe discloses, 'Everything' in her past life is 'painful or lost', and she and Baby Suggs have tacitly agreed 'that it [is] unspeakable' (p.58). Sethe has never told these stories to Denver or Paul D, but she willingly shares them with Beloved, who feeds on a diet of Sethe's past and serves as the materialization of Sethe's memory.

Beloved also acts as a catalyst for Paul D's recollection of his past. Although she has no particular knowledge of his past, his contact with her brings unpleasant memories to the surface of his consciousness. As Paul D says, Beloved 'reminds me of something. Something, look like, I'm supposed to remember' (p.234). Despite the characters' efforts to diffuse the power of the past, the ghost baby, like the traumatic nightmare, intrudes on the present, forcing Sethe and Paul D to remember what they have tried unsuccessfully to forget.

Beloved represents African American history or collective memory as much as she does Sethe's or Paul's individual memory.[37] The narrative merges Beloved's memories of death with the histories of women who endured the Middle Passage, where the institutionalized rape of enslaved women began. Both Sethe's mother and her mother's friend Nan are violated en route to North American slavery. Beloved remembers and recounts their horror: 'dead men lay on top of her. . . . she had nothing to eat. Ghosts without skin stuck their fingers in her and said beloved in the dark and bitch in the light' (p.241).

Morrison has explained in an interview that Beloved speaks 'the language of both experiences – death and the Middle Passage' in this section and that the language 'is the same' for both.[38] But Beloved is also speaking a revised language of rape structured by the historical narratives of rape in slavery. In Beloved's language *white* and *black* are nouns rather than modifiers. Largely about men and women, the available idiom of rape in American culture has obfuscated the centrality of race. For instance, there is no widely recognizable story of white men's rape of black women, and narratives of homosexual rape are even less visible when the victim is black. The only recognizable narrative of interracial rape is what Angela Davis has called 'the myth of the black rapist'.[39]

Morrison powerfully narrates the rape of black women and of black men by white enslavers. As Morrison has commented, slave narratives are often silent about 'proceedings too terrible to relate'.[40] Harriet Jacobs's *Incidents in the Life of a Slave Girl* is notable for taking sexual exploitation as its explicit subject, and Morrison gestures toward Jacobs's text by violently articulating the history Jacobs delicately describes.[41] Morrison revises the conventional slave narrative by insisting on the primacy of sexual assault over other experiences of brutality.

Beloved embodies the recurrent experience of a past that the community of women in the novel wants to forget. The women take responsibility for exorcizing Beloved. But Ella, whose life has been irrevocably marked by 'the lowest yet', is the most determined to eradicate the violation Beloved represents. Ella has refused to nurse a baby conceived through rape; that child represents a monstrous sign of past horror, and Ella staunchly maintains that such horrors must not intrude on the community's present. Yet through Beloved the women also confront their memories and wounded histories. This attempt to know the incomprehensible trauma done to them is a step toward healing.[42] I say 'a step' because Beloved never definitively leaves, not even at the end of the novel. Characters continue to encounter traces of her – footprints that 'come and go', the sound of skirts rustling, and the sensation of 'knuckles brushing [their] cheek[s]', as they wake from sleep (p.275). The insistent crisis of trauma is 'truly gone. Disappeared, some say, exploded right before their eyes.' But Beloved is more than her manifestation. What she represents is always there to be survived. Significantly, 'Ella is not so sure' that Beloved is not 'waiting for another chance' (p.263).

'Like a Bad Dream': Beloved and Supernatural Assault

At the end of the novel, Beloved seems to disappear, and the towns-people forget her 'like an unpleasant dream during a troubling sleep' (p.275) – indeed, like a nightmare. In *On the Nightmare* Ernest Jones outlines the derivation of the word *nightmare* from the Anglo-Saxon word for 'succubus' or 'incubus', *mara*. Jones notes that 'from the earliest times the oppressing agency experienced during sleep was personified'.[43] Before the community forgets Beloved 'like a bad dream', Paul D and Sethe experience her as a sexually menacing nightmare figure (p.274). After Paul D is forced out of Sethe's bed and from room to room, Beloved visits him in the cold house. He tries to resist her sexual coercion, and he is frightened when she lifts her skirts and pronounces, 'You have to touch me. On the inside part.' He silently lists the things he must not do if he is to be safe (p. 117). When Paul D does reach the inside part, the act is described as occurring against his will. He finds himself 'Fucking her when he [is] convinced he [doesn't] want to' (p.126). He says there is 'nothing he [is] able to do about it' though 'he trie[s]' (p.126). He imagines telling Sethe, 'it ain't a weakness, the kind of weakness I can fight 'cause 'cause something is happening to me, that girl is doing it . . . she is doing it to me. Fixing me. Sethe, she's fixed me and I can't break it' (pp. 126–27). Near the end of the novel, Paul D remembers this nightmarish experience, but in 'daylight he can't imagine it. . . . Nor the desire that drowned him there and forced him to struggle up, up into that girl like she was the clear air at the top of the sea. . . . It was more like a brainless urge to stay alive.' He had 'no more control over it than over his lungs' (p.264). The visitation scene ends with Paul D crying out so that he wakes Denver and then himself (p.117). He survives, and he wakes from his sexual assault as if from a nightmare.

Beloved attacks her mother, Sethe, in a form that more closely resembles that of a vampire. 'The Vampire superstition', Jones writes, 'is evidently closely allied to that of the Incubus and Succubus. . . . Just as Incubi suck out vital fluids and thus exhaust the victim . . . so do Vampires often lie on the breast and induce suffocation.'[44] The vampire is 'a blood-sucking ghost or re-animated body of a dead person [. . .] believed to come from the grave and wander about by night sucking the blood of persons asleep, causing their death.'[45] Beloved is the re-animated body of Sethe's murdered baby, and she metaphorically drains Sethe's vitality.

Within moments of being discovered at 124 by Sethe, Paul D, and Denver, Beloved drinks glass after glass of water as water correspondingly gushes from Sethe in a supernatural birthing. The connection between Sethe's body and Beloved's is also evident at the novel's end – Beloved ingests while Sethe is drained. Like the 'mossy-toothed' boys who assault Sethe in the barn, Beloved also sucks Sethe dry. Although Sethe is initially thrilled to realize that Beloved is her dead daughter returned, she and Beloved soon enter into a struggle for survival, 'rationing their strength to fight each other' (p.239) – a struggle that Beloved seems to win. As Sethe grows so thin that the flesh between her forefinger and thumb fades, Beloved eats all the best food and grows a 'basket-fat' stomach (p.243). Beloved animates her ghostly flesh with food but also with Sethe's life: 'Beloved [eats] up [Sethe's] life, [takes] it, swell[s] up with it, gr[ows] taller on it' (p.250).

Like the succubus, the vampire drains its victims of fluid in an attack with sexual resonances. H. Freimark writes, 'Though it is not an absolute rule, still it can be observed that in most cases women are constantly visited by male Vampires, and men by female ones. . . . The sexual features characterize the Vampire belief as another form of the Incubus-Succubus belief – it is true, a more dangerous one.'[46] The vampire trope is usually played out in the heterosexual paradigm of the earlier nightmare figures, but the vampire figure in *Beloved* enacts an incestuous, homosexual desire. Paul D remarks that Beloved is constantly aroused, but he knows she is not 'shining' for him. Rather, her appetite is for Sethe, who is 'licked, tasted, eaten by Beloved's eyes' (p. 57). Beloved tells Paul D, 'You can go but she is the one I have to have' (p. 76). Sethe experiences Beloved's attentions as a night visitation: Sethe is 'sliding into sleep when she [feels] Beloved touch her. A touch no heavier than a feather but loaded, nevertheless, with desire' (p. 58). When Beloved kisses Sethe's neck in the clearing, Sethe is transfixed but suddenly becomes aware that the act is inappropriate. Perhaps she also senses the danger of a kiss on the neck as a prefiguration of a vampiric attack. This haunting is marked by an infantile sexual desire for the mother, as Sethe's reprimand suggests: 'You too old for that' (p. 98).

As Beloved drains Paul D and Sethe, her animated ghostly frame becomes an embodiment of the traumatic past and the embodied threat of that past's intrusion on the future. By the end of the novel, Beloved has 'taken the shape of a pregnant woman' (p. 261), a manifestation that derives from the medieval belief that 'a succubus, or demon masquerading as a voluptuous woman, molested men, while an incubus, a demon masquerading as a man, molested women'. It was thought that the two could work in tandem to impregnate sleeping women: 'Though sterile, the incubi were said to be able to impregnate women with semen collected from the nocturnal emissions of men.'[47] In Reginald Scot's *The Discoverie of Witchcraft* (1584), 'The divell plaieth *Succubus* to the man and carrieth from him the seed of generation, which he delivereth as *Incubus* to the woman' (*OED*, s.v. *succubus*). Beloved, who plays succubus and incubus, collects sperm from Paul D to impregnate herself, then uses the life force of her mother's body to sustain her spawn. When Ella and the neighborhood women come to drive out the 'devil-child' (p. 261) they notice her 'belly protruding like a winning watermelon' (p. 250). An effect of heterosexual assault on Paul D, Beloved's pregnancy is a figure for one function of rape in slavery: multiplying human beings as property. But the pregnancy also means that the past of rape threatens to intrude on the future. Beloved's child would represent for the community of women something they wish to exorcize, something they will not tolerate in the future – the memory of children forced on their bodies in the past.

'Mossy Teeth, an Appetite': Sexual Violence, Sucking, and Sustenance

Like Beloved, the other rapists in Morrison's novel attempt to annihilate their victims – sexual violence is figured as eating one's victim up. Beloved embodies the particular violations Sethe and Paul D have suffered, violations characterized by sucking (being sucked or being forced to suck). Through this trope of eating, which links sexual violence with vampirism, a human being becomes the source of another's sustenance. The link to the institution of slavery is clear.

The first assault in the novel, which Sethe tries to forget, appears as a 'picture of the men coming to nurse her' (p. 6). The boys cruelly mock the maternal associations of nursing by treating Sethe as an animal to be milked. They enact an assault of the kind perpetrated by alps, the German nightmare figures that suck milk rather than semen or blood.[48] In recollection, Sethe expresses the horror of this violence, which, as the loss of a life-sustaining fluid, prefigures and even structures Beloved's vampiric attack. In other references to rape, Sethe often speaks of appetite. When the white girl Amy finds her lying in the wild onion field and approaches her, Sethe believes she is about to be discovered by another white boy with 'mossy teeth, an appetite' (p. 31). And when Sethe has sex with the engraver to pay for the name on her baby's gravestone, the engraver's son looks on, 'the anger in his face so old; the appetite in it quite new' (p. 5).

The eating imagery associated with Sethe's rape reappears in the morning ritual of Alfred, Georgia, where prisoners are forced to fellate prison guards. After the prisoners line up, they must kneel and wait 'for the whim of a guard, or two, or three. Or maybe all of them wanted it' (p. 107). That whim is announced with taunts such as 'Breakfast? Want some breakfast, nigger?' and 'Hungry, nigger?' which deflect the guards' appetite onto the prisoners and force the prisoners to name it as their own in their reply: 'Yes, sir' (pp. 107, 108). Lee Edelman argues in *Homographesis* that by forcing the prisoners to express homosexual desire, the guards symbolically 'castrate' them. This violence is both racist and homophobic: 'white racists (literally) *castrate others* while homosexuals (figuratively) *are castrated themselves*'.[49] Edelman argues that this scene, where the prisoners are marked with homosexuality, figures the 'violent disappropriation of masculine authority that underlies the paranoid relation of black and white in our modern, "racially" polarized, patriarchal social formation'.[50]

In racist American culture the black man signifies the 'hole', the 'absence of all that constitutes manhood', and thus social domination of black men is often figured as sexual domination of black men by white men.[51] This conflation of sexual and racial domination is a product of a prevailing definition of black masculinity as interchangeable with black male sexuality. When black masculinity is not called on to signify excessive virility, it paradoxically often suggests emasculation or social impotence. This discursive formation partly dictates the form of the prisoners' violation. Symptomatically, the prisoners are emasculated by passive homosexuality – they are forced to 'go down',[52] to express their social subordination as desire for penetration, and to assume the 'faggot' identity.[53] The degradation of being forced to voice desire for one's own rape echoes in Paul D's terrible experience of Beloved. He says he is humiliated by her power to move him from Sethe's bed and by his own uncontrollable 'appetite' for her (p.126).

In Morrison's novel, even a satisfied appetite has negative connotations. When Paul tells Sethe about Halle's breakdown, she likens contemplating painful information to gorging:

I just ate and can't hold another bite[.] I am full God damn it of two boys with mossy teeth, one sucking on my breast the other holding me down. . . . I am still full of that, God damn it, I can't go back and add more. (p. 70)

Fullness is dangerous for Sethe. During the beating she bites her tongue and fears that she may 'eat [herself] up', finishing the job that the boys have started (p.202). When she imagines that she is about to be discovered by a 'hungry' white boy, she thinks of biting him, eating him violently: 'I was hungry . . . just as hungry as I could be for his eyes. I couldn't wait. . . . so I thought . . . I'm gonna eat his feet off. . . . I was hungry to do it. Like a snake. All jaws and hungry' (p.31). Sethe links appetite with the desire to annihilate, figuring the attack she plans and her own violation in the same terms.

'The Last of the Sweet Home Men': Manhood and Naming

When Paul D realizes the sexual punishment he will suffer on the chain gang, he vomits. Earlier, after an aborted escape attempt, he has endured the horror of being forced to suck an iron bit. These experiences are two of the horrible contents sealed in the tobacco tin Paul D substitutes for his heart. He does not want anyone to get a 'whiff of [the tin's] contents' because such a disclosure would 'shame him' (p.73). Thus he places his painful memories 'one by one, into the tobacco tin lodged in his chest. By the time he [gets] to 124 nothing in this world [can] pry it open' (p.113).

But Beloved is not of 'this world', and she has the power to force the box open by traumatizing Paul D. Valerie Smith argues that 'the act of intercourse with Beloved restores Paul D to himself, restores his heart to him'.[54] Late in the novel Paul does express a bewildered and confused gratitude, but what Smith calls a 'bodily cure'[55] I view as rape. And yet without this nightmare experience, Paul D would not be able to overcome his numbing defense mechanisms or perform the necessary exorcism. Beloved forces Paul D to reexperience sexual violation; ironically, he might heal if he can assimilate the previously unknowable trauma. Because of the humiliation of succumbing to Beloved, Paul D confronts the pain that he has locked away. As he nears climax, the tobacco tin bursts open and he cries out, 'Red heart. Red heart. Red heart' (p. 117). As much as it hurts to feel his heart again, he needs it if he is to love. Unfortunately, Paul D's attempted 'incorporation of trauma into a meaningful (and thus sensible) story' does not promote healing.

The subordination Paul D experiences at Beloved's hands, at Sweet Home, and on the chain gang tests his conviction of his own masculinity. He is the only principal character who must deal with two forced sexual encounters, and these encounters are central to his constant meditation on the meaning of his manhood. Paul D is introduced as 'the last of the Sweet Home men' (p. 6). Garner, the master of Sweet Home, brags about his 'men', but the term seems to be a self-fulfilling designation for the men's productivity. Thus encouraged by Garner, they work hard to make the plantation more productive and thus to make him more prosperous. With the exception of Sixo, the Sweet Home men take pride in their name until they learn, after Garner's death, that they are 'only Sweet Home men at Sweet Home' (p. 125). Though free, Paul D continues to ask, 'Is that where the manhood lay? In the naming done by a whiteman who was supposed to know?' and to wonder whether Garner was 'naming what he saw or creating what he did not' (pp. 125, 220). Paul D is certain that Sixo and Halle are men regardless of Garner, but 'concerning his own manhood, he [can] not satisfy himself on that point' (p. 220).

Paul D believes that he cannot stop Beloved's assault because he is not 'man enough to break out'. He needs Sethe even though 'it shame[s] him to have to ask the woman he want[s] to protect to help him' (p. 127). But the shame is too great, and rather than ask for help he reverts to anxious assertions of his masculinity. Instead of explaining, 'I am not a man', he tells Sethe he wants her pregnant with his child: 'suddenly it was a solution: a way to hold onto her, document his manhood and break out of the girl's spell' (p. 128). The connection is clear – he must 'document his manhood' because he is a victim of a supernatural rape that he feels has emasculated him just as the guards in Alfred, Georgia, have.

Paul D and his fellow prisoners must choose between saying 'Yes, sir' and death, but they articulate the choice as a choice between manhood and impotence. Stamp Paid says that he 'hand[s] over' his wife, Vashti, 'in the sense that he did not kill anybody, thereby himself, because his wife demanded that he stay alive' (pp. 184–85). But in fact he had no power to offer or deny her body to the white man who enslaved them both. Halle, who sees the attack on Sethe from the loft, is in a similar quandary. He does not fight the attackers, because he hopes to escape with his family. Like Paul D and Stamp, Halle is rendered powerless and ostensibly passive, and Paul D and Stamp both view that position as emasculating. Because the conceptual categories and language Paul D and Stamp know for masculinity cannot account for men oppressed by slavery, both consider their powerlessness a sign of their failure as men. Furthermore, Paul D has been raped, and he cannot speak of that experience in a language that does not account for the sexually victimized male body or that casts that body as feminized. Though he is victimized as a black man in a racist system, he articulates his sexually subordinate position in terms of gender. Thus he struggles alone in the church basement with painful feelings and memories, but he will never be able to confront them publicly or with the help of the community because his shame as a male rape victim is too great. He cannot join the community of women that finally challenges and exorcizes Beloved and what she represents, and his violation remains unspeakable or incomprehensible.

Notably, critics who do refer to Paul D's experience of rape are also confounded by the 'unspeakability' of his story, and many write of his violation euphemistically if at all. Although Paul D is distressed by Beloved and unwilling to have sex with her, the incident, because of its supernatural quality, is not easily recognizable as rape, a term bound by legal definitions. But critics treat even Paul D's experience on the chain gang as unrelatable. Valerie Smith describes Paul D as having 'endured the hardships of the chain gang';[56] Marilyn Sanders Mobley refers to the 'atrocities such as working on the chain gang';[57] Sally Keenan mentions the 'story of the prison farm' as something Paul D cannot speak aloud.[58] Mae Henderson acknowledges that the boys' assault on Sethe is her primary violation but equates the assault with Paul D's experience of wearing the horse's bit in his mouth, neglecting to mention the final trauma to his hurting heart – 'breakfast' in Alfred, Georgia.

Paul D's experience is unrelatable because it exceeds American understandings of rape and gender, but it is also unspeakable because it is dehumanizing. Morrison challenges Paul D's and Stamp's conceptions by emphasizing that Halle's destruction goes beyond his destruction as a man. Halle is reduced to utter madness. When Paul D sees him for the last time, Halle is sitting at the churn, his face smeared with butter – a substance associated with his wife's stolen milk and indicating Halle's relational identification with his family. Halle is primarily a human being who loves, not specifically a man. When Paul D recounts being shackled with a bit in his mouth, he tries to explain to Sethe that the greatest humiliation of all was 'Walking past the roosters looking at them look at me' (p.71). Paul D believes that the cock, which, significantly, is named Mister, has smiled at him. This episode makes Paul D feel that he is 'something else' and that 'that something [is] less than a chicken sitting in the sun on a tub' (p.72). Because Paul D recognizes Mister as nothing more than a chicken, the scene is unequivocally one of dehumanization rather than of emasculation.[59] Moreover, Paul D understands that the guards in Alfred, Georgia, are 'not even embarrassed by the knowledge that without gunshot fox would laugh at them' (p.162). Morrison suggests that both rapist and victim are dehumanized – the victim left feeling reduced as a human being, the rapist aligned with the animal.

Reinventing the Discourse of Gender and Rape

Beloved explodes the dichotomies not only, as Valerie Smith argues, 'between life and afterlife, living and dead, oral and written, self and other, and so on'[60] but also between male and female, rapist and victim. Morrison challenges the idea that sexually subjected bodies fall within clear gender and heterosexual parameters. In reworking Harriet Jacobs's text, Morrison suggests that sexual exploitation is not only the black woman's story of slavery. The gendered discourse of rape, as well as feminist literary criticism that has sought to recover women's lost texts and stories, has unwittingly veiled Paul D's brutalization. Moreover, it seems inconceivable for Beloved to figure as a female rapist because twentieth-century notions of women and rapists exclude the assaultive agency of the succubus.[61] Morrison foregrounds the variability and historicism of the gendered discourse of rape and thus the mutability of seemingly entrenched conceptualizations.

Beloved serves as a powerful reminder that rape was and often still is a racial issue, that it is not, as Susan Brownmiller has asserted, 'a process of intimidation by which *all men* keep *all women* in a state of fear'.[62] While *male* and *female* do not formulaically describe rapist and victim in the novel, *white* and *black* almost always do. Beloved is a black perpetrator, but she embodies memories of whites' assaults on blacks. Morrison depicts rape as a process by which some white men keep some black women and even some black men in a state of fear. In this way she constructs a discourse for the rape of black women and men that has been largely absent in twentieth-century America and thus asserts the complex and various powers that structure rape.[63]

In the novel, free African American men and women have survived rape and slavery but they are not free of the recurrent experience of trauma. They can neither contain nor repress their memories, and hence survival is, as Caruth says, a kind of crisis. However, the novel suggests that the community might survive at least a gradually mitigating crisis. Once Beloved emerges from the darkness of private dreams and becomes a communal memory, only traces of her remain. Indeed, the last paragraph of the novel claims that 'By and by all trace is gone'. Yet the closing sentences carry those denied traces. Morrison writes that 'The rest is weather. Not the breath of the disremembered and unaccounted for. . . . Certainly no clamor for a kiss.' These deliberate negations are mobilized against a persisting presence. Similarly, the narration repeatedly insists, 'they forgot her', the repetition signaling that the memories can never be 'disremembered and unaccounted for' (p.275). Ella warns that Beloved 'Could be hiding in the trees waiting for another chance' (p.263), and the novel's conclusion suggests that Beloved will get that chance should the community fail to realize that forgetting, not communal memory, is the condition of traumatic return. □

CHAPTER FOUR

'This Is Flesh I'm Talking About':
Language, Subjectivity and the Body

■ There is no selfhood apart from the collaborative practice of its figuration. *The "self" is a representational economy*: a reification continually defeated by mutable entanglements with other subjects' histories, experiences, self-representations; with their texts, conduct, gestures, objectifications. □

Debbora Battalgia[1]

A S THE recent work of cultural critics and post-colonial theorists has demonstrated, whiteness – the fact of having white skin – has been associated historically with a certain invisibility, regarded simply, in Hazel Carby's words, as a 'normative state of existence: the (white) point in space from which we tend to identify difference'.[2] Yet even as whiteness has typically sought to mask and efface itself by an appeal to the 'normative', white power, by contrast, engages constantly in the project of rendering itself visible, quite literally disporting itself, in the context of *Beloved*, upon the enslaved black body by means of physical violence. These processes of inscription and marking – 'with whips, fires, and ropes'[3] – are perhaps given most spectacular form, in Morrison's text, in the 'revolting clump of scars' (p. 21) that Sethe bears on her back as a result of a beating received from schoolteacher's nephews while she is pregnant with Denver at Sweet Home.

White power is asserted and maintained not only through physical violence, however, but also by recourse to other instruments of subjection – particularly language and discourse. Each of the following three extracts differently addresses this interplay between the somatic and linguistic/discursive in the shaping and unshaping of black subjectivities.

The first extract, given with minimal cuts, is from David Lawrence's 'Fleshly Ghosts and Ghostly Flesh: The Word and the Body in *Beloved*', first published in *Studies in American Fiction* (1991) and more recently reprinted in an anthology of critical essays on Morrison's fiction edited by David L. Middleton (1997). Like numerous critics, Lawrence emphasises the role of memory in *Beloved* and draws attention to the continuities between past and present, life during and life after slavery. His main focus is on how the black body is regulated as much through the discursive constructions deployed by 'Whitepeople' (p.198) as by the more obviously brutal technologies of subjugation at slavery's disposal. Whether as slave or ex-slave, Lawrence argues, the black subject occupies the position of 'the other in the discourse of the dominant ideology', and comes to see his or her own body from the perspective of the white gaze, in a way that leads, in its turn, to alienation from the possibilities of desire and relationship that the body carries within itself. What is at once most striking and most disturbing about the mutually supportive economy of linguistic and bodily disempowerment, Lawrence contends, is the ongoing fragmentation that it produces within the black community. Those figures (such as Baby Suggs) who struggle to step outside the white codes that the community has internalised are reprimanded and rejected, with devastating consequences: the ostracising of Baby Suggs results, albeit indirectly, in Sethe's murder of her daughter.

That which enslaves at the same time contains the potential, however, for liberation, as various acts of language (both individual and collective) are shown to be integral to the possibility of recovering aspects of bodily and subjective experience repressed by slavery: even as Beloved is 'Disremembered and unaccounted for' at the end of the novel (p.274), it is not before the codification of the black body by white culture has been largely dismantled, a process in which Beloved herself is the chief catalyst.

■ In William Faulkner's *Light in August*, Byron Bunch reflects that no matter how much a person might 'talk about how he'd like to escape from living folks . . . it's the dead folks that do him the damage'.[4] The damage done by dead folks in Toni Morrison's *Beloved* points to the central position accorded to memory, the place where these dead folks are kept alive, in this novel of futile forgetting and persistent remembrance. Operating independently of the conscious will, memory is shown to be an active, constitutive force that has the power to construct and circumscribe identity, both individual and collective, in the image of its own contents. Sethe's 'rememory', in giving substance to her murdered daughter and to the painful past, casts its spell over the entire community, drawing the members of that community into one person's struggle with the torments of a history that refuses to die.

In portraying the capacity of the past to haunt individual and community life in the present, *Beloved* brings into daylight the 'ghosts' that are harbored by memory and that hold their 'hosts' in thrall, tyrannically dictating thought, emotion, and action. The stories of the tightly woven network of characters culminate in a ritualistic sacrifice of Beloved, a ceremony that frees the community from this pervasive haunting. The supernatural existence of Beloved, who acts as a scape-goat for the evils of the past, threatens the naturalized set of inherited codes by which the community defines itself. The climactic scene shows how a culture may find it necessary in a moment of crisis to exorcise its own demons in order to reaffirm its identity.

Morrison first exposes, however, the workings of the internal mechanisms that have generated the need for exorcism in the first place. A deeply encoded rejection of the body drives the highly pres-surized haunting in *Beloved*. The black community of Cincinnati is caught in a cycle of self-denial, a suffocating repression of fundamen-tal bodily needs and wants. The inability to articulate such embodied experience, to find a text for the desiring body within communal codes, obstructs self-knowledge and does violence to the fabric of community. Woven into the dense texture of the novel, into what Morrison has called the 'subliminal, the underground life of a novel',[5] the interaction of language and body underlies the collective con-frontation with the ghosts of memory. In her representation of this psychic battle, Morrison fashions word and flesh as intimate allies in the project of constructing a domain in which body and spirit may thrive. The exorcism of Beloved, an embodiment of resurgent desire, opens the way to a rewording of the codes that have enforced the silencing of the body's story, making possible a remembering of the cultural heritage that has haunted the characters so destructively. In the end, the communal body seems ready to articulate a reinvigorated language that, in returning to its roots in the body, empowers its speakers to forge a more open, inclusive community.

In a novel that examines the dehumanizing impact of slavery, one might expect that the white man, the monstrous enforcer of slavery's brutality, would haunt the black community. The haunting occurs, however, within a social structure relatively insulated from the white community and, in its most intense form, springs from the 'rememory' of an ex-slave in the form of one victimized by slavery. There is nothing mysteriously threatening about whites; on the contrary, 'white folks didn't bear speaking on. Everybody knew' (p.53). Of course, whites 'spoke on' their slaves tirelessly, and, in the exploration of political power in the novel, ownership of body and authorship of language are shown to be insidiously linked. Under the regime of white authority, the 'blackness' of the slave's body represents for 'whitefolks' an animal savagery and moral depravity that, ironically, ends up remaking them in the image of their own fears:

> Whitepeople believed that whatever the manners, under every dark skin was a jungle. Swift unnavigable waters, swinging screaming baboons, sleeping snakes, red gums ready for their sweet white blood. . . . But it wasn't the jungle blacks brought with them to this place from the other (livable) place. It was the jungle whitefolks planted in them. And it grew. It spread. In, through and after life, it spread, until it invaded the whites who had made it. . . . The screaming baboon lived under their own white skin; the red gums were their own. (pp. 198–99)

This 'belief', which underlies the chilling scientific rationality of schoolteacher, abstracts the human corporeality of the slave into a sign for the other in the discourse of the dominant ideology. Further, such invasive signifying upon the black body generates a self-fulfilling prophecy, as blacks find themselves unable to assert an identity outside the expectations imposed upon them: 'the more [colored people] used themselves up to persuade whites of something Negroes believed could not be questioned, the deeper and more tangled the jungle grew inside' (p. 198).

In *Beloved*, the question of authority over one's own body is consistently related to that of authority over discourse; bodily and linguistic disempowerment frequently intersect. At Sweet Home, Sethe makes the ink with which schoolteacher and his nephews define on paper her 'animal characteristics'; the ink, a tool for communication produced by her own hands, is turned against her as ammunition for their 'weapons' of torture, pen and paper.[6] Shocked, she asks Mrs. Garner for the definitions of 'characteristics' and 'features', vainly attempting to assert control over the words that have conscripted her body in a notebook (pp. 194–95). The terror she feels at seeing herself defined and divided (animal traits on the left, human on the right) concludes her list on ways whites can 'Dirty you so bad you forgot who you were' (p. 251); the litany of brutality – decapitations, burnings, rapes – she provides Beloved as 'reasons' for killing her ends with this bottom line: 'And no one, nobody on this earth, would list her daughter's characteristics on the animal side of the paper. No. Oh no' (p. 251).

As Stamp Paid, the community's literate newsbearer, reads about the post-Civil War violence against his people, he can 'smell' the bloody brutality in the very words that attempt to communicate that violence in digestible form:

> The stench stank. Stank up off the pages of the *North Star*, out of the mouths of witnesses, etched in crooked handwriting in letters delivered by hand. Detailed in documents and petitions full of *whereas* and presented to any legal body who'd read it, it stank. (p. 180)

The primary means of entry into the realm of the written word for blacks is the atrocity that is inflicted upon them or that they inflict upon others. Looking at Sethe's picture in Stamp's newspaper clipping relating the story of Sethe's 'crime', Paul D knows that 'there was no way in hell a black face could appear in a newspaper if the story was about something anybody wanted to hear' (p. 155).

Even on Sweet Home, where Garner believes he allows his slaves to be men, the power of naming remains with the white master.[7] Paul D wonders years later, 'Is that where the manhood lay? In the naming done by a whiteman who was supposed to know?' (p.125). Of course, schoolteacher, Garner's successor, destroys even this precarious sense of identity. Sethe recalls how schoolteacher asserted his authority as 'definer' after Sixo had dexterously challenged an accusation of theft. Sixo's rhetorical artistry – stealing and eating the shoat is 'improving property' since such apparently transgressive behavior actually will increase his productive capacity – is futile: 'Clever, but schoolteacher beat him anyway to show him that definitions belonged to the definers – not the defined' (p. 190). Sethe tells Denver that what 'tore Sixo up. . . . for all time' was not the beatings but the questions that schoolteacher asked them, presumably as part of his research into their animal nature. According to Sethe, it is the notebook schoolteacher carries with him containing the answers that destroys Sixo, not the gunshots that eventually end his life (p. 37).

Finally, in the first pages of the novel, Sethe remembers how she had to exchange 'ten minutes' of sex with the engraver for the 'one word that mattered' – Beloved (p. 5). In order to acquire the inscribing power of the white man's chisel, she must transform her body into a commodity; he will grant the cherished script provided he first be granted the right of sexual inscription. Thus Sethe must temporarily 'kill off' her own body (she lies on a headstone, 'her knees wide open as any grave', [p. 5]) to purchase the text that she thinks will buy her peace. The debt owed to her murdered daughter, however, is not to be so 'easily' paid.

As Sethe lies in the Clearing where her mother-in-law, Baby Suggs, used to preach the Word, she thinks about how her month of 'unslaved life' made her realize that 'Freeing yourself was, one thing; claiming ownership of that freed self was another' (p. 95). This striving to claim ownership links Sethe's own horrifying story to the story of the entire community. Central to the pursuit of self-ownership is the articulation of a self-defining language that springs from the flesh and blood of physical experience and that gives shape to the desire so long suppressed under slavery. Baby Suggs discovers such self-definition immediately upon gaining her freedom. After she experiences the wonder of possessing her own body, of recognizing the pounding of 'her own heartbeat' (p.141), she renames herself 'Suggs' (her husband's name), forcefully rejecting Garner's uncomprehending defense of the 'legal' name on her bill of sale, Jenny Whitlow. She thus begins to fill with 'the roots of her tongue' (p.141) that 'desolated center where the self that was no self made its home' (p.140).

Of course, it is precisely this kind of 'self-generating' language that has been stifled by the mortifications of flesh endured under slavery. In defending itself against the bodily depredations of enslavement, the community has learned to choke off its capacity for pleasure and love, for the experience of jouissance. 'Baby Suggs, holy', the 'unchurched preacher' (p.87), tries to revise this legacy of self-denial in her self-loving exhortations, devoting 'the roots of her tongue' to calling the Word. Eschewing such confining abstractions as sin and purity, Baby Suggs grounds her words in the earthly, sensual realm through which the body moves: 'She told them that the only grace they could have was the grace they could imagine. That if they could not see it, they would not have it' (p.88). Rather than a divine state of being that descends from above, grace is a humanly conceived, embodied experience. In the oral text of her 'sermon', which Baby Suggs draws from the powerfully felt fact of being alive within a body, 'grace' is both noun and verb, a blessed touching of one's own body: 'Here . . . in this here place, we flesh; flesh that weeps, laughs; flesh that dances on bare feet in grass. Love it. Love it hard. . . . grace it, stroke it and hold it up' (p.88). In this open-ended, organic religion, Baby Suggs taps a bodily 'organ music', imploring her listeners to love their 'dark, dark liver' and 'life-giving private parts' (pp.88–89). And when her words cease, Sethe recalls, she 'danced with her twisted hip the rest of what her heart had to say while the others opened their mouths and gave her the music' (p.89). Using her own disfigured body as an instrument, Baby Suggs talks through dance to find the language adequate to the demands of their bodies: 'Long notes held until the four-part harmony was perfect enough for their deeply loved flesh' (p.89). Her speech, both literally and metaphorically, comes from her 'big old heart', providing a kind of scaffolding for the reconstitution of the damaged communal body. The members of the community must put themselves back together – re-member themselves – so that they can remember that the heart 'is the prize' (p.89).

Sethe recalls how this 'fixing ceremony' (p.86) had begun the work of asserting self-defined ownership: 'Bit by bit . . . along with the others, she had claimed herself' (p.95). But the unwritten codes of the community cannot yet entirely accommodate such joyous self-celebration. After Baby Suggs hosts a spontaneous feast to mark the arrival of her daughter-in-law, the community finds itself resenting what they perceive as her prideful behavior. She has crossed the boundary of permissible pleasure: 'Her friends and neighbors were angry at her because she had overstepped, given too much, offended them by excess' (p.138). Her former guests transfer their self-despising outrage at the poverty of their own lives onto the person who dares to dispense such a rare commodity as love with 'reckless generosity': 'Loaves and fishes were His powers – they didn't belong to an ex-slave' (p.137). Ironically, the communal voice that Baby Suggs 'hears' the morning after the feast plays, in effect, the role of the white master by reprimanding the 'slave' who has violated the code of acceptable behavior. The oppression enforced by slaveowners is now perpetuated by the oppressed themselves. As a unit, the community itself remains an 'ex-slave', unable to define itself outside the parameters of the slave experience.

To be sure, Morrison makes it clear that under slavery the self-imposed prohibition on 'reckless generosity' worked as a necessary survival strategy, an indispensable means of self-defense. Paul D learned 'to love just a little bit; everything, just a little bit, so when they broke its back, or shoved it in a croaker sack, well, maybe you'd have a little love left over for the next one' (p.45). Loving 'big', according to Paul D, 'would split you wide open', so 'you protected yourself and loved small' (p.162). On the chain gang in Alfred, Georgia, Paul D and the men vent their rage in songs, fictions that permit them to act out through their labor their desire to 'kill[ ] the boss' as well as 'the flirt whom folks called Life for leading them on' (p.109). But this life-killing strategy of self-defense has become, after slavery, a deadly form of self-destruction. Listening to Sethe's own story of desperate self-defense (her 'explanation' of why she had to kill her children in order to protect them), Paul D reflects upon the need to find a space for uninhibited love: 'to get to a place where you could love anything you chose – not to need permission for desire – well now, *that* was freedom' (p.162). Freed from slavery, the community must now learn to permit itself the freedom to desire. The denial of this permission to Baby Suggs, apparently an act of collective self-assertion, only implicates the community in Sethe's self-destructive defense of her own flesh and blood. Because her neighbors are furious at Baby Suggs' presumption, they do not send someone to warn her of schoolteacher's approach, a warning which might have prevented the slaughter of one of their own by one of their own.

Having moved from 'the center of things' (p.137) to the margins of the community, 124 is haunted, its residents three phantoms (after Sethe's sons run away) and a ghost. Baby Suggs, her heart 'collapsed' and her voice silenced, spends the last eight years of her life contemplating the colors on her quilt. Sethe devotes herself to beating back the past that is 'still waiting' (p.42) for Denver, who goes deaf rather than remember the dark time she spent with her mother in prison (p. 104). They lead sterile, isolated lives, the ghost the only member of the family who seeks the intimacy of physical contact.

But Paul D's arrival eighteen years after 'the Misery' (p. 171), disturbs the unhealthy equilibrium at 124. In evicting the ghost and touching Sethe, he initiates the process of articulating 'word-shapes' (p. 99) for the past that still imprisons them. The marks of violence and humiliation must be 'read', translated into a shared understanding, before that body language called by Baby Suggs in the Clearing can be rediscovered and respoken. With instinctive compassion, Paul D goes straight to the source to learn of Sethe's suffering, the network of scars inscribed by schoolteacher's nephews that has numbed her entire back: 'He rubbed his cheek on her back, and learned that way her sorrow, the roots of it; its wide trunk and intricate branches' (p. 17). The sexual union that allows Sethe to 'feel the hurt her back ought to' (p. 18) also brings about a psychic union; they silently recall, in tandem, the safe memory of love at Sweet Home. Morrison's narrator creates seamless transitions between their separate but simultaneous memories of Sethe and Halle's first lovemaking in the cornfield. The recollection culminates in the shared trope for sexual arousal and fulfillment expressed in the husked corn: 'How loose the silk. How quick the jailed-up flavor ran free' (p. 27). This convergence of sexuality, memory, and poetic figure beautifully illustrates the intimate communion of linguistic and bodily experience enacted in the text of the novel.

As Sethe and Paul D 'make talk' (p. 20), what had previously been 'unspeakable' begins to be speakable: 'Her story was bearable because it was his as well – to tell, to refine and tell again. The things neither knew about the other – the things neither had word-shapes for' (p. 99). In his presence, Sethe rediscovers her own capacity for bodily sensation and reestablishes contact with the outside world that induces such sensation: 'Emotions sped to the surface in his company. Things became what they were. . . . Windows suddenly had view' (p. 39). After a day spent at the carnival enjoying Paul D's gregarious companionship, Sethe allows herself to imagine that the three hand-holding shadows she observes on their return will shortly be a fully fleshed unit. The desire that Paul D stirs up, however, taps a reservoir of repressed feeling that seems to trigger Beloved's emergence from Sethe's rememory. The spoken text of their love cannot accommodate Beloved, and their storytelling intimacy is soon broken by the ghost's return in full-grown, fleshly form.

Beloved acts as an embodiment of uninhibited desire, projecting a 'bottomless' 'longing' (p. 58) for love that places impossible demands upon the human body. Her appearance at 124 fresh from the waters of the Ohio causes Sethe to run desperately for the privy to relieve the incredible pressure of her own waters, an emergency evacuation re-enacting Beloved's natural birth. Her touch, 'no heavier than a feather but loaded, nevertheless, with desire' (p. 58), dissolves the 'tobacco tin' into which Paul D has crammed his painful, humiliating memories, moving him involuntarily from the house he thought he had claimed. She absorbs Denver's devotion only to give her more strength for consuming Sethe's love: 'Sethe was licked, tasted, eaten by Beloved's eyes' (p. 57). Her appetite is an insatiable 'life hunger' (p. 264), a 'downright craving to know' (p. 77) the life and love that was denied her. Like a vampire, she sucks out Sethe's vitality, fattening on her mother's futile attempts to 'make her understand', to explain and justify the necessity of murdering her own child to save her from the murder of slavery.[8]

When Stamp Paid approaches the newly haunted 124, he hears 'a conflagration of hasty voices' speaking a language incomprehensible save for the word *mine* (p. 172). He senses that this is the 'roaring' of 'the people of the broken necks, of fire-cooked blood and black girls who had lost their ribbons' (p. 181). Beloved magnetizes 124, attracting all that lost life now returning to lay claim to its own. The impossibility of articulating such possessive claims in an 'earthly' language suggests the life-threatening potency of Beloved's desire. As an infant in a nineteen-year-old body, Beloved has not yet learned the codes that give shape to and control desire. Her unadulterated narcissism permits her to 'seduce' her mother in the Clearing, an impulsive sensuality that probably derives from her memory of breastfeeding. Here, though, the libidinal element in normal breast-feeding becomes dominant, as Beloved's tender kisses entrance Sethe until she finds herself forced against the wall of the incest taboo: 'You too old for that' (pp. 97–98). Beloved recognizes no social bounds, showing a resistance to conventional form that is registered in the disturbing 'cadence' (p. 60) of her own words. While she craves adult language, particularly those stories that 'construct out of the strings' of Denver and Sethe's experience 'a net' to hold her (p. 76), she is incapable of such construction herself.

The sections of the novel dominated by Beloved's voice reflect her lack of a socially circumscribed identity; her 'word-shapes' embody her tenuous physical and psychical shape. Before she finds 'the join' with Sethe that enables her to escape the 'dark place' (pp. 210–13), her 'units' of self-representation are fragmented memories, word-pictures, and sensations, articulated without clearly established frames of reference – inside and outside, past and present, cause and effect. Even the gaps on the printed page suggest the danger of the disintegration of her being.[9] After she assumes physical form (pp. 214–17), her self-projection in language integrates itself syntactically but continues to obfuscate the boundary between self and other; Beloved's image of her mother's face – 'She smiles at me and it is my own face smiling' (p.214) – suggests her inability to distinguish her own body from that of her mother.

At the end of the sections expressing the 'unspeakable thoughts, unspoken' of 'the women of 124' (p.199), the voices of Sethe, Denver, and Beloved merge into a single chorus that effaces individual identity in a possessive love sounded by the refrain

> You are mine
> You are mine
> You are mine. (p.217)

The fusion of identity expressed in this refrain can only be destructive, as Sethe and Denver lose themselves in the overpowering 'mine' asserted by Beloved. In the end, their 'conversation' is a monologic discourse dictated by a fleshly ghost, a univocal tyranny silencing any attempt at dialogic communication. In her insistence on absolute possession of her mother, Beloved resurrects the slavemaster's monopoly over both word and body, enforcing the internalized enslavement that has become a legacy of institutionalized slavery.[10]

In order to free itself of the haunting past embodied in 124, the community must tap a deeper level of language, a more primitive source of cultural experience that creates communal bonds rather than destroying them. When Paul D's chain gang rescues itself from the muck flooding their below-ground cages, it discovers this kind of instinctive communication in the chain that binds them together: 'They talked through that chain like Sam Morse and, Great God, they all came up' (p.110). This 'talking' is born out of the ooze, a pre-Genesis chaos – 'All Georgia seemed to be sliding, melting away' (p.111) – from which the human community is delivered. Ironically, the 'best hand-forged chain in Georgia' (p.107) acts as a linguistic tool for forging the communal identity that enables each one of them to survive the flood. Conversely, as Paul D reflects, had just one not 'heard' the message, they all would have perished. Individual and community survival are thus inseparable; the trials of one body are, in some form, the trials of everybody.

This unity of the one with the whole is reaffirmed when the townswomen, alerted by Denver, come to rescue Sethe. The community resuscitates itself by again giving voice to the power of the life-affirming language that Baby Suggs had called out in the Clearing and that now demands the complete devotion of their bodily efforts. Eighteen years ago, the community, outraged at Sethe's prideful self-possession, had turned its back to her as she rode off to prison. The narrator observes that, had Sethe not been so seemingly convinced of her rectitude, 'a cape of sound would have quickly been wrapped around her, like arms to hold and steady her on the way. As it was, they waited till the cart turned about, headed west to town. And then no words. Humming. No words at all' (p. 152). The people withhold the support that their songs would have bodied forth, their words disdaining to touch the offending flesh. Now, however, the community, led by Ella, tries to sing Sethe back into its embrace. Like the singing of Paul D's chain gang and that of Sixo just before he is shot to death, the human voice in song is a potent material force. Sixo's song, triumphant because the Thirty-Mile Woman has escaped with his 'blossoming seed', culminates in a laugh 'So rippling and full of glee it put out the fire' (p. 229).

But when the women's singing prayer does not have the power to make contact with the 'roaring' around 124, they must go all the way back to the first page of the text in their collective memory: 'In the beginning was the sound, and they all knew what that sound sounded like' (p. 259). This familiar, original sound precedes and overwhelms words,[11] revitalizing Sethe's body and allowing her to break the lock Beloved has had upon her:

> For Sethe it was as though the Clearing had come to her with all its heat and simmering leaves, where the voices of women searched for the right combination, the key, the code, the sound that broke the back of words. Building voice upon voice until they found it, and when they did it was a wave of sound wide enough to sound deep water and knock the pods off chestnut trees. It broke over Sethe and she trembled like the baptized in its wash. (p. 261)

This preverbal language seems to flex its muscles as it bursts forth from the deepest roots of human knowing, tapped by the 'Building' of a chorus of individual voices. Unleashed, Sethe rushes toward Bodwin (mistaking him for schoolteacher) with ice pick raised, her body partially transformed into the shape of the weapon she must use to protect her daughter: 'The ice pick is not in her hand; it is her hand' (p. 262). But the reconstituted community intervenes, absorbing her in what Beloved sees as a 'hill of black people, falling' (p. 262). Now that Sethe and Denver have both reentered the communal fold, Beloved senses she has been left behind 'Alone. Again.' (p. 262), and the 'devil-child' (p. 261) vanishes.

In the aftermath of her baptism, though, Sethe is devastated, her 'best thing' taken from her a second time. She has taken a crucial step towards self-ownership in directing her protective violence against the oppressor (schoolteacher in the form of Bodwin) instead of against her own flesh and blood, but, alone, she cannot recuperate from the tragic repetition of her loss. To open the way to such recuperation, Paul D's own story of self-recovery is reunited with Sethe's. After he first leaves 124, ostensibly in horror at the news of Sethe's murderous past, he retreats into isolation, drinking alone in the cold church.[12] When Stamp Paid visits him, Paul D resists his attempts to humanize Sethe's actions. But when Stamp asks whether he might have been 'run off' 124 by Beloved, not Sethe, he is shocked into recognizing that his condemnation of Sethe's shameful act actually covered his own shame at his emasculation in Beloved's company (pp. 234–35). Now, returning to 124 to check on Sethe, he recalls his peculiar lovemaking with Beloved:

> Coupling with her wasn't even fun. It was more like a brainless urge to stay alive. Each time she came, pulled up her skirts, a life hunger overwhelmed him and he had no more control over it than over his lungs. And afterward, beached and gobbling air, in the midst of repulsion and personal shame, he was thankful too for having been escorted to some ocean-deep place he once belonged to. (p. 264)

His gratitude suggests a recognition that his rival for Sethe's affections had actually started the work of prying open his rusty tobacco tin and restoring to him the pulse of his 'Red heart' (p. 117).

Paul D must discover this 'life hunger' within himself by sounding that 'ocean-deep place' that the community tapped into in exorcising Beloved. To find that place 'he once belonged to', he must begin drawing a 'map to discover' himself (p. 140), one charting those regions of memory that block the way to the ocean-deep self. Standing over the half-conscious Sethe, not knowing what to make of this powerful woman, he suddenly recalls how Sixo described his love for the Thirty-Mile Woman: '"She is a friend of my mind. She gather me, man. The pieces I am, she gather them and give them back to me in all the right order. It's good, you know, when you got a woman who is a friend of your mind"' (pp. 272–73). Then, 'thinking about her wrought-iron back', that map of Sethe's sorrow and suffering, he remembers a moment that previously had been 'packed away', in his tobacco tin:

> The mean black eyes. The wet dress steaming before the fire. Her tenderness about his neck jewelry – its three wands, like attentive baby rattlers, curving two feet in the air. How she never mentioned

or looked at it so he did not have to feel the shame of being collared like a beast. Only this woman Sethe could have left him his manhood like that. He wants to put his story next to hers (p. 273).

This remembering of his haunting past is constructive rather than destructive, giving him the freedom, finally, to choose his own desire. In effect, he regains the authorship of his own text; he wants to put the story of his body, as well as the body of his story, alongside Sethe's. The next words inscribed into that text, communicated through the 'holding fingers' (p. 273) of Paul D's 'educated hands' (p. 99), begin the restoration of Sethe's own self-authorship: 'You your best thing, Sethe. You are.' Her wondering response, 'Me? Me?', implies its own affirmation (p. 273). Reviving her with the knowing touch of his words, Paul D rescues Sethe from mute oblivion, reconnecting her with the talking spirit of companionship and community.

In the end, Beloved again becomes one of the 'Disremembered and unaccounted for' (p. 274),[13] lurking in the liminal space of communal memory perhaps, but not a part of that community's consciousness. As Morrison's narrator puts it, 'Remembering seemed unwise', for Beloved's story 'was not a story to pass on' (pp. 274–75). Her demonic 'life hunger' simply cannot be encompassed within the 'word-shapes' of the community's storytelling language. Provoked by Beloved's intrusion, the neighborhood has widened the circle of community to reincorporate Sethe and 124, but that circle must exclude the unassimilable otherness of Beloved.

Having accomplished its spontaneous 'fixing ceremony', the kind Baby Suggs had led in the Clearing, the community is free to lay down 'the heavy knives of defense against misery, regret, gall and hurt' (p. 86), those weapons of self-defense that had turned against them as weapons of self-denial and self-destruction. Morrison has commented on the need for the novel as a way of dispensing 'new information': 'It should have something in it that enlightens; something in it that opens the doors and points the way. Something in it that suggests what the conflicts are, what the problems are. But it need not solve those problems because it is not a case study, it is not a recipe'.[14] In *Beloved*, Morrison suggests a way through the door of memory, even if that way entails a precarious balancing act between the danger of forgetting a past that should not be forgotten and of remembering a past that threatens to engulf the present. While the painful heritage of slavery cannot simply 'pass on', cannot die away (to use another meaning suggested by that ambiguous phrase), enslavement to that heritage, Morrison implies, must 'pass on', must die away, in order to undertake the task of remembering and re-articulating the individual and the communal body. ☐

The next extract is taken from the third section of April Lidinsky's 'Prophesying Bodies: Calling for a Politics of Collectivity in Toni Morrison's *Beloved*', which originally appeared in Carl Plasa and Betty J. Ring's *The Discourse of Slavery: Aphra Behn to Toni Morrison* (1994). Influenced by the work of Michel Foucault in particular, Lidinsky aims, in the essay as a whole, to show how *Beloved* challenges, as she puts it:

■ the 'naturalness' of the established discursive, disciplinary techniques that historically have produced not only the enslaved proprietary body as an owned 'object', but also the viciously individuated Cartesian 'subject', which operates through a similar proprietary model of one's body as simply the property of the self.[15] ☐

Nowhere is this challenge more forcefully pronounced than in the visionary spirituality of Baby Suggs, whose Call in the Clearing to 'Love' (on which Lawrence also comments in detail) constitutes both a reimagining of the self and its communal relations and a way of effecting a movement towards collective political action. While Baby's liberative energies draw upon nineteenth-century holiness currents of Methodist and African Methodist Episcopal churches, they resonate also, Lidinsky shows, with post-modern theories of the construction – and possible reconstruction – of embodied subjectivity in and through discourse.

This aspect of Lidinsky's argument perhaps looks back to Morrison's own reflections on the preveniently post-modern condition of nineteenth-century black women in the exchange with Paul Gilroy in chapter one above. It also intersects with the position of bell hooks in 'Postmodern Blackness' (1990). In this essay hooks suggests, on the one hand, that black intellectuals and writers should entertain a degree of suspicion towards 'postmodern critiques of the "subject" [since] they surface at a historical moment when many subjugated people feel themselves coming to voice for the first time'.[16] Yet, on the other hand, hooks argues that 'postmodernist thought is useful for African-Americans' who, like the Morrison of *Beloved*, in Lidinsky's reading, are 'concerned with reformulating outmoded notions of identity'.[17]

In the extract from the essay reprinted here, Lidinsky moves away from the question of 'matrilineal connections' in *Beloved* which, as she notes, has been the focus of much critical attention (including the pieces from Horvitz and House in chapter three above). Her primary concern, instead, is to consider the ramifications of slavery upon the body of the black male subject. At the centre of this exploration is a particularly vivid analysis of Paul D's experiences on the coffle, or chain-gang, in Alfred, Georgia, where the status of Paul and the other slaves as properties owned by white masters is made graphically evident through the repetitive actions that their bodies are made to perform.

For Lidinsky – as for Lawrence – the disciplined body can, however, also be un- or redisciplined and it is this process of resistance and transformation that she traces in the second part of the extract, by showing how Paul D begins tentatively to reclaim an alternative corporeal knowledge to that imposed by slavery and moves, subsequently, across the gender-line to assist Sethe in her struggle with the same project: both figures, according to Lidinsky, reach empowerment not only by fashioning sympathetic and collectivised relations with others but also by dint of an 'empathy for the "others in themselves"'.

■ While most critics have emphasized the matrilineal connections in *Beloved*,[18] Morrison's text is also richly suggestive with regard to the various effects of slavery's disciplinary tactics on *masculinity*, at the same time exploring ways that the 'boundaries' of gender [. . .] can be tested and crossed. I will move on accordingly – briefly – to the figure of Paul D, the Sweet Home man who becomes Sethe's lover after the war. His experience of brutality – and the resistance to it – on a coffle, after schoolteacher sells him from Sweet Home, perhaps best illustrates the disciplinary and gestural *propriety* that produces the bodily discourse of *property* which speaks in turn through an enslaved person until those gestures can be unlearned. Paul D's coffle-experience details, then, the disciplinary model to which all the characters are subjected, and literally traces methods of resistance.

While the actual chains ordering the bodies of the men in the coffle must be categorized in terms of force rather than disciplinary power, the narrator suggests that the 'miracle of their obedience' is due less to a physical binding than to the discipline of dressage or training. The repetitive performance of the chain gang announces Paul D's identity as property with equal clarity whether the chain is on or off:

All forty-six men woke to rifle shot. All forty-six. Three whitemen walked along the trench unlocking the doors [of their cages] one by one. No one stepped through. . . . another rifle shot signaled the climb out and up to the ground above, where one thousand feet of the best hand-forged chain in Georgia stretched. Each man bent and waited. The first man picked up the end and threaded it through the loop on his leg iron. He stood up then, and, shuffling a little, brought the chain tip to the next prisoner, who did likewise. (p. 107)

Soldier-like discipline seems, more than rifle shots, to be the 'miracle' enabling three white guards to achieve such control that forty-six prisoners mechanically chain themselves at a signal each morning. [. . .] this discipline is effected through a vertical organization of power which radically partitions these men (via spaces on the chain by day and separate cages by night) in order to eliminate the possibility of collective identity and agency. For a time, Paul D incorporates the gestural training with such devastating thoroughness that his body seems to lose whatever knowledges it might draw on for resistance or even preservation. His hands and legs that are so 'steady' and disciplined while going through the motions of coffle-work are no longer trained for – nor do they seem to contain knowledge of – any other use:

> when they shoved him into the box and dropped the cage door down, his hands quit taking instruction. On their own, they traveled. Nothing could stop them, or get their attention. They would not hold his penis to urinate or a spoon to scoop lumps of lima beans into his mouth. The miracle of their obedience came with the hammer at dawn. (p.107)

From this most concretely realized illustration of the devastating effects of discipline, however, comes an equally concrete example of how a horizontal redirection of power at the level of the gesture can enable precisely the collective disposition that the coffle-masters fear. This redirection begins, just as Baby Suggs preaches, with the men being moved to 'listen' to the body's alternative knowledges, since disciplinary partitioning eliminates the possibility of meaningful speech. As in spiritual doctrine, visual literacy takes on new meaning. 'The eyes had to tell what there was to tell: "Help me this mornin; 's bad"; "I'm a make it"; "New man"; "Steady now steady"' (p.107). Once the men begin 'listening each other into speech', according to the spiritual model, collective action becomes a possibility, and not simply for inventing a collective and private glossolalia of 'tricking the words [of their songs] so their syllables yielded up other meanings'. Through the guidance of Hi Man, who serves as the Baby Suggs figure on the coffle and similarly knows 'what was enough, what was too much, when things were over, when the time had come' (p.108), the men develop yet another discourse of motion and emotion – a series of tugs and pulls with which 'They talked through that chain like Sam Morse', thereby transforming the very device that keeps them partitioned into a mechanism for collective agency. This passage crystallizes the politics and Holiness spirituality of Baby's Call for connection: 'For one lost, all lost. The chain that held them would save all or none, and Hi Man was the Delivery' (p.110). This gestural discourse of conflated motion and emotion enables the men to swim simultaneously, blindly, out of the deadly muck which crushes and loosens their cages in a cataclysmic rain-storm, and to escape northward as a collective, their bodies no longer speaking the mastered, proprietary discourse, but instead beginning to articulate new identities.

This gestural retraining demands repetition, however, and Paul D survives the powerful experience of connection without entirely learning to 'love' and 'listen to' his heart, which remains a 'tobacco tin lodged in his chest' (p.113), perhaps because he is inscripted with specifically masculine cultural discourses of individuation – discourses built on the same proprietorial tropes found in Douglass's culturally central narrative. What makes Sweet Home so exceptional under the Garners, after all, is Garner's willingness to call his slaves 'men' – a naming that re-inscribes Garner's own manhood, for it proves to himself he is 'tough enough and smart enough to make and call his own niggers men' (p.11). Yet Garner undermines the nominal power of substituting 'men' for 'niggers' with the disciplinary logic revealed in his proprietary terms of 'making' 'his own' men. On this point Paul D reflects, 'Is that where the manhood lay? In the naming done by a whiteman who was supposed to know?' 'Suppose Garner woke up one morning and changed his mind?' (pp.125, 220). No matter how seemingly noble Garner's intention, his naming and 'making' of these men does not challenge their proprietary objectification, nor does it undo the power of ownership central to masculinist models of selfhood like Douglass's. When schoolteacher, as the very letter of the law, takes over the farm after Garner's death, Paul D is renamed or produced as something animal-like, even 'less than a chicken' whose freedom taunts him on the farm – a chicken named, with telling mockery, 'Mister' (p.72).

Beloved does, then, explore the specifically gendered trauma of certain effects of slavery's degradation, such as the reification and undermining of cultural concepts of 'manhood' at Sweet Home, and the stealing of Sethe's milk by schoolteacher's boys, but the bodily effects of enslavement on both men and women are linked through images of 'animality' and 'iron', suggesting that Sethe and Paul D must alike unlearn the mechanization of slavery's signifying disciplines of dressage, metallically incorporated into each of them (both figuratively and literally). Like the iron bit schoolteacher forces Paul D to wear, concretizing the horse-like dressage of slavery, Sethe's 'iron eyes and backbone to match' (p.9) are linked to his M/master inscription of her enslaved body as half-consisting of animal characteristics. Paul D must unlearn the sensation of the coffle-irons – incorporated as the 'tin' of his heart – as part of the process of redirecting power's flow, just as Sethe must unlearn the choke-hold of the 'circle of iron' (p. 101) around her throat that is both the collectively rememoried sensation of the Middle Passage and the somatic effect of Beloved's rage. Instead, Sethe learns to incorporate Baby's Call to 'love [her] neck; put a hand on it, grace it' (p. 88) – to 'listen' its somatic knowledges into speech through connection, as Paul D learns somatically the language of the numb 'ironsmith's' scar on Sethe's back through precisely these spiritually connecting gestures of love and grace:

> He rubbed his cheek on her back and learned that way her sorrow, the roots of it; its wide trunk and intricate branches. Raising his fingers to the hooks of her dress, he knew without seeing them or hearing any sigh that the tears were coming fast. (p. 17)

Images of liquidity, of somatic movement, mark Paul D's growing ability to produce in 124 a 'listening quiet' (p.15) that summons into speech these fluxuating, nonmechanized bodily knowledges which, like Baby Suggs's Call, cross gender boundaries through a kind of spiritual 'blessing':

> Not even trying, he had become the kind of man who could walk into a house and make the women cry. . . . There was something blessed in his manner. Women saw him and wanted to weep – to tell him that their chest hurt and their knees did too. Strong women and wise saw him and told him things they only told each other. (p.17)

As when he enters 124, a 'wave of grief soak[ing] him so thoroughly he wanted to cry' (p. 9), Paul D's growing ability to move both others and himself to new somatic knowledges and connections later becomes such a threat to Beloved's own connection to Sethe that Beloved 'moves' Paul D right back – blurring inner and outer effects to force him right out of the house. Similarly, like the 'closed portion' of Paul D's head that 'opened like a greased lock' (p.41), Sethe's own increasing ability to 'listen' her own alternative bodily knowledges into speech is figured in terms of the mechanized 'iron' of her body opening to spatial rememories. For example, while Sethe initially does not recognize her daughter in the figure of the adolescent Beloved, her own body marks this knowledge through a gush of water whose meaning Sethe must learn to 'read' in the manner of an alternative spiritual discourse. Significantly, her reading moves first through slavery's readily available discourse of objectification (figured as animality), and then beyond it to her own life-affirming birthing experience:

> She never made the outhouse. Right in front of its door she had to
> lift her skirts, and the water she voided was endless. Like a horse,
> she thought, but as it went on and on she thought, No, more like
> flooding the boat when Denver was born. (p. 51)

Later in the 'poetic' chapters in which Sethe's subject-positions blur
with those of Beloved, Sethe reads her body's discourse yet more
complexly, as the text merges these 'birth' waters with Beloved's act of
drinking:

> I would have known who you were right away because the cup
> after cup of water you drank proved and connected to the fact that
> you dribbled clear spit on my face the day I got to 124. (p. 202)

Whether operating on the small-scale dialogism of Sethe's gestural
readings of her own body's rememories, or on the larger call-and-
response connection between Paul D and Sethe, the collective identity
enabled by the horizontal redirection of power's flow works discur-
sively, through both new somatic literacies and the practices of
collaborative storytelling. History's presence in their very bodies
causes these characters to be moved – physically and emotionally – not
just by a sympathy for others, but by empathy for the 'others in themselves', despite divisive enculturated lines of identity.[19] Men like Paul
D and Stamp Paid are moved across gender lines to collaborate with
Sethe and Baby on events about which 'nobody knows' a totalising
narrative. Similarly, Amy Denver, the runaway 'whitegirl' (p. 8) who
midwives Denver's birth, is moved to cross lines of race in order to
mother Sethe and collaborate on class-based experiences of abuse and
creative survival that are eventually woven into the discursive fabric
of 124 through repeated stories of her nursing and her dreams of buy-
ing velvet, as through the very name carried on by Sethe's second
daughter, Denver. Once gesturally 'listened' into eloquence, then,
rememory dissolves power's vertical compartmentalization of
knowledge, temporality and identities. [. . .] □

The third and final extract in this chapter comes from Kristin Boudreau's
highly original 'Pain and the Unmaking of Self in Toni Morrison's
Beloved', published in *Contemporary Literature* in 1995. In Boudreau's
analysis, Morrison's text constitutes, above all, a powerful challenge to a
model of suffering and pain that characterises two ostensibly divergent
cultural traditions – those of Anglo-European Romanticism, on the one
hand, and African-American blues, on the other – as respectively
exemplified in the writings of John Keats and James Baldwin. Both
derived in turn from traditions of Christian contemplation, Romanticism

and the blues are linked, Boudreau argues, by a mutual investment in suffering/pain as a pivotal experiential process 'whereby one gains one's full humanity'.[20] Within such a process, the role of aesthetic representation is paramount, possessing the capacity, as it does, to transform 'the horrific into the tragically beautiful'.[21]

Having established the context for her reading of *Beloved* in these terms, Boudreau goes on, in the extract below, to illustrate the ways in which suffering/pain is figured somewhat differently in Morrison's text, using Elaine Scarry's reflections on torture in *The Body in Pain* (1985) as a theoretical point of reference. In contrast to the roles they play in the Romantic and blues traditions, suffering and pain, in *Beloved,* 'unmake' language, exceeding representation and communicability. Yet what is most radical about Morrison's novel, Boudreau suggests, is its dramatisation of the ways in which language itself has the potential to unmake selfhood or identity: Paul D's troubled question, 'Did a whiteman saying it make it so?' (p. 220) is one that Boudreau answers emphatically in the affirmative. Indeed, she concludes that the power of language to make and unmake the self is not exclusive to 'slaveholders and school-teachers', but in fact available to 'anyone who threatens individual autonomy by including the individual in his or her language and gaze'. Beloved thus emerges as a typical rather than anomalous figure, literalising the painful dilemmas of embodied subjectivity because to be human, in this text, is indistinguishable, Boudreau ultimately shows, from the condition of being ghostly or spectral.

■ Most readings of *Beloved* suggest that suffering can heal and humanize, provided that one can reorganize the painful events of the past and retell them in one's own language. A crucial problem arises, however, when these readings must confront the narrative's emphatic final assertion: 'This is not a story to pass on' (p. 275). Most critics resolve the problem by claiming that the story should, in fact, be passed on.[22] But why not take the narrative at its word and heed its caution that this story should *not* be passed on? Why not ask what accounts for its untenability? Contrary to most readings of *Beloved* – and contrary even to some of Morrison's own comments on the novel – that suffering makes one real, suffering in fact makes one a great deal less than real.[23] Suffering, as *Beloved* seems to cry in repeated anguished moments, *unmakes* the self and calls violent attention to the practice of making and unmaking selves.[24]

The most extreme condition of physical and psychological pain is, of course, the pain of torture. As Elaine Scarry claims in her remarkable discussion of this particular category of physical pain, torture destroys both the subject and his or her body:

what the process of torture does is to split the human being into two, to make emphatic the ever present but, except in the extremity of sickness and death, only latent distinction between a self and a body, between a 'me' and 'my body'. The 'self' or 'me', which is experienced on the one hand as more private, more essentially at the center, and on the other hand as participating across the bridge of the body in the world, is 'embodied' in the voice, in language. The goal of the torturer is to make the one, the body, emphatically and crushingly *present* by destroying it, and to make the other, the voice, *absent* by destroying it.[25]

I consider Scarry's analysis of torture an appropriate point of departure for a discussion of a novel that has located its narrative space in the memories of slavery. *Beloved* returns repeatedly to sites of physical, psychological, and sexual victimization, suggesting that these characters, scarred in an unfolding variety of ways, represent the product of a system of torture. Unlike the slave narrative, which typically presents a reasoned argument in favor of abolition – punctuated, of course, by scenes of violence, but seldom deviating from logical and rhetorically controlled condemnations of slavery – the characters in Morrison's novel have no access to the methods of ordered narrative.[26] Their language, their reasoning powers, even their sense of self have been dismantled by the process of torture. Because it acknowledges the incapacitating effects of slavery, the novel refuses to celebrate the pain that has produced these fragmented figures.

Slavery, of course, did not affect all African Americans in the same way, and we should be careful not to overstate the destructive power of the institution. Indeed, as Eugene Genovese and others have shown, much independent and original production took place even under the burden of slavery. But it is also clear that *Beloved* takes to task any nostalgia about slavery days. One need not grant absolute authority to the oppressiveness of slavery, but *Beloved* cautions us against confusing gestures of creativity and self-reliance on the part of slaves with the extremely different act of romanticizing the ugliness of slavery.

Certainly *Beloved* offers moments in which it approaches a romantic, beautified version of pain. Remembering her last days at Sweet Home, Sethe finds, to her dismay and astonishment, that the violent events on the slave plantation have no place in her memory, replaced, as they are, by a pastoral vision of Sweet Home:

Nothing else would be in her mind. . . . Nothing. Just the breeze cooling her face as she rushed toward water. . . . and suddenly there was Sweet Home rolling, rolling, rolling out before her eyes,

and although there was not a leaf on that farm that did not make
her want to scream, it rolled itself out before her in shameless
beauty. . . . Boys hanging from the most beautiful sycamores in the
world. It shamed her – remembering the wonderful soughing trees
rather than the boys. Try as she might to make it otherwise, the
sycamores beat out the children every time and she could not
forgive her memory for that. (p. 6)

The problem is not, as we later discover, that Sethe beautifies the
pains that she herself does not experience. Even the sign of her own
pain presents itself to Sethe in 'shameless beauty': she cannot help
repeating a white girl's vividly beautiful description of the lash marks
on her back. 'I've never seen [the scar] and never will', Sethe tells Paul
D, 'But that's what she said it looked like. A chokecherry tree. Trunk,
branches, and even leaves. Tiny little chokecherry leaves' (p. 16). Even
Sethe's mother-in-law, Baby Suggs, arrives at a similar, aesthetically
charged description of the wound when she observes 'Roses of blood
blossom[ing] in the blanket covering Sethe's shoulders'. But Baby
Suggs 'hid her mouth with her hand' (p. 93), as if to suggest that she,
unlike Sethe, cannot find 'shameless beauty' in this sight. And Paul D,
taken in at first by Sethe's metaphorical description of her scar, soon
rejects that description. The mark, he decides, is 'in fact a revolting
clump of scars. Not a tree, as she said. Maybe shaped like one, but
nothing like any tree he knew because trees were inviting; things you
could trust and be near; talk to if you wanted to as he frequently did
since way back' (p. 21). The novel, in fact, quickly chastises its own
impulse to beautify pain. Even momentary attempts to recuperate a
violent past for the sake of transcendence are met with the implied
accusation that such interpretive gestures occlude the horrific
moments of slavery.

Likewise, the novel raises the possibility of communicating pain
only to mock that attempt. In a Baldwinian moment Sethe suggests
that pain can, in fact, be articulated, and that the effort to communicate
pain can heal rifts between individuals. To acknowledge and examine
pain, as Baldwin implies – as well as to convey that pain – might
rescue these people from what Baldwin calls the 'limbo' of their failed
lives. Such, at least, is Sethe's feeling when she voices a hope for her
murdered child's return: 'if she'd only come, I could make it clear to
her' (p. 4). But this opening announcement – that the novel will
dramatize the communication of pain – is belied repeatedly by the
dizzying effects of the narrative. Pain communicates nothing if not its
own incommunicability.

Not only is pain ineffable, but, as Sethe should know, the experience of vivid pain dismantles language itself, so that pain results in

the impossibility of any intelligible utterance. After Sethe sees the body of her dead mother, lynched and burned, her language breaks down and remains incapacitated for a number of years: 'Stuttered after that. Didn't stop it till I saw Halle' (p.201). One might argue that Sethe stutters still – indeed, that the novel itself stutters in its [. . .] struggle to render pain linguistically. Sethe's own attempt to communicate her pain to Paul D mirrors the larger narrative, made 'recognizable but undecipherable' (p.199) to those who have not participated in the particular pain being uttered:

> It made him dizzy. At first he thought it was her spinning. Circling him the way she was circling the subject. Round and round, never changing direction, which might have helped his head. Then he thought, No, it's the sound of her voice; it's too near. Each turn she made was at least three yards from where he sat, but listening to her was like having a child whisper into your ear so close you could feel its lips form the words you couldn't make out because they were too close. He caught only pieces of what she said. (p.161)

Sethe tells her tale because she's convinced that 'the words [in the newspaper] she did not understand hadn't any more power than she had to explain' (p.161). But in fact her own word, unsupported by the authority of the newspaper, is pallidly impotent: 'Sethe knew that the circle she was making around the room, him, the subject would remain one. That she could never close in, pin it down for anybody who had to ask. If they didn't get it right off – she could never explain' (p.163). Although Paul D cannot read words, he understands the language of newspapers, a language whose dangerous conventions carry a force for him that Sethe's own words cannot:

> there was no way in hell a black face could appear in a newspaper if the story was about something anybody wanted to hear. A whip of fear broke through the heart chambers as soon as you saw a Negro's face in a paper, since the face was not there because the person had a healthy baby, or outran a street mob. Nor was it there because the person had been killed, or maimed or caught or burned or jailed or whipped or evicted or stomped or raped or cheated, since that could hardly qualify as news in a newspaper. It would have to be something out of the ordinary – something whitepeople would find interesting, truly different, worth a few minutes of teeth sucking if not gasps. (pp.155–56)

If the spoken word of individual experience offers an alternative center of meaning, Paul D nonetheless refuses that alternative in favor of an apparently more objective account: rightly or wrongly, Sethe has already been judged by the community of whitepeople and nothing she tells Paul D can commute that judgment. Having heard Sethe's story and accepted the newspaper's unreadable 'signs' rather than Sethe's own account, Paul D passes his own judgment and leaves.

Beloved challenges the romantic notion of beautiful, communicable, and humanizing pain by calling attention to the role of pain in unmaking language – not just the language of pain, but any language whatsoever. But if pain cannot be clearly conveyed, can it at least be examined privately, in order to validate the self to itself? If not publicly utterable, can suffering be comprehended and contemplated? The novel suggests a vexed relation between memory and desire, an interaction that makes contemplation all but impossible. When Stamp Paid attempts to tell Paul D of Sethe's violent past – to tell the very story she can render only in vertiginous language – he falters at the sight of Paul D's desire for an uncomplicated past. The problem for Stamp Paid – who had been present at the event – is not how to tell the story to Paul D, but finally, and more unsettlingly, how to remember it at all: 'Stamp looked into Paul D's eyes and the sweet conviction in them almost made him wonder if it had happened at all, eighteen years ago, that while he and Baby Suggs were looking the wrong way, a pretty little slavegirl had recognized a hat, and split to the woodshed to kill her children' (p. 158). In the blues tradition, Sethe's call and Paul D's response would lead to a dialogue of shared and transcended pain. But here, the anticipated response not only silences any articulation of pain but also dissolves the memory bearing these blues. If desire alters once vivid memories here, at other times it is unable to keep memory at bay. When Paul D calls attention to the inaccuracy of language, reminding Sethe that Sweet Home 'wasn't sweet and it sure wasn't home', Sethe answers, 'But it's where we were. . . . Comes back whether we want it to or not' (p. 14). Sethe has already shown us that her memory is *not* accurate – that the 'Sweet Home' that returns unbidden to her imagination is not the Sweet Home she had occupied during slavery – and now, in announcing that memory competes with desire, she suggests the impossibility of contemplation as well. Contemplation, that is, demands a sequestered space, remote from the conflicted workings of desire and denial. In figuring her memory as a battleground between desire and 'factual' accuracy, Sethe calls attention to the futility of reflection. Not only is she unable to gain access to whatever painful events she has endured in the past, but her memory – far from healing and reordering the pain of her Sweet Home days – merely replicates the violence of that past.

The unmaking of language and memory, however, points to a more alarming unmaking of selfhood and signals Morrison's most radical revision of romantic, 'humanizing' accounts of pain. *Beloved* persistently asks its readers where selfhood is located and seems to imply that language and memory, already dissolved by pain, bear responsibility for constructions of self. As Paul D puzzles over the source and status of his manhood, he wonders whether it wasn't invented and destroyed in the language of white men:

> Was that it? Is that where the manhood lay? In the naming done by a whiteman who was supposed to know? Who gave them the privilege not of working but of deciding how to? No. In their relationship with Garner was true metal: they were believed and trusted, but most of all they were listened to. (p. 125)

Manhood is constituted, Paul D concludes, not in language but in the 'metal' of reality; language merely represents that metal. But after Garner's death and schoolteacher's arrival at Sweet Home, Paul D learns differently. After all, as schoolteacher makes clear, 'definitions belonged to the definers – not the defined' (p. 190). Only when Paul D arrives at Sethe's home and cannot help being seduced by a young girl does he begin to doubt the metal of his manhood: 'If schoolteacher was right it explained how he had come to be a rag doll – picked up and put back down anywhere any time by a girl young enough to be his daughter. Fucking her when he was convinced he didn't want to' (p. 126). His inability to resist this young girl drives him to interrogate the process whereby he inherited his 'manhood', and finally to doubt the very metal of that manhood:

> Now . . . he wondered how much difference there really was between before schoolteacher and after. Garner called and announced them men – but only on Sweet Home, and by his leave. Was he naming what he saw or creating what he did not? . . . It troubled him that, concerning his own manhood, he could not satisfy himself on that point. Oh, he did manly things, but was that Garner's gift or his own will? . . . Did a whiteman saying it make it so? (p. 220)

Paul D discovers, then, that his identity is produced in the perceptions of others and rendered 'real' to him through linguistic mechanisms – a slaveholder's descriptions, definitions, and boasts about his slaves. If his manhood seemed more stable and authentic when he was owned by the fair-minded Garner, that very stability was a fiction produced by consistent linguistic references to manhood. He only comes to doubt his manhood when those consistent signs are supplanted by a different rendering of the slave self. 'Suppose Garner woke up one morning and changed his mind?' Paul D wonders, 'Took the word away' (p.220). The self, he comes to understand, is located in the word, so that when that word changes, so, too, does identity.

Can freedom replace that instability with consistency and restore the fiction of autonomous selfhood? Baby Suggs, at one time a convincing advocate of self-reliance, learns the futility and slipperiness of such fictions. Just released from slavery and become a self-ordained preacher, she speaks for an almost Emersonian belief in the self: 'She told them that the only grace they could have was the grace they could imagine. That if they could not see it, they would not have it' (p.88).[27] But self-reliance requires a self, and Baby Suggs soon discovers that imagination is impossible without this self, which she has never been granted:

> the sadness was at her center, the desolated center where the self that was no self made its home. Sad as it was that she did not know where her children were buried or what they looked like if alive, fact was she knew more about them than she knew about herself, having never had the map to discover what she was like. (p.140)

Baby Suggs's slippery language betrays the unlocatable status of selfhood: because she cannot decide whether hers is a self, no self, or an undiscoverable self, she cannot accurately say that she has a self at all, or if self can exist without being identified or identifiable. Would she recognize her children if she saw them? Would she recognize her *own* self if she could see it? If she can neither see nor recognize her own interiority, how does she know she is a self at all? Baby Suggs's skepticism about her own selfhood presages the failure of her doctrine of self-reliance.[28] Denver tells the story of Baby Suggs's disillusionment, of 'how she made a mistake. That what she thought about what the heart and the body could do was wrong. The whitepeople came anyway. In her yard. She had done everything right and they came in her yard anyway' (p.209). Like Paul D, seduced against his will by a young girl, Baby Suggs discovers that even the 'grace [she] could imagine' is impossible because her 'desolated center' is no self at all. The violence of slavery, like the changing linguistic code at Sweet Home, has unmade her fiction of autonomous selfhood.

Having discovered the process whereby self is unmade, are we to trust the remaking of self? Morrison offers us the possibility of recuperating the self when, near the close of the novel, Denver discovers herself in her family's dependence on her:

> Somebody had to be saved, but unless Denver got work, there would be no one to save, no one to come home to, and no Denver

either. It was a new thought, having a self to look out for and preserve. And it might not have occurred to her if she hadn't met
Nelson Lord leaving his grandmother's house as Denver entered it
to pay a thank you for half a pie. All he did was smile and say,
'Take care of yourself, Denver,' but she heard it as though it were
what language was made for. The last time he spoke to her his
words blocked up her ears. Now they opened her mind. (p. 252)

Nelson's words 'opened her mind': how are we to read this passage?
Do Nelson's words, as Denver believes, call attention to a self that had
been present all along, the mere idea of which 'might not have
occurred to her'? Does his language represent the 'metal' of selfhood, a
real presence to which Denver had previously been blind? Or should
we rather believe, to modify Paul D's insight, that a young boy's
'saying it makes it so'? In Denver's experience we see the real
significance behind Paul D's: the power of self-definition does indeed
reside with the definers, not the defined, and the definers are not necessarily white folks. As Denver fails to recognize, but the novel seems
to insist, identity is located in the perceptions and definitions of anyone or anything external to the self. Even without language or cultural
power, the rooster named Mister fills the role of definer, as Paul D
discovers:

'He sat right there on the tub looking at me. I swear he smiled. My
head was full of what I'd seen of Halle a while back. I wasn't even
thinking about the bit. Just Halle and before him Sixo, but when I
saw Mister I knew it was me too. . . . I was something else and that
something was less than a chicken sitting in the sun on a tub.'
(p. 72)[29]

In seeing a 'free' rooster smile at him, Paul D discovers his own con-
trasting enslavement and arrives at a definition of himself imposed by
his internalization of the rooster's gaze. 'Mister was allowed to be and
stay what he was', Paul D says. 'But I wasn't allowed to be and stay
what I was' (p. 72). Paul D resents not so much the particular definition of selfhood imposed by the rooster and the master but, more
precisely, the transient, shifting definitions of self that depend upon
the gaze of his audience: 'When he looks at himself through Garner's
eyes, he sees one thing. Through Sixo's, another. One makes him feel
righteous. One makes him feel ashamed' (p. 267). Though we might
be tempted to believe in either Paul D's 'righteous' or Denver's newly
discovered self, the novel cautions against such a reading. Identity,
constructed according to one's audience, is liable to shift as soon as the
audience changes. The self remade in admiration and kindness,

though more palatable, is no more real than the self made in violence, and one can only believe in it at the peril of forgetting how easily self is made and unmade. [. . .]

Indeed, Paul D attempts to protect a fictional self from the violent remaking of this (perhaps sympathetic) audience. For this reason, he cuts short his account of Mister, even though Sethe, victim to pains of her own, has offered a nonjudgmental hearing. 'Saying more might push them both to a place they couldn't get back from. He would keep the rest where it belonged: in that tobacco tin buried in his chest where a red heart used to be. Its lid rusted shut' (pp. 72–73).

If he has no heart, Paul D implies, he at least has a heartless self that needs protecting, a self composed of unspeakable memories: 'Alfred, Georgia, Sixo, schoolteacher, Halle, his brothers, Sethe, Mister, the taste of iron, the sight of butter, the smell of hickory, note-book paper' (p. 113). But when, in a lonely moment, 'His tobacco tin, blown open, spilled contents that floated freely and made him their play and prey' (p. 218), the contents of the tin are revealed to be nothing but a metaphor for what Baby Suggs has called 'the self that was no self'. The tin opens, finally, to release not a self but merely a scattering of dry tobacco leaves (p. 218). To protect the self from its audience, we learn, is to cause the disintegration of that self.

What, then, can we say about pain? Sethe wants to grant a reality to her painful memories, if only to invest them with meaning:

> If a house burns down, it's gone, but the place – the picture of it – stays, and not just in my rememory, but out there, in the world. What I remember is a picture floating around out there outside my head. I mean, even if I don't think it, even if I die, the picture of what I did, or knew, or saw is still out there. Right in the place where it happened.
> . . . Someday you be walking down the road and you hear something or see something going on. So clear. And you think it's you thinking it up. A thought picture. But no. It's when you bump into a rememory that belongs to somebody else. (p. 36)

If selfhood is rendered a fiction, Sethe wants to believe, at least the experience of suffering can be invested with meaning and made substantial. Sethe offers this reading of pain as an alternative to romanticism, as a means of making pain mean something, as Emerson says, 'to court suffering, in the hope that here at least we shall find reality, sharp peaks and edges of truth'.[30] If the self is neither real nor permanent, perhaps the pains endured by that 'self' can be experienced empirically. If language cannot render the experience of suffering, at least, Sethe believes, that experience can continue to occupy physical space in the world, so that a stranger may 'bump into a rememory that belongs to somebody else'.

Sethe's reified memory merely highlights the tenuous status of selfhood: her memory is more real, more present and lasting, than the agent of that memory. Likewise, the reified desire embodied by Beloved points to the fictionality of subjectivities. The question posed by the novel's conclusion is not why Beloved disappears, but rather how anything short of disappearance could be possible for an individual who loses her desirability. Beloved, it must be noted, appears only after Sethe expresses a desire for the return of her dead child. 'But if she'd only come', Sethe says, 'I could make it clear to her' (p.4). Beloved's disappearance only literalizes what happens to all selves: constructed in terms of audience, she can exist only as long as her audience chooses to acknowledge her:

> Everybody knew what she was called, but nobody anywhere knew her name. Disremembered and unaccounted for, she cannot be lost because no one is looking for her, and even if they were, how can they call her if they don't know her name? Although she has claim, she is not claimed. In the place where long grass opens, the girl who waited to be loved and cry shame erupts into her separate parts, to make it easy for the chewing laughter to swallow her all away. (p.274)

Like the 'self that was no self' until constituted in language and acknowledged by an audience, this 'self' disappears when the people among whom she lived no longer look for her or call her name. If the people in this community enjoy any agency over their lives, that agency consists of the ability to choose their own point of focus, to look away when desire dissipates or fear becomes too oppressive. Beloved's literal, corporeal disappearance prefigures her disappearance from memory – the vehicle of the real, according to Sethe:

> They forgot her like a bad dream. After they made up their tales, shaped and decorated them, those that saw her that day on the porch quickly and deliberately forgot her. It took longer for those who had spoken to her, fallen in love with her, to forget, until they realized they couldn't remember or repeat a single thing she said, and began to believe that, other than what they themselves were thinking, she hadn't said anything at all. So, in the end, they forgot her too. (p.274)

Beloved, I would argue, is a model for all selves: if she is ghostly and ephemeral, she only literalizes what occurs to all other characters in

Morrison's novel. They, like Beloved, exist at the pleasure of other selves. Once one takes the word away, selfhood inevitably vanishes. The definers are not simply slaveholders and schoolteachers, but anyone who threatens individual autonomy by including the individual in his or her language and gaze. And to revoke name and gaze, further, is to abolish the self.

Pain, finally, cannot make us real: if empirical reality is reserved for (re)memory and desire, it can, like the acknowledgment of a self's existence, be revoked at any time. The most pain can do, as the novel suggests, is call attention to the violent and necessary process whereby self is constructed by other. If we choose to seize on more attractive versions of self and believe them to be 'real' – or, in the romantic account, 'fully human' – we take the dangerous risk, in Emerson's words, of 'court[ing] suffering' in order to verify our humanity. Of course, healthy-minded denials of pain pose an opposite threat to our conceptions of history, and perhaps the [romantic and blues] traditions [. . .] have gained such ground precisely as a corrective to healthy-mindedness. However, if we wish to persist in our belief that pain does make us fully human, we need to reevaluate our definition of 'human'. Perhaps here we find Morrison's most radical reevaluation of Baldwin and other voices from the blues heritage. To be human, *Beloved* suggests, is no different from being ghostly: to be human means to be as likely spectral as substantial, fictional as real, and to be ontologically as well as emotionally contingent on one's audience, to occupy an ever shifting identity. □

CHAPTER FIVE

'It's Not Over Just Because It Stops': Post-colonialism, Psychoanalysis, History

■ The accounts of race and nation that were implicated in the institution of slavery have not disappeared in a grand narrative which charts emancipation. On the contrary, the metaphors and categories intrinsic to the post-enlightenment imagination, and which shaped the slavery debate, are present in our own thought. □

Isobel Armstrong

■ To articulate the past historically does not mean to recognise it "the way it really was". It means to seize hold of a memory as it flashes up in a moment of danger. □

Walter Benjamin[1]

THE TWO extracts that make up this final chapter illustrate approaches to *Beloved* that, on the face of it at least, appear to be quite different from one another. The first – fairly long – extract is taken from Sally Keenan's '"Four Hundred Years of Silence": Myth, History, and Motherhood in Toni Morrison's *Beloved*', itself a lengthy essay published in *Recasting the World: Writing after Colonialism*, edited by Jonathan White in 1993. Comparable in some respects to Deborah Horvitz's reading of *Beloved*, Keenan's approach is distinctive for the manner in which it locates Morrison's novel in an overtly post-colonial context. The second extract is much briefer but at the same time much more theoretically dense and consists of the second and fourth sections of Peter Nicholls's 'The Belated Postmodern: History, Phantoms, and Toni Morrison', an essay that uses psychoanalytic theory to read both *Beloved* and, in its fifth and final section, Morrison's *Jazz* (1992). This piece is to be found in *Psychoanalytic Criticism: A Reader*, edited by Sue Vice in 1996, for which it was specially commissioned. (The first four sections of the essay also appeared, in the same year, in *A Practical Reader in Contemporary Literary Theory*, edited by Peter Brooker and Peter Widdowson.) Notwithstanding their differences of approach, however, both extracts concern themselves with the questions of history that *Beloved* raises and, as such, provide further perspectives on an issue that has been variously addressed in much of the critical material covered so far.

Despite the importance of the place that Morrison's text so clearly occupies in the theoretical reflections of post-colonial critics such as Paul Gilroy and Homi K. Bhabha,[2] Keenan's inclusion of *Beloved* under the rubric of the post-colonial is relatively unusual within criticism on the novel, though it has been usefully developed in readings of the text by Lynda Koolish and Eleni Coundouriotis.[3] Indeed, as Keenan herself begins by pointing out, it is not just *Beloved* that remains largely under-theorised by post-colonial critics, but African-American (as well as Native American) writing as such. To use Keenan's own word, this situation is, historically speaking, 'curious': even as America came into being as a post-colonial nation by liberating itself from British rule in 1776, it was constituted out of and remained spectacularly implicated in forms of colonial oppression – from the attempted genocide of indigenous peoples to the enslavement of Africans – which, *inter alia*, continue to exert their effects today. This point is driven home by Ruth Frankenberg and Lata Mani in a powerful vision of America past and present:

■ USA: Here, the term "postcolonial" sticks in our throats. White settler colony, multiracial society. Colonization of Native Americans, Africans imported as slaves, Mexicans incorporated by a border moving south, Asians imported and migrating to labour, white Europeans migrating to labour. US imperialist foreign policy brings new immigrants who are "here because the US was/is there", among them Central Americans, Filipinos, Vietnamese and Cambodians . . . the serious calling into question of white/Western dominance by the groundswell of movements of resistance, and the emergence of struggles for collective self-determination most frequently articulated in nationalist terms.[4] □

Yet if the 'post' in 'post-colonial', as applied to America (as elsewhere) is 'prematurely celebratory', in Anne McClintock's phrase,[5] a post-colonial approach to *Beloved* is nonetheless illuminating, enabling Keenan, as it does, to show how the question of history in Morrison's text stretches beyond the specificities of slave-oppression in America and out towards the African diaspora itself. In the course of making this argument, Keenan also adopts a feminist perspective, foregrounding gender issues and the role of mother-daughter relations in the novel, in particular. Thus the linkages and sunderings of Sethe's relation to Beloved provide an analogy for the relation of African-Americans to a history that has been radically fractured by the Middle Passage. Equally, however, Keenan is careful to stress that the metonymic dimensions of the mother/daughter relation must not be effaced, for it is precisely the bodily proximities and emotional connections between mother and daughter that slavery sought to negate. The act of breaking them (through infanticide) becomes the anguished ground of black maternal resistance.

■ Until recently studies of postcolonial and Third World literatures have not customarily addressed themselves to the writing of Native or African Americans.[6] On reflection this must appear surprising, given the extreme forms of 'colonialist' subjection which have marked their respective histories: genocide and slavery at the hands of European imperialist powers. This lack of attention can be explained in part by the complex character of the United States's emergence as a nation, in which it played the role both of the colonized, fighting a war of independence from European control, as well as that of the colonizer of an indigenous population and of African slaves. That the inclusion of Native and African American histories in postcolonial discourse has not been axiomatic in the past signals a failure to address the processes of colonization on which the foundation of the United States rests. That it is a postcolonial society can no longer be in question. Furthermore, in the United States, as elsewhere, the *post-* of that term should not be regarded as a sign that the processes of colonialism have ended; rather, their legacy continues to exist as a lived reality for many citizens.

The writing of African American women, which has been so prolific over the last two decades, has done much to highlight the postcolonial condition of the contemporary United States. Moreover, this body of writing has made a significant contribution to the revisioning of North American history, a recasting of our understanding of the past which resonates beyond the borders of that continent. Toni Morrison's *Beloved* provides an exemplary instance of this revision.

When *Beloved* won the Pulitzer Prize in 1988 Morrison's work finally received the recognition by the literary establishment which many writers and critics in the African American community believed it had long deserved.[7] Was this a sign that black American women writers had finally made the move from the margins to the center of North American cultural and intellectual life which had been promised by the success of Alice Walker's *Color Purple* five or so years before? Or are Morrison and Walker merely token figures used by the literary/publishing establishment to provide not only a highly profitable product but also the illusion that the publishing world in the United States does not still exercise discrimination against the work of large numbers of writers from the so-called margins of North American culture? I suspect that Morrison herself, although no doubt pleased with the accolade of a Pulitzer Prize, might agree that there is an element of tokenism here, having described the sense of responsibility she feels as an editor in a New York publishing house who often finds herself insisting on the acceptance of work by black writers, against a belief that there isn't room in the catalog for more than one or two. But then Morrison, despite her success, would not agree that she has moved from the margins to the center of cultural life, for, as she has said, 'There's nothing remotely marginal about being a black woman.'[8] Such an assertion, I believe, lies embedded in her novel's dramatic evocation of what it might have meant to be both a slave and a mother.

Even before winning the literary establishment's most prestigious prize, *Beloved* had assumed a central place within current writing by African Americans which insists on an examination of U.S. culture and history, one that takes account of the processes of 'internal colonization'.[9] I believe, however, that Morrison's novel can also be read as contributing in a wider sense to contemporary postcolonial discourse, as it offers a perspective on African American history and literature which refuses to place its origins in the institution of slavery but, instead, situates that history within the larger context of the African diaspora. It is significant too that the novel has rapidly become established in the academic curriculum at the very moment that a debate is raging concerning the traditional canon of literature studies in U.S. universities and the value of Western culture foundation courses for undergraduates is coming under attack.[10]

In this essay I want to examine what I consider to be both timely and different about Morrison's *Beloved* – that is, its placing of the issue of motherhood and female resistance to slavery at the heart of an exploration of the processes of memory, recovery, and representation of African American history and the dilemma that has long faced African Americans of finding a language to speak and write about their past. Morrison's narrative, I will argue, exposes with painful clarity that the ambiguities of connection and separation between the slave mother and child bear some correlation with the contradictions that mark the relationship of African Americans to their history. If, in psychoanalytical terms, the mother as source, or origin, is problematic and irrecoverable, so too African Americans, perhaps above all peoples, have learned through their particularly fractured past that history is problematic and often irrecoverable. I do not wish to suggest that the idea of motherhood can function as some kind of all-embracing metaphor for that history – far from it – but that the mythologizing that black women as mothers have been subjected to is a crucial part of the mythologizing of African American history as a whole, whether that be the enabling myths that have helped black culture to survive or the disenabling mythologies imposed by white culture and threatening to that survival. If feminist writing and postcolonial writing are said to 'have strong parallels',[11] Morrison's text delineates an area in which they intersect. At the same time *Beloved* extends the limits of previous histories and autobiographical writings on slavery through its exploration of the ways subjectivity might be established and inscribed by those who have been denied its possibility.

At the opening of *Beloved* Baby Suggs, the grandmother of an ex-slave family, has finally laid down the burden of her 'intolerable' life and retired to bed. 'Suspended between the nastiness of life and the meanness of the dead, she couldn't get interested in leaving life or living it' (pp. 3–4). It is clear in these opening pages that all the inhab-itants of her home at 124 Bluestone Road are also suspended between the past and the present, the living and the dead, the presence of the latter most vociferously signified by the baby ghost who haunts the house, furious 'at having its throat cut' (p. 5) before it was two years old. The ghost has chased off Baby Suggs's grandsons, and the memory of the manner of its death has cut the family off from their community of freed and former slaves.

Morrison's narrative pivots around the contradiction implied in living with impossible memories, the need to remember and tell and the desire to forget, memories with an inexhaustible and monstrous power to erupt and overwhelm the mind but which must somehow be laid aside if life is to continue; it is a life that is structured around each 'day's serious work of beating back the past' (p. 73). Denver, however, the last living child remaining in the family, born outside slavery while the mother, Sethe, was on her fugitive's flight to freedom, desires to know 'all what happened', the story of the past having been told and retold in part but always cut off at a point in the narrative 'beyond which [her mother] would not go' (pp. 36, 37). Her sister, the baby ghost, Beloved, represents the insistent claims of that forbidden or hidden part of the family's history, and Beloved, as both text and figure in the text, becomes in the course of the narrative a complex metaphor for black America's relationship with its enslaved past. If Beloved's spectral return into the slave family represents within the narrative the eruption of that which has lived on as memory but has remained unspoken, the text, *Beloved*, signals a current discursive renegotiation with their history by African Americans which amounts to a contestation of the ways that past has been erased by or subsumed within the historical discourse of the hegemonic culture. The writer

Sherley Anne Williams says, 'Afro-Americans, having survived by word of mouth – and made of that process a high art – remain at the mercy of literature and writing; often these have betrayed us.'[12] It has become an imperative for black Americans in the post-civil rights period of the 1970s and 1980s to write their own histories, in order to negotiate that difficult relation between past and present, a necessity of the postcolonial present that Morrison's ex-slave protagonists are depicted as negotiating in the colonial past. [. . .]

I wish to suggest that the text functions on an axis that is simultaneously metaphoric and metonymic. Recent literary criticism has picked up on the challenges put forward by both Jacques Derrida and Paul de Man to the Western tradition of privileging metaphor over metonymy as the trope 'revealing unexpected truth'.[13] Donna Stanton, for instance, has critiqued the maternal metaphors in the feminist texts of Julia Kristeva, Hélène Cixous, and Luce Irigaray, suggesting that the totalizing tendency of this metaphorization could be replaced by exploring the maternal via metonymy, which, because of its associations with contiguity, is context bound and therefore exposes specific cultural values, prejudices, and limitations.[14] Homi Bhabha also argues that metonymy is a preferable trope through which to read postcolonial literatures because, unlike metaphor, which tends to universalize and thus to ignore cultural specificity, metonymy can be employed to symptomatize the social, cultural, and political forces that traverse those texts.[15]

I believe, however, that *Beloved* is a text that privileges neither the one nor the other but, rather, reveals an interrelation of both these tropes. Morrison creates a subjective language of enslavement which articulates the metonymic relation between the bodies of mothers and daughters which the institution of slavery would deny. Her text, however, does not simply rest with the reversal of a rhetorical trope, and it does not settle for a privileging of the reconnection of mother and daughter in the history of slavery but, instead, echoes out into the stories of all slaves, male as well as female. By focusing her narrative of slavery on motherhood, she is able to delineate the particular interrelation between maternity and the history of African Americans and to undo the stereotypical mythologizing of black women's identities. At the same time the struggles of her protagonists to find a way to speak about their past, and thus to confront its horror, function metaphorically to suggest the historical dilemma of African Americans of finding a means to write their own history outside the rhetoric and disenabling mythologies of the hegemonic culture.

Beloved is a story that revolves around contradiction: a story of an infanticide motivated by the mother's fierce love, a story that is itself about a preoccupation with storytelling. Moreover, it is not just one story but many, involving the personal histories of the protagonists, which, in the telling, become representative of the history and culture of the tribe, stories that bind the group together but which also have a violent potential to destroy those bonds. These contradictions are textually embodied in the figure of the baby Denver, who takes in her mother's milk along with her sister's blood. An analogy between feeding and storytelling is drawn repeatedly throughout the narrative, suggesting that the culture's history and the myths created out of it are its sustenance, its means of survival, especially since that history is constantly under threat of erasure.

Out of these many stories I want to focus on three that are bound into one. They are all the mother's story, but two of them are also the daughters': there is the story of Sethe's life at Sweet Home, the fragile creation of the small slave community of one woman and five men, and its catastrophic conclusion; then there is the story of the escape, which is also the story of Denver's birth, and Sethe's frantic journey to get her breast milk to the older baby, Beloved; finally, there is the story of Beloved's death and the mystery of her return, the fearful, locked-away story around which the narrative circles and which Paul D's return releases. But this is also ultimately the story of Denver's survival. Each story unfolds in fragments of narration, picked up by different narrative voices, a sign that each is too painful to be delivered whole, as Sethe puts it, 'like a tender place in a corner of her mouth that the bit left' (p.58), but also emblematic of the fractured nature of that past.

The second story, Sethe's escape and Denver's birth, is the first to be spoken of, as Sethe relates it to Paul D while she rolls out dough for bread: 'I was pregnant with Denver but I had milk for my baby girl. ... All I knew was I had to get my milk to my baby girl. Nobody was going to nurse her like me' (p.16). But it is also Denver's story, the friendly, magical story of her birth, of the white woman, Amy Denver, who helped her fugitive mother in labor and whom she was named after. It is the story her imagination is ever hungry for: 'Denver hated the stories her mother told that did not concern herself, which is why Amy was all she ever asked about. The rest was a gleaming, powerful world made more so by Denver's absence from it' (p.62). The gleaming powerful world consists, in fact, of the other two stories that frame this one, the story that precedes it, the violent ending of Sweet Home life, and the one that followed it, the killing of Beloved, the story that Denver literally turns deaf to when she first hears it.

If the story of escape and birth is the one around which Denver exclusively binds her identity, it is also the story she uses to bind to herself the miraculously returned sister, Beloved: 'She swallowed twice to prepare for the telling, to construct out of the strings she had heard all her life a net to hold Beloved' (p. 76). As she responds to Beloved's plea to 'Tell me how Sethe made you in the boat' (p. 76), the naive metaphor of making the child is echoed in the way the story is molded by Denver's telling and Beloved's listening:

> Denver was seeing it now and feeling it – through Beloved. Feeling how it must have felt to her mother. Seeing how it must have looked. . . . she anticipated the questions by giving blood to the scraps her mother and grandmother had told her – and a heart-beat. The monologue became, in fact, a duet as they lay down together, Denver nursing Beloved's interest like a lover whose pleasure was to overfeed the loved. . . . Denver spoke, Beloved listened, and the two did the best they could to create what really happened, how it really was, something only Sethe knew because she alone had the mind for it and the time afterward to shape it: the quality of Amy's voice, her breath like burning wood. (p. 78)

In recreating the story together, the daughters produce a subjective discourse for the mother as pregnant fugitive; the image of giving lifeblood and a heartbeat to the story is the trope whereby that subjectivity is actualized, just as the blood and heartbeat of the unborn baby pumps inside the mother's womb and the milk destined for the other baby seeps from her breasts. The storytelling process mimicked here takes on the resonance of mythmaking. It shifts from a monologue to a duet, from the individual to the communal; it is represented as mythic story in the process of becoming, Denver lovingly embellishing its details as she tells it, continuous, never complete, always capable of repetition and expansion. The mythic quality exists in its meaning as well as in its telling, for it is a heroic story of female liberation from slavery: the mother's death-defying flight is a venture not only to ensure her own survival but also that of the daughter inside her and the one who was sent ahead. And it images the absolute identification of the three, mother and two daughters, an identification figured narratively in the plot and figuratively and literally in the mother's body, one baby inside and nipples seeping milk for the other.

Morrison here, I suspect, defies the limits of empirical history. Deborah Gray White points out that some of the reasons why women were underrepresented among fugitive slaves had to do with child-bearing. Runaways were mostly between the ages of sixteen and thirty-five, and most slave women of this age were pregnant, nursing, or had children, and few would leave without them.[16] But the very extraordinariness of Morrison's tale is part of its compelling and mythic power; in combining in one event both the woman slave's fierce desire for freedom and the fierce devotion to her children, she figures something that the historiography has largely been unable to represent.

The significance of the story, however, resonates beyond heroic myth. As the only story of the past Denver wants to hear and as the story of her own birthing, it is synonymous with her identity: she is this story. But it is a story about a moment of transition, between the there of slavery and the here of freedom, between the past and the future. Especially, as I have indicated, it exists between one barely speakable moment of violence and another that is utterly unspeakable. Denver and the mythic story of liberation are locked in by two moments of pain which cannot be purged, because to purge them would be to kill off the only precious thing that remains, the trace of what has been lost, the child returned from the dead. Thus, the heroic myth of liberation can ultimately be seen to entrap, a trap both of history and of personal identity. As the narrative unfolds, it becomes clear that the mother and daughters are locked together in a circular narrative from which the heroic myth is not sufficient to liberate them.

When Denver does ask for more of the story of the past – 'You never told me all what happened. Just that they whipped you and you run off, pregnant. With me' – the answer is: 'Nothing to tell except schoolteacher' (p. 36), and Sethe provides a glimpse of life turned sour at Sweet Home after Garner dies and schoolteacher, the brother-in-law, the small, polite man with book learning takes over. 'He liked the ink I made. . . . he preferred how I mixed it and it was important to him because at night he sat down to write in his book' (p. 37). This is the book, she is to discover later, in which he records the 'animal' and 'human' characteristics of his slaves; it contains the lessons in slave 'nature' and 'behavior' which he passes on to his nephews. It is the sudden realization of what these lessons signify, for which Garner's 'soft' treatment had not prepared them, which prompts Sethe to agree to the escape plan, her recognition of what slavery really meant to the slave owners, that is, the absolute appropriation of the slave, body and mind, which renders him or her inert matter on which the master writes his own script.

It is through this, the story of the ink that Sethe made with her own hands and her discovery of its purpose, that Morrison weaves into her text the problematic relation of the slave to the master's tools: reading and writing and the way that learning was used to inscribe its own economy on the body of the slave mother. Barbara Omolade writes that to the master the slave woman was 'a fragmented commodity':

> Her head and her heart were separated from her back and her hands and divided from her womb and vagina. Her back and muscle were pressed into field labor where she was forced to work

with men and work like men. Her hands were demanded to nurse and nurture the white man and his family. . . . Her vagina, used for his sexual pleasure, was the gateway to the womb, which was his place of capital investment – the capital investment being the sex act and the resulting child the accumulated surplus, worth money on the slave market.

The totalitarian system of slavery extended itself into the very place that was inviolable and sacred to both African and European societies – the sanctity of the woman's body and motherhood within the institution of marriage.[17]

Morrison represents this dissection of the woman's body both in schoolteacher's 'book learning' (p.36) and in the punishment his nephews give Sethe after the first attempt to escape: they milk her like a cow, taking away her baby's milk. Then they whip her on the back while her stomach is placed in a pit to protect the fetus. Jacqueline Jones writes that this punishment was commonly used against pregnant and nursing slave mothers and adds, 'Slave women's roles as workers and as childbearers came together in these trenches, these graves for the living, in southern cottonfields.'[18] After the whipping Sethe bears on her back a scar so deep and elaborate that it looks like a tree, which ensures that the slave owner's inscription of her identity is not only held in her 'rebellious brain' (p.70), which would not let her forget, but is also carved permanently into her flesh.

In this representation of the maternal body carved up (breasts for milk, back for whipping) and carved into, Morrison figures the reductive metonymy through which the institution of slavery signified slave women. Sethe's own definition of motherhood involves a rejection of that metonymic division and the construction of her own metonymic relation located in a conception of maternal responsibility and connection between the maternal body and the child's body: 'The best thing she was, was her children. Whites might dirty *her* all right, but not her best thing, her beautiful, magical best thing – the part of her that was clean. . . . And no one, nobody on this earth, would list her daughter's characteristics on the animal side of the paper' (p.251). Sethe's maternal subjectivity is figured in this defiant claim to her own definition of motherhood, motherhood being not a state she finds herself subjected to for someone else's economic advantage but, rather, the part of herself which exceeded the bounds of slavery, which refused its limits and thus her own means of self-inscription. The narrative makes clear, however, that this definition of a female self within slavery was not entirely a matter of choice, that is to say, that many slave women did not have the choice. Baby Suggs reminds Sethe that she is lucky even to have any children with her at all: 'Be thankful, why don't you? I had eight. Every one of them gone away from me. . . . My first-born. All I can remember of her is how she loved the burned bottom of bread. Can you beat that? Eight children and that's all I remember' (p. 5).

In the community of former slaves there is Ella, the root woman, who spent her puberty locked in a house and shared by a father and son, whom she called 'the lowest yet'. 'Ella had been beaten every way but down. . . . She had delivered, but would not nurse, a hairy white thing, fathered by "the lowest yet"' (pp. 258–59). Ella's rejection of enforced motherhood is echoed in Sethe's faint memory of her own mother's life, a woman she hardly knew, the only sign of recognition she could recall being the brand in her flesh – a woman whose story stretches back to her capture in Africa and the horrors of the Middle Passage and who bore children to the crew on the ship and to other white men but 'threw them all away' (p. 62), keeping only Sethe, the child she conceived with a black man. So Ella and Sethe's mother did exercise a choice of sorts, one that provokes in Sethe a wave of anger and shame that she cannot quite comprehend. Thus, Sethe's definition of motherhood is a defiant answer to slavery's brutal destruction of maternal connection. Maternity is, therefore, not a fixed or naturalized category. Sethe's response is one extreme point in a range of possibilities in which mothering or the rejection of it becomes a register of female resistance to the condition of enslavement and the commodification of the female body. It is also a radical assertion of the bonds of the slave family and the bond between the slave mother and the father.

Despite this radical resistance, however, Sethe is haunted by the smell of the ink she made out of cherry gum and oak bark; it was the ink made with her hands which was used in schoolteacher's book to place her characteristics 'on the animal side of the paper'. Somehow the inscription of that ink cannot be erased but is, instead, engraved in the memory as well as on the page. This is Sethe's secret shame, her innocent complicity with the violence of schoolteacher's letter, his assumption of the power to name and to brutalize with that naming.

If Sethe's double act of flight and infanticide was her way of renaming herself, not animal but mother, for the other survivors – Paul D, Baby Suggs, and Stamp Paid – the question of identity and self-naming remains problematic. For Baby the only name she knows is the endearment her husband gave her, and she never acquired 'the map to discover what she was like' (p. 140). Stamp Paid, the name he gave himself, carried within it the sacrifice he had made in allowing his wife to become the mistress of his master's son, without killing either her or himself. And Paul D is haunted by his title, 'The last of the Sweet Home men', so named by Garner but unnamed and unmanned by schoolteacher with the bit he put in his mouth: 'Was that it? Is that where the manhood lay? In the naming done by a whiteman who was supposed to know? . . . It was schoolteacher who taught them otherwise. A truth that waved like a scarecrow in rye: they were only Sweet Home men at Sweet Home' (p.125).

But embedded in the stories of two who did not survive school-teacher's brutality, Sixo and Halle, there exist alternative responses to the violence of the slave owner's power to name. Sixo, the wild man, the Indian, 'Indigo with a flame-red tongue' (p.21), who danced alone at night among the trees 'to keep his bloodlines open' (p.25), the spiritual connection with his people, is in many respects a male counter-part to Sethe. Like her, he radically refuses the white man's definitions and rejects the master's tools; as the man most acutely aware of the white man's power to brutalize them, he stops speaking English and refuses to learn the master's numbers because 'it would change his mind' (p.208). But he is also a nurturing man who helps Sethe with her children, cooks potatoes for the other slaves, travels thirty miles overnight to see his woman, and is the one who provides the others with the knowledge of an escape route. Halle embodies a different response, as the one who learns to write and to count. However, he puts the master's knowledge to his own use: he buys his mother's free-dom, and his knowledge of the land ensures that his wife and children can escape.

In Halle's acceptance of the learning Garner offers him Morrison's text touches on the debate in literary criticism and historiography con-cerning the slave community's response to reading and writing. Hazel Carby points out that most contemporary literary critics regard the slave's acquisition of literacy, especially as it is figured in the auto-biographical slave narratives 'as a means of asserting humanity'. But she argues that historians of the WPA interview material suggest a different response to literacy among the slaves. In particular, she cites Arna Bontemps, who edited a collection of these interviews and wrote a historical novel about slavery, *Black Thunder*, in which it is clear that literacy was the slave's path to resistance and revolution and was regarded as such by many.[19] Sixo and Halle represent two possible revolutionary responses to enslavement on the part of the slave man; neither can be read as an assertion of their humanity, as that was never in question. Sixo's resistance is an assertion of his cultural difference and a selfhood marked as cultural (communal) connection; Halle's resistance is a means to find a way out of enslavement. And both, in their different ways, assert the possibility of a future for the enslaved beyond slavery.

The issue for Morrison's survivors is somewhat different. It is not so much whether or how the master's tools can be stolen from him in order to read and write one's way to freedom and self-inscription;

rather, it is a question of how to live with a past too terrible to remember, let alone to tell or record. The question that haunts the narrative is, how did the individual and the community of slaves deal with their own history? How, for instance, could they speak of their history without being forced to relive its horror and its indignities (in the case of Paul D), or how was it possible for those who refused that horror to persuade the others to accept the enormous price exacted by that refusal (in Sethe's case)? Paul D's story of the prison farm in Georgia is locked away in the little rusty tin that contains his lost heart; Sethe's story of infanticide, although comprehensible to herself, is locked away in her mind because it is unbearable for everyone else. The danger involved even in telling each other is suggested in Paul D's response when Sethe finally tells him her story; his response threatens to return them to the brutality they had escaped: '"What you did was wrong, Sethe. . . . You got two feet, Sethe, not four," he said, and right then a forest sprang up between them; trackless and quiet. . . . How fast he had moved from his shame to hers' (p. 165).

The difficulties of approaching Sethe's story of infanticide are replicated textually in Morrison's narration. Although hints of the story are woven through the narrative, it is not fully told until midway into the text, and what is more, it is first approached from the perspective of the slave catchers, schoolteacher and his nephews, the only moment in the text which is focused from their viewpoint. Thus, the first picture the reader receives of Sethe in the woodshed with the slaughtered baby is presented through the discourse of the slavers. The effect is one of shock, profound disturbance, but it enables the reader to register the distance between their perspective and that of the mother herself. But before Sethe tells the story herself it is filtered through the perspectives of the other witnesses, first Baby Suggs then Stamp Paid, emphasizing again and again the pain involved in its telling. When it is finally told by Sethe she too finds it difficult to express, because she cannot be sure that it will be understood:

> Sethe knew that the circle she was making around the room, him, the subject, would remain one. That she could never close in, pin it down for anybody who had to ask. If they didn't get it right off – she could never explain. Because the truth was simple. . . . Little hummingbirds stuck their needle beaks right through her headcloth into her hair and beat their wings. And if she thought anything, it was No. No. Nono. Nonono. Simple. She just flew. Collected every bit of life she had made, all the parts of her that were precious and fine and beautiful, and carried, pushed, dragged them through the veil, out, away, over there where no one could hurt them. (p. 163)

Why did Morrison choose this story of infanticide on which to base her novel, one might ask, particularly since the research of historians such as Eugene Genovese and Deborah Gray White seems to show that it was not an especially prevalent phenomenon in slave life? Perhaps that is the point. [. . .] it is the scandalous nature of the slave mother's resistance, its transgression of conventional moralities, which provides the measure of the intolerable contradictions of her position. How could Morrison hope to reproduce in her late-twentieth-century readers that experience of scandal, of shock? But what issue could have more emotional and political resonance in the contemporary United States than a representation of infanticide at a moment when a vociferous debate is raging regarding abortion and the rights of the fetus over those of the mother? In focusing her story of a mother killing her own child, an event still with the power to shock an audience blunted by pervasive representations of violence, Morrison is able to capture the horrific contradiction of the slave mother, a contradiction signified in her maternal body, caught between the image of brood mare (which the nephews' act of milking her and their protection of her unborn baby emphasized) and that of the mother desperately trying to get her milk to her hungry baby. This intolerable contradiction finds its logical consequence in Sethe's appalling act.

It is the return of that story in the ghostly form of Beloved which finally brings all the horror to the surface again and causes it to be spoken of so that it can be confronted. Who or what Beloved signifies, whether she is just the ghost of the dead daughter or represents something more is a question that dwells on the minds of the other protagonists as well as the reader. Discussions of the psychoanalytic implications of the narrative tend to regard the figure of Beloved as the return of Sethe's repressed, which she 'must "conjure up" . . . and confront . . . as an antagonist.'[20] Beloved is clearly a cathartic force, a 'materialization' of Sethe's memory.[21] However, I would like to offer a variant reading of the text's psychoanalytic implications, since, in my view, to read Beloved as primarily the return of Sethe's repressed somewhat elides the full political significance of Morrison's text and her evocation of the history of black women in general.

To speak of repression is to speak of what is unconscious or unacknowledged, a trace of the past which remains in the present in disguised form. But Sethe has not forgotten either her daughter or the fact that she killed her. Nor are any of the other ex-slaves surprised by Beloved's reappearance, since, as Baby Suggs says, 'Not a house in the country ain't packed to its rafters with some dead Negro's grief. We lucky this ghost is a baby' (p.5), suggesting that remembering or acknowledgment is not the problem but, rather, how to forget, how to lay the past to rest, is. Sethe is trapped in the past and cannot go forward. She is locked into what she remembers, not a process of disavowal or unconscious repetition of what she has forgotten. Beloved is not a 'detour-return'.[22] The bind that entraps Sethe is the contradiction that slavery imposed on a woman who acted out her sense of maternal responsibility to its logical conclusion and who, in the face of slavery's destruction of the mother-child relationship, insisted upon its indissolubility. The daughter's return constitutes the fulfillment of the mother's desire for that unbreachable bond and the remembering of the maternal body. What separates Sethe from the other ex-slaves and isolates her from them is that she had the mind to commit an act that encompassed the enormity of slavery's contradiction and to take responsibility for it.

The climactic realization of this desire in the text is the epiphanic moment when the three women are skating on a frozen creek: 'Holding hands, bracing each other, they swirled over the ice' (p. 174). It is a magical moment of fulfilled desire; the refrain that punctuates the scene, 'Nobody saw them falling' (p. 174), suggests the absolute identification of the three, not split into subject or object, gazer or gazed upon, an idealized moment of absolute unity, as fragile as the ice they skate upon.

In the three women's interior monologues that follow Morrison creates a subjective discourse of motherhood, daughterhood, and sisterhood, a discourse that the institution of slavery would ignore or deny. Sethe's monologue is a reverie on the day of her flight and the day of Beloved's death, on the milk her daughter was being deprived of and of Beloved's blood, which she shed. The boundaries between life (milk) and death (blood) are broken down, as are the boundaries between the mother's identity and the daughter's. This fluidity of identity is expressed in Sethe's memory of the baby's face being blotted out by the sun, but it is still a face she recognizes: 'when I tell you you mine, I also mean I'm yours. I wouldn't draw breath without my children' (p. 203). Her reverie also constitutes a rebellious rewriting of her own experience as a daughter born into slavery who had hardly tasted her mother's milk and who wouldn't recognize her mother's face.

Denver's monologue expresses not identity with her mother but, rather, with the lost sister returned, who embodies all the losses she has suffered, of the father she never knew and the brothers and grandmother who left her. In Denver the mother's milk and the daughter's blood come together: 'Beloved is my sister. I swallowed her blood right along with my mother's milk' (p. 205). But her monologue also heralds a break in that magic circle of identification. She fears the mother love that can kill and identifies with the father for whom she has waited all her life.

Beloved's monologue reasserts the indivisibility of the mother-child bond from the daughter's perspective: 'I am not separate from her there is no place where I stop   her face is my own and I want to be there in the place where her face is' (p. 210). It is a surreal mixture of densely packed allusions, providing a sense of the child in purgatory trying to reach the mother's face, but also there are references that resonate beyond the tragedy of Sethe and Beloved, an amalgam of the experiences of all other slaves who died, stretching back in time to the Middle Passage. The figure of Beloved, therefore, is not only the lost daughter, but she is also all the dead victims of slavery, reaching out to the living, demanding to be remembered. The voices of all those dead gather around the house, 'voices that ringed 124 like a noose'(p. 183), merging with those of the three women and providing an ominous warning of the battle to come.

The verbal battle between Sethe and Beloved which follows, a battle for survival, marks the cost of Sethe's radical assertion of her own subjectivity in terms of the absolute identification between mother and daughter. I want to suggest that this battle can be read from a double perspective, simultaneously historical and psychological, which is figured on that metaphoric-metonymic axis I have previously mentioned. Once Sethe has acknowledged Beloved as the returned daughter, she becomes locked in a cycle of impossible atonement and expiation. She embarks on an orgy of giving food, clothes, and games. As Beloved's demands grow with the gifts, the mood of their exchange shifts from pleasure to resentment, and Sethe is caught in an unending bind in which she attempts to explain and justify the killing: 'Anything she wanted she got, and when Sethe ran out of things to give her, Beloved invented desire' (p. 240). This process of giving and taking is materialized in the women's bodies: the mother begins to starve herself in order to feed the daughter, so that her body withers, while the daughter 'was getting bigger, plumper by the day' (p. 239). Thus, the story that began with the mother's impassioned loving gift of her body to her daughter turns into a story of the daughter voraciously devouring that body; the mother and daughter's desire for the other has grown monstrous, like an incubus feeding on itself.

This situation can be read on a psychoanalytical level, the two locked into an unfinished story, the child's process of separation having been untimely cut off by her death, before she has discovered that, 'if it completely devours or controls the other, it can no longer get what it originally wanted'.[23] This is a stage in the child's development when she cannot recognize the possibility of the mother's subjectivity independent of itself: 'Beloved accused her of leaving her behind. . . . She said they were the same, had the same face, how could she have left her?' (p.241). Sethe's act has meant the relinquishing of any possible subjectivity outside of that prescribed by the mother-daughter bond. The killing of Beloved was the only means left to her to resist the deathly metonymy inscribed with schoolteacher's ink, whereby her own and her daughter's bodies existed as merely sites of the production of capital which ensured the survival of slavery. Sethe rewrote that metonymic connection, based on maternal love and connection in the milk she finally got to the daughter and the blood that placed that daughter beyond the slave owner's reach. But in defining those connections as indissoluble – mother/daughter, milk/blood, life/death – the mother and daughter became locked in another kind of bondage, a psychological trap that sets in motion an eternal repetition of the past, an endless reassertion of the necessity of that loving murder.

Sethe's act is also a radical assertion of the inseparability of the personal and the political, emphasizing, I believe, how crucial the parent-child bond is to any reading of slavery, historical or literary. As Morrison suggested in her analysis of Willa Cather's literary evocation of slavery, it is a story that could not be acknowledged so long as Euro-America continues to interpret that past in terms of the slave's subjective dependence on the masters. It seems to me that, in focusing on the mother-daughter relation in particular, Morrison's text focuses on a crucial area of resistance to that inscription of the female body. This is figured in Baby Suggs's words to Denver: 'Slaves not supposed to have pleasurable feelings on their own; their bodies not supposed to be like that, but they have to have as many children as they can to please whoever owned them. . . . She said for me not to listen to all that. That I should always listen to my body and love it' (p.209).

Yet the bondage that Sethe and Beloved become locked into signifies a rejection of any idealization of motherhood.[24] It is a site of resistance and of subjective expression for the slave woman, but it exposed her to the threat of another form of bondage. The mother cannot speak to the daughter, cannot get her to understand, because the daughter cannot hear. Beloved is a figure from the past, locked in the past: 'Beloved wasn't interested. She said when she cried there was no one. That dead men lay on top of her. That she had nothing to eat. Ghosts without skin stuck their fingers in her and said beloved in the dark and bitch in the light' (p.241). Therefore, even in the verbal battle with Sethe there are echoes in Beloved's curses of other histories, other torments, beyond those of the dead baby girl. The 'ghosts without skin' are presumably white men who fingered her lovingly at night but with hatred in the day; this is suggestive of the experience of many slave women, as Barbara Omolade describes it, a split between their daytime and nighttime lives. Of the white slave owner Omolade writes: 'He would never tell how he built a society with the aid of dark-skinned women, while telling the world he did it alone. . . . History would become all that men did during the day, but nothing of what they did during the night.'[25]

Denver later acknowledges to Paul D these echoes that reverberate in the figure of Beloved after she has disappeared:

'You think she sure 'nough your sister?'
. . . 'At times. At times I think she was – more.' (p. 266)

Thus, the battle between mother and daughter figures, metonymically, the complexities of gender identity within slavery and, metaphorically, the difficulties for African Americans both in telling the story of their past and in releasing themselves from it. If Beloved represents all the dead of the past, then she also represents the threat of being engulfed by that past. Morrison has created a fiction out of a fragment of recorded history. In so doing she has also created a myth, in the sense that it is not just a fiction that attempts to bear witness to historical event but also a story that embodies a particular historical contradiction, that is to say, the desire and necessity to remember and honor the past and the dangers of becoming locked in it. The stories of the two daughters represent a double movement: the story of Beloved, a pulling back into the past; the story of Denver, a pulling forward into the future. [. . .] □

If post-colonial perspectives are relatively rare within criticism on *Beloved*, psychoanalytic readings, by contrast, are much more pervasive and include, amongst the best examples, essays by Jennifer Fitzgerald and Jean Wyatt.[26] In one sense, this kind of theoretical emphasis is hardly surprising for, as Nicholls himself begins by noting in the first section of his essay, the issues of 'time, memory and mourning' with which Morrison's fiction as a whole is recurrently concerned are also very much the grist of psychoanalysis.[27] In another sense, however, the project of deploying psychoanalyis as a means of reading *Beloved* might seem unpromising since psychoanalysis, as Wyatt puts it, 'is based on assumptions about family and language grounded in Western European patriarchal culture, while Morrison's novel comes out of African and African American oral and written narrative traditions'.[28]

It is with regard to questions concerning psychoanalysis and its use as a reading strategy for *Beloved* that the essays by Keenan and Nicholls might be said to enter into dialogue with one another: even as Keenan argues that viewing Beloved as 'the return of Sethe's repressed' threatens to diminish the political force of Morrison's text and that Beloved is not a 'detour-return', it is precisely in these terms that Nicholls wants to frame the Sethe/Beloved relation, while complicating and finessing them at the same time. His exploration of the vicissitudes of the subject in *Beloved* is not, however, simply an end in itself. It is linked, rather, to a larger enquiry into the nature of historical memory in contemporary American culture. For Nicholls – *contra* Keenan – a psychoanalytic approach to Morrison's text neither blocks nor reduces its political implications but is a particularly powerful way of opening them up.

As a means of theorising what he calls 'psychic life' in *Beloved*, Nicholls invokes the Freudian concept of *Nachträglichkeit* or 'deferred action', discussing it in detail in the second section of his essay. This concept is formulated by Freud in the course of his case history of the so-called 'Wolf Man' (1914) as a way of thinking about traumatic experience.[29] What is distinctive about the process of *Nachträglichkeit* is the way in which it challenges conventional or common sense perceptions of time, entailing, as it does, a reinscription or revision of past experience in the light of later events. Indeed it is only with the advent of those later events that the full significance of the past first emerges: the subject becomes traumatised after the fact, as it were. As Linda Ruth Williams puts it, commenting on the case of the 'Wolf Man', analyst and analysand look back to a moment in the past that 'is [. . .] destined to be left unresolved until the future, as a loop of trauma is set up'.[30]

Nicholls develops these arguments by suggesting that the relations between Morrison's text and the history of enslavement to which it returns can themselves be construed in terms of Freud's reflections on *Nachträglichkeit*. As he puts it, *Beloved* effects a 'refiguring of "History" along the lines of a psychic temporality for which memory is less a matter of cultural allusion than of shock and trauma'.[31] In other words, the history that comes back in Morrison's novel does not do so as a full presence that was once lost, but as an eruption into a present enabled by that present.

Nicholls's examination of the relevance of Freud for a reading of *Beloved* leads him in turn to the proposal that Morrison's novel should be thought of as post-modern. On the one hand, the 'exercises in aimless self-reflexivity'[32] with which post-modern writing is often charged have little to do with the kind of 'passionate historical imagination'[33] by which Morrison's text is animated. Yet on the other hand, much post-modern thought – from Jacques Derrida to Jean-François Lyotard – is concerned to disrupt a metaphysical conception of history as 'a sort of container in which events are serially disposed'.[34] As Nicholls demonstrates in his essay's third section, such thought can indeed – like *Beloved* itself – be usefully set in relation to Freud's insights into the time of the subject. He goes on, in section four, to focus specifically on *Beloved* and the ways in which subjective time is patterned according to Freud's strange logic of belatedness. The essay's discussion of *Beloved* concludes with a consideration of how Morrison's text might be further illuminated by recourse to the distinctions between the psychoanalytic categories of 'incorporation' and 'introjection', as developed by Nicolas Abraham and Maria Torok.

This is the essay's second section:

■ 'The narrative into which life seems to cast itself surfaces most forcefully in certain kinds of psychoanalysis'.[35] How, though, might the intimacies of the analyst's couch provide us with a way of talking about a history no longer grounded in metaphysics? One tempting answer to that question is to invoke Freud's concept of the 'return of the repressed', as Mae G. Henderson has done in one of the best discussions of *Beloved*.[36] The danger here, though, is that we begin to think of the 'repressed' as simply a lost fact or datum, a link which once restored will return us to a form of historical continuity. Yet psychoanalysis is concerned not so much with the discovery of a hidden content as with, in the words of Laplanche and Leclaire, 'an interpretive elaboration or working through whose role is to weave around a rememorated element an entire network of meaningful relations that integrate it into the subject's explicit apprehension of himself'. From this point of view, then, 'the Freudian experience of "memory" has less to do with the recollection of an "event" than with the repetition of a structure'.[37] And for psychoanalysis, of course, memory leads a double life since it is (in David Krell's words) both 'the source of the malady with which it is concerned and the *therapy* it proffers'.[38] To remember is thus not simply to restore a forgotten link or moment of experience, nor is it unproblematically to 'repossess' or re-enact what has been lost.[39] That idea of recovering an occluded or 'buried' past derives from a traditional association of knowledge with recollection and depends on a thoroughly metaphysical 'presencing' of what is absent. The development of Freud's theory of memory is actually away from this phantasmatic form of recollection, and while his use of 'acting out' (*Agieren*) in therapy might seem tied to a form of 'presence', this is complicated, as Dominick LaCapra has argued, by a concept of memory which 'allowed for the distinction between mnemic trace and phantasm'.[40]

The distinction is a momentous one, connecting a major strand of Freud's thought to subsequent poststructuralism and to a certain theory of the postmodern for which concepts of time and memory are of central importance.[41] In the wake of Lacan, attention has recently been focused on a related concept of deferral in Freud's theory which is codified in the word *Nachträglichkeit*, 'belatedness', or, in its usual technical translations, 'deferred action' and 'retroaction'. The concept is best known from the case history of the Wolf Man, though it is foreshadowed in the *Studies on Hysteria* and in some of Freud's early letters to Wilhelm Fliess. The Wolf Man, we recall, witnesses at the age of one and a half an act of sexual intercourse between his parents but the shock of this impression is deferred until some sexual understanding of its import is possible. As Freud puts it:

> At the age of one and a half the child receives an impression to which he is unable to react adequately; he is only able to understand it and to be moved by it when the impression is revived in him at the age of four; and only twenty years later, during the analysis, is he able to grasp with his conscious mental processes what was then going on in him.[42]

As Lacan observes, 'the event remains latent in the subject',[43] thereby giving rise to a complex temporality in which the subject is always in more than one place at any time. Deferred action is, then, a product of the excessive character of the first event which requires a second event to release its traumatic force ('only the occurrence of the second scene can endow the first one with pathogenic force').[44] John Forrester neatly defines this movement as 'the articulation of two *moments* with a time of delay'.[45] It is not simply a matter of recovering a lost memory, but rather of the restructuring which forms the past in retrospect as 'the original site [. . .] comes to be reworked'.[46]

What is involved, then, is not just a time-lapse between stimuli and response, but, as Laplanche and Pontalis are careful to point out, a particular kind of 'working over', a 'work of recollection'.[47] So too *Nachträglichkeit* must be distinguished from Jung's theory of 'retrospection' (*Zurückfantasieren*), for, as Laplanche explains, while the latter

> simply means the fact of creating a past to meet current needs, perhaps in an attempt to avoid present difficulties and to conceal them from oneself [. . .] Freud insists upon the tension between the old scene and the recent scenario.[48]

It is this 'tension' which implies a radical unsettling of that 'philosophy of representation – of the original, the first time, resemblance, imitation, faithfulness'[49] which postmodernism will also seek to disrupt. *Nachträglichkeit* calls into question traditional notions of causality – the second event is presented now as the 'cause' of the first[50] – and its retroactive logic refuses to accord ontological primacy to any originary moment. Since the shock of the first scene is not felt directly by the subject but only through its later representation in memory we are dealing with, in Derrida's words, 'a past that has never been present'.[51] Belatedness, in this sense, creates a complex temporality which inhibits any nostalgia for origin and continuity – the 'origin' is now secondary, a construction always contained in its own repetition (as Andrew Benjamin puts it, 'The original event is thus no longer the same as itself. The effect of the present on the past is to cause a repetition of the "event" within which something new is taking place').[52] □

Here is section four of Nicholls's essay:

■ This [. . .] cannot but remind us of Morrison's *Beloved*, the text in which Morrison has explored most vividly what we might call the insistence of historicity in the self. There is a ghost here and a persistent haunting, as Morrison uncovers the intricate relations between love and possession, using the resources of fiction to free us from a metaphysical History.

The theme of possession, of a force invading the self, has itself haunted postmodern American writing, being first definitively broached in William Burroughs' *The Naked Lunch* (1959) and operating as a persistent metaphor of social control in experimental fiction of the last three decades.[53] Yet while *Beloved* also explores ways in which the body can be possessed by something external to it, Morrison tends to see the workings of power as inseparable from the disjunctive operations of a 'belated' temporality. This is the full force of 'unspeakable thoughts, unspoken' (p.199), for feeling, understanding and speaking never seem to occur in the same moment. The fluid shifts between different times in this novel [. . .] thus do not work to enforce some deterministic reading of the past's effects upon the present, but rather to evoke the traumatic force of a historicity which splits the subject, compelling it to live in different times rather than in a secure, metaphysical present.

Who is Beloved? A revenant, someone who comes back, she seems to offer precisely what we have always yearned for, the past made good, an origin restored, 'my girl come home' (p.201), with 'new skin' (p.50) to match her 'new shoes' (p.66). But she is not that; or at least she is always more than that, at once Sethe's daughter and an African lost in the Middle Passage – and even as Sethe's daughter, she is not what she was, but grown to the age she would have been, her neck bearing 'the little curved shadow' left by the handsaw (p.239). This play of contradiction seems now the very mark of the postmodern, issuing in an insistence that something (someone) can be two things at once, that two things can occupy the same space, that the origin is irreducibly doubled.

And there is more: for this haunting is but one of many (as Baby Suggs points out, 'Not a house in the country ain't packed to its rafters with some dead Negro's grief. We lucky this ghost is a baby' [p.5]), and the voices heard in 124 are quickly understood by Stamp Paid: 'although he couldn't cipher but one word, he believed he knew who spoke them. The people of the broken necks, of fire-cooked blood and black girls who had lost their ribbons. What a roaring' (p.181). So Beloved is also a figure of thwarted love, of the body literally possessed by others, of the entire tragedy of slavery which cannot adequately be spoken. Her belated appearance is traumatic in Freud's sense precisely because it embodies an overwhelming desire, a now unrepresentable excess of the emotional need suppressed under slavery ('to love anything that much was dangerous' [p.45], and 'not to need permission for desire – well now, *that* was freedom' [p.162]).[54]

Beloved returns, then, *nachträglich*, but she will be forever 'unaccounted for' (p.275), impossible to memorialize in some metaphysical History. In her figure, historicity comes back with all the force of bewildering, unfulfilled desire, playing havoc with temporal and symbolic schemes. That force permeates the texture of Morrison's writing which [. . .] makes powerful use of retroactive effects, embedding signs and images which will only become clear at a later stage. In some cases these are darkly proleptic of a story to be filled in later; in others Morrison constructs a complex sequence of displaced affect – early on we hear, for example, that Sethe's hurt 'was always there – like a tender place in the corner of her mouth that the bit left' (p.58), but it is not until we have penetrated further into the narrative that we associate this portentous but unlocated image with the suffering of both Sethe's mother and Paul D. The distinctive rhythms of Morrison's prose create an intricate cross-weaving of times in which each moment comes to signify only in relation to at least one other. To re-read *Beloved* forewarned of this is to become increasingly attuned to the flickering trail of such emotional intensities, one illuminating another in a time which can never constitute a full present. This brief exchange between Denver and Beloved, for example:

'What is it?' asks Denver.
'Look,' she points to the sunlit cracks.
'What? I don't see nothing.' Denver follows the pointing finger. (p.124)

But Beloved does, as we later know: 'at night I cannot see the dead man on my face   daylight comes through the cracks and I can see his locked eyes' (p.210). This is not some facile trick of composition, one time 'rhyming' with or passively echoing another;[55] rather, Morrison evokes the texture of a temporality which makes anachronism the condition of the psychic life, embedding its effects in the very detail of narration ('Sethe feels her eyes burn and it may have been to keep them clear that she looks up' [p.261]).

If belatedness is a condition recognized in the local detail of the writing, it also frames the larger movement of the narrative. Beloved first exists in 124 as a troublesome ghost, 'not evil, just sad' (p.8). Whereas the community tends to assume that 'the haunting was done by an evil thing looking for more', 'None of them knew the downright pleasure of enchantment, of not suspecting but *knowing* the things behind things' (p.37). It is Paul D who 'beat[s] the spirit away', but 'in its place he brought another kind of haunting' which seems to conjure up the full horror of slavery (p.96). 'Paul D ran her off so she had no choice but to come back to me in the flesh' (p.200), and it is in this new embodiment that Beloved begins to play her ambiguous role in the narrative. At first she is a 'sweet, if peculiar guest' (p.57) but as the very incarnation of a boundless desire (p.58) she soon imposes intolerable demands upon Sethe.

The partial demonizing of Beloved runs parallel to a shifting conception of memory in the novel. In the opening stages, Sethe is troubled by frozen images of the past – 'I was talking about time. It's so hard for me to believe in it. Some things go. Pass on. Some things just stay' (p.35) – and the 'glittering' headstone which is her memorial to Beloved seems a way of 'keeping the past at bay' (p.42). With the 'miraculous resurrection' (p.105) of her lost daughter, however, Sethe begins to remember 'something she had forgotten she knew' (p.61). Yet the process of remembering is at once a release and a bondage, snaring the mind in a deadly repetition even as it brings a part of the psyche back to life ('Anything dead coming back to life hurts' [p.35]). The danger becomes clearer as the novel proceeds and the narcissistic identification with Beloved becomes stronger: 'But her brain was not interested in the future. Loaded with the past and hungry for more, it left her no room to imagine, let alone plan for the next day' (p.70). With her recognition of Beloved, Sethe is finally freed from the need to remember and left 'smiling at the things she would not have to remember now' (p.182). But this release from 'rememory' is another kind of prison, bringing a claustrophobic introversion ('The world is in this room' [p.183]) and leaving Sethe 'wrapped in a timeless present' (p.184).[56]

Now we begin to see the darker effects of the 'miraculous resurrection', for having dropped her defences on the departure of the 'chastising ghost' (p.86),[57] Sethe is, as it were, invaded by the spirit of her murdered daughter. It is the violence of this intrusion of one world into another which will later appal the pragmatic Ella:

> As long as the ghost showed out from its ghostly place – shaking stuff, crying, smashing and such – Ella respected it. But if it took flesh and came in her world, well, the shoe was on the other foot. She didn't mind a little communication between the two worlds, but this was an invasion. (p.257)

The force of Beloved's desire, strongly marked by a language of orality and ingestion (chewing and swallowing), threatens to consume Sethe from within. 'Beloved ate up her life, took it, swelled up with it, grew taller on it' (p. 250), and the momentum of this desire, excessive and unspeakable because so long pent up by slavery, begins to carry us back into the past. If the novel opens with a grim rewriting of the primal scene (here a *dead* child witnesses the sexual act), now an equally macabre reversal takes place as 'Beloved bending over Sethe looked the mother, Sethe the teething child' (p. 250). To complete this traumatic looping back of the narrative we have the final sight of Beloved facing the singing women:

> The devil-child was clever, they thought. And beautiful. It had taken the shape of a pregnant woman, naked and smiling in the heat of the afternoon sun. Thunderblack and glistening, she stood on long straight legs, her belly big and tight. (p. 261)

Pregnant with . . . Paul D's child? Or – the suggestion is ludicrous – with Sethe herself?

Perhaps one way of understanding this peculiar moment in the novel is to consider more closely the work of mourning which frames the story. Sethe's initial attempt to 'keep [. . .] the past at bay' is in one sense a refusal to mourn which we might understand with the help of a distinction drawn by Nicolas Abraham and Maria Torok between 'incorporation' and 'introjection'.[58] Whereas introjection assimilates to the self what is lost, incorporation perpetuates the existence of the lost object as something alive and foreign within the self. As Derrida explains in his introduction to Abraham and Torok's study of the Wolf Man:

> Sealing the loss of the object, but also marking the refusal to mourn, such a maneuver [incorporation] is foreign to and actually opposed to the process of introjection. I pretend to keep the dead alive, intact, *safe (save) inside me*, but it is only in order to refuse, in a necessarily equivocal way, to love the dead as a living part of me, dead *save in me*, through the process of introjection, as happens in so-called normal mourning.[59]

The dead person is thus not an object of identification but a phantasmatic presence within the self which gives rise to a topography which Abraham and Torok call the 'crypt':

> Grief that cannot be expressed builds a *secret vault* within the subject. In this crypt reposes – alive, reconstituted from the memories of

words, images, and feelings – the objective counterpart of the loss, as a complete person with his own topography, as well as the traumatic incidents – real or imagined – that had made introjection impossible.[60]

This 'crypt' is equivalent to 'a split in the Ego',[61] a rift from which emerges 'a false unconscious filled with phantoms – to wit, fossilized words, live corpses, and foreign bodies'.[62] The lost object is thus incorporated as something live and present, 'fantasmatic, unmediated, instantaneous, magical, sometimes hallucinatory'.[63] The terms Derrida uses here are certainly suggestive in the context of *Beloved*, and indeed Morrison herself has spoken of her novel in a way which further confirms the relevance of this idea of incorporation as some sort of fragmentation of the self. In an interview with Gloria Naylor given when she was at work on *Beloved*, Morrison spoke of her interest in a theme connecting two stories (one was that of Margaret Garner, model for Sethe, the other would form the basis of Dorcas's story in *Jazz*):

Now what made those stories connect, I can't explain, but I do know that, in both instances, something seemed clear to me. A woman loved something other than herself so much. *She had placed all of the value of her life in something outside herself.* That the woman who killed her children loved her children so much; they were the best part of her and she would not see them sullied.[64]

Is this, then, the major theme of *Beloved* [. . .] ? If the crypt is a split in the ego, then Morrison's account suggests that [. . .] the central problem for Sethe is to come to terms with 'what it is that really compels a good woman to displace the self, her self'.[65] Morrison explains to Naylor:

So what I started doing and thinking about for a year was to project the self not into the way we say "yourself", but to put a space between those words, as though the self were really a *twin* or a thirst or a friend or something that sits right next to you and watches you, which is what I was talking about when I said "the dead girl".[66]

So for Morrison, it seems, the genesis of *Beloved* lay partly in that sense that 'the best thing that is in us is also the thing that makes us sabotage ourselves, sabotage in the sense that our life is not as worthy, or our perception as the best part of ourselves'.[67] Beloved has striven to destroy the boundaries of her mother's self ('I want the join' [p.213]), seeking now to possess – to incorporate – Sethe.[68] If Sethe's only hope lies in 'claiming ownership of [her] freed self' (p.95) it is ultimately by managing, as Derrida puts it, to 'love the dead as a living part of me, dead *save in me'* that she will do so (Morrison has described the main problem in *Beloved* as 'how to own your own body and love somebody else').[69] The crucial recognition then will be Paul D's, that 'You your best thing, Sethe. You are' (p. 273).

But as Morrison emphasized in a recent talk,[70] something remains after the end of this particular story ('There is a loneliness that can be rocked . . .' [p. 274]). In the gap between Sethe's final words ('Me? Me?') and the name which closes the narrative ('Beloved') the contradictions reappear. Beloved is exorcized, but in the last two pages of the novel she returns (again). This particular haunting is not over:

> Down by the stream in back of 124 her footprints come and go. They are so familiar. Should a child, an adult place his feet in them, they will fit. Take them out and they disappear again as though nobody ever walked there. (p. 275)

'Familiar', familial: this ghost seems the product of what Abraham and Torok term 'transgenerational haunting' in which something repressed is transmitted across several generations.[71] This phantom, writes Abraham, 'is not related to the loss of a loved one, it cannot be considered the effect of unsuccessful mourning, as is the case of melancholics or all those who carry a tomb within themselves'.[72] In line with his theory of 'transgenerational haunting', Abraham concludes instead that

> It is the children's or descendants' lot to objectify these buried tombs through diverse species of ghosts. What comes back to haunt are the tombs of others. The phantoms of folklore merely objectify a metaphor active within the unconscious: the burial of an unspeakable fact *within the loved one.*[73]

The desire to forget is strong, but while 'This is not a story to pass on' (p. 275) the memory of *'Sixty Million and more'* is somehow encrypted within us, in our time and in our bodies:

> So they forgot her. Like an unpleasant dream during a troubling sleep. Occasionally, however, the rustle of a skirt hushes when they wake, and the knuckles brushing a cheek in sleep seem to belong to the sleeper. Sometimes the photograph of a close friend or relative – looked at too long – shifts, and something more familiar than the dear face itself moves there. They can touch it if they like, but don't, because they know things will never be the same if they do. (p. 275)[74] □

NOTES

INTRODUCTION

1 The epigraph to this chapter is taken from an interview given by Morrison to Paul Bailey, BBC Radio 3, 14 August 1982, cited in Olga Kenyon, *Writing Women: Contemporary Women Novelists* (London and Concord, MA: 1991), p. 98.

2 See Trudier Harris, 'Toni Morrison: Solo Flight Through Literature into History', *World Literature Today*, 68 (1994), p. 9.

3 *The Oprah Winfrey Show*, Sky 1, 14 November 1997.

4 Nancy J. Peterson, 'Introduction: Canonizing Toni Morrison', *Modern Fiction Studies*, 39 (1993), p. 465.

5 Peterson, p. 464.

6 Despite its usefulness as a shorthand, the term 'non-white', it should be stressed, remains problematic, 'as if', to cite Richard Dyer, 'people who are not white only have identity by virtue of what they are not'. See Richard Dyer, *White* (London and New York: Routledge, 1997), p. 11.

7 On this point see Carl D. Malmgren, 'Mixed Genres and the Logic of Slavery in Toni Morrison's *Beloved*', *Critique: Studies in Contemporary Fiction*, 36. 2 (Winter 1995), p. 100: 'If *Beloved* is both a ghost story *and* a historical novel, it can also be characterized as a love story, exploring what it means to "be-loved."'

8 Catherine Belsey, *Desire: Love Stories in Western Culture* (Oxford and Cambridge, MA: Blackwell, 1994), p. 92.

9 Belsey, p. 93.

10 Gayatri Chakravorty Spivak, *The Post-Colonial Critic: Interviews, Strategies, Dialogues*, ed. Sarah Harasym (New York and London: Routledge, 1990), pp. 62–63.

11 For an excellent broad discussion of the inherently politicised nature of reading (taking Morrison's 1982 experimental short story, 'Recitatif', as its point of departure), see Elizabeth Abel, 'Black Writing, White Reading: Race and the Politics of Feminist Interpretation', *Critical Inquiry*, 19 (1993), pp. 470–98. Relevant also is Kristine Holmes's consideration of her own position as an Anglo-American feminist reader of African-American fiction in '"This is flesh I'm talking about here": Embodiment in Toni Morrison's *Beloved* and Sherley Anne Williams' *Dessa Rose*', *LIT: Literature Interpretation Theory*, 6 (1995), p. 134.

12 Linden Peach, *Toni Morrison* (Basingstoke and London: Macmillan, 1995), pp. 11–12.

13 For an alternative account of the genealogy of critical theory linking, in particular, the emergence of post-structuralism in the West in the late 1960s to processes of Third World decolonisation, see Robert Young, *White Mythologies: Writing History and the West* (London and New York: Routledge, 1990), p. 1: 'If [. . .] "so-called poststructuralism" is the product of a single historical moment, then that moment is probably not May 1968 but rather the Algerian War of Independence – no doubt both itself a symptom and a product.'

14 Barbara Christian, 'Fixing Methodologies: *Beloved*', *Cultural Critique*, 24 (Spring 1993), p. 5.

15 Christian, p. 8.

16 Jacqueline de Weever, *Mythmaking and Metaphor in Black Women's Fiction* (New York: St. Martin's Press, 1991), p. 22. Cited in Peach, p. 12.

17 See Caroline M. Woidat, 'Talking Back to Schoolteacher: Morrison's Confrontation with Hawthorne in *Beloved*', *Modern Fiction Studies*, 39 (1993), pp. 527–46 and Charles Lewis, 'The Ironic Romance of New Historicism: *The Scarlet Letter* and *Beloved* Side by Side', *Arizona Quarterly: A Journal of American Literature, Culture, and Theory*, 51. 1 (Spring 1995), pp. 32–60.

18 See Richard C. Moreland, '"He Wants to Put His Story Next to Hers": Putting Twain's Story Next to Hers in Morrison's *Beloved*', *Modern Fiction Studies*, 39 (1993), pp. 501–25 and Sylvia Mayer, '"You Like Huckleberries?": Toni Morrison's *Beloved*

and Mark Twain's *Adventures of Huckleberry Finn*', in *The Black Columbiad: Defining Moments in African American Literature and Culture*, ed. Werner Sollers and Maria Diedrich (Cambridge, MA and London: Harvard University Press, 1994), pp. 337–46.

19 Kari J. Winter, *Subjects of Slavery, Agents of Change: Women and Power in Gothic Novels and Slave Narratives, 1790–1865* (Athens, GA: University of Georgia Press, 1992), p. 13.

20 This prophetic phrase was, of course, originally made famous by W. E. B. Du Bois in his 1903 proclamation that 'The problem of the twentieth century is the problem of the color-line'. See W. E. B. Du Bois, *The Souls of Black Folk*, ed. Candace Ward (New York: Dover Publications, 1994), p. 9.

21 Kenneth W. Warren, *Black and White Strangers: Race and American Literary Realism* (Chicago: University of Chicago Press, 1993), p. 10.

22 Henry B. Wonham's phrase in the 'Introduction' to *Criticism and the Color Line: Desegregating American Literary Studies*, ed. Henry B. Wonham (New Brunswick: Rutgers University Press, 1996), p. 3.

23 Stanley Crouch, *New Yorker*, 6 November 1995, p. 96.

24 Morrison's phrase, used in an interview with Christopher Bigsby, *Kaleidoscope*, BBC Radio 4, 23 February 1988. Cited in Kenyon, p. 91.

25 Toni Morrison, *Beloved* (London: Vintage, 1997), pp. 154–58. All subsequent references are to this edition and included in parenthesis in the text.

26 Henry Louis Gates, Jr., *Loose Canons: Notes on the Culture Wars* (New York and Oxford: Oxford University Press, 1992), p. 146.

27 Toni Morrison, interview with Olga Kenyon, Institute of Contemporary Arts, 23 February 1988. Cited in Kenyon, p. 92.

CHAPTER ONE

1 Robert Allen, Maya Angelou, Houston A. Baker, Jr., *et al*, 'Black Writers in Praise of Toni Morrison', *New York Times Book Review*, 24 January 1988.

2 Walter Goodman, 'The Lobbying for Literary Prizes', *The New York Times*, 28 January 1988, p. C28.

3 John Wideman, cited in Marilyn Judith Atlas, 'Toni Morrison's *Beloved* and the Reviewers', *Midwestern Miscellany*, 18 (1990), p. 45.

4 Richard Todd, 'Toni Morrison and Canonicity: Acceptance or Appropriation?', in *Rewriting the Dream: Reflections on the Changing American Literary Canon*, ed. W. M. Verhoeven (Amsterdam: Rodopi, 1992), p. 43.

5 Toni Morrison, 'Unspeakable Things Unspoken: The Afro-American Presence in American Literature', *Michigan Quarterly Review*, 28 (1989), p. 8.

6 This epigraph is taken from Atlas, p. 46.

7 T. S. Eliot, 'Tradition and the Individual Talent' in *Selected Essays*, ed. Frank Kermode, 3rd enlarged edn, (London and Boston: Faber and Faber, 1951), p. 15.

8 Toni Morrison, *Playing in the Dark: Whiteness and the Literary Imagination* (Cambridge, MA and London: Harvard University Press, 1992), pp. 4–5.

9 *Playing in the Dark*, p. 5.

10 Kate Ferguson Ellis, *The Contested Castle: Gothic Novels and the Subversion of Domestic Ideology* (Urbana: University of Illinois Press, 1989), p. 3.

11 Barbara Christian, 'Fixing Methodologies: *Beloved*', *Cultural Critique*, 24 (Spring 1993), p. 9.

12 Christian, p. 6.

13 Christian, pp. 7–8.

14 Christian, p. 7.

15 Stanley Crouch, 'Aunt Medea', *New Republic*, 19 October 1987, p. 39.

16 Nancy J. Peterson, 'Introduction: Canonizing Toni Morrison', *Modern Fiction Studies*, 39 (1993), p. 463.

17 Peterson, p. 463.

18 Atlas, p. 50.

19 Peterson, p. 464.

20 Paul Gilroy, *The Black Atlantic: Modernity and Double Consciousness* (London and New York: Verso, 1993), p. 217.

21 This epigraph is taken from the interview between Morrison and Marsha Darling that forms the basis for the first extract in this section of the chapter. See Marsha Darling, 'In the Realm of Responsibility: A Conversation with Toni Morrison', *Women's Review of Books*, March 1988, p. 6.

22 Christian, p. 7.

CHAPTER TWO

1 The epigraph to this chapter is taken from Lynn Hunt, 'History as Gesture; or, The Scandal of History', in *Consequences of Theory*, ed. Jonathan Arac and Barbara Johnson (Baltimore and London: Johns Hopkins University Press, 1991), p. 103.

2 For other examples of this approach, see Bernard W. Bell, '*Beloved*: A Womanist Neo-Slave Narrative; or, Multivocal Remembrances of Things Past', *African American Review*, 26 (1992), pp. 7–16 and Molly Abel Travis, 'Speaking from the Silence of the Slave Narrative: *Beloved* and African-American Women's History', *Texas Review*, 13 (1992), pp. 69–81.

3 For detailed discussions of the importance of Margaret Garner to the conception of *Beloved*, see Cynthia Griffin Woolf, '"Margaret Garner": A Cincinnati Story', *Massachusetts Review*, 32 (1991), pp. 417–40, Ashraf H. A. Rushdy, 'Daughters Signifyin(g) History: The Example of Toni Morrison's *Beloved*', *American Literature: A Journal of Literary History, Criticism, and Bibliography*, 64 (1992), pp. 567–97 and Paul Gilroy, *The Black Atlantic: Modernity and Double Consciousness* (London and New York: Verso, 1993), pp. 64–68.

4 Dominick LaCapra, *History and Criticism* (Ithaca: Cornell University Press, 1985), p. 128. Cited in Travis, p. 69.

5 Linda Hutcheon, *The Politics of Postmodernism* (London and New York: Routledge, 1989), pp. 81–82.

6 Nancy J. Peterson, 'History, Postmodernism, and Louise Erdrich's *Tracks*', *PMLA*, 109 (1994), p. 984.

7 Peterson, p. 984.

8 Frederick Douglass, *Narrative of the Life of Frederick Douglass*, in *The Classic Slave Narratives*, ed. Henry Louis Gates, Jr. (New York: Mentor, 1987), p. 294.

9 Betty J. Ring, '"Painting by Numbers": Figuring Frederick Douglass', in *The Discourse of Slavery: Aphra Behn to Toni Morrison*, ed. Carl Plasa and Betty J. Ring (London and New York: Routledge, 1994), p. 118.

10 For Derrida's elaboration of the notion of supplementarity, in the context of the work of Jean-Jacques Rousseau, see Jacques Derrida, *Of Grammatology*, trans. Gayatri Chakravorty Spivak (Baltimore and London: Johns Hopkins University Press, 1976), pp. 141–64.

11 Judith Thurman, 'A House Divided', *New Yorker*, 2 November 1987, p. 175.

12 Quoted in the opening epigraph of *The Slave's Narrative*, ed. Charles T. Davis and Henry Louis Gates, Jr. (New York: Oxford University Press, 1985).

13 *The Black Book*, comp. Middleton A. Harris [ed. Toni Morrison], (New York: Random House, 1974).

14 Toni Morrison, 'Behind the Making of *The Black Book*', *Black World*, February 1974, pp. 86–90. Compiled by Middleton A. Harris, *The Black Book* does not identify Morrison as its editor. In this article, however, she not only discusses her role as editor, but describes the project of producing the book as an act of professional service and personal mission: 'I was scared that the world would fall away before somebody put together a thing that got close to the way we really were' (p. 90). Ironically, although *The Black Book* omits any mention of Morrison as its editor, it names her parents, Ramah Wofford and George Carl Wofford, in the acknowledgments, as two of the people who contributed to the text 'with stories, pictures, recollections and general aid'.

15 See Amanda Smith, 'Toni Morrison',

Publishers Weekly, 21 August 1987, p. 51. This article is a report on an interview with Morrison a month before the publication of *Beloved*.

16 See Harris, p. 10.

17 *Black Women Writers at Work*, ed. Claudia Tate (New York: Continuum, 1984), p. 122.

18 The term 'narrative intervention' is one I borrow from Hazel Carby's analysis of the uses of fiction in moments of historical crisis. See Hazel V. Carby, *Reconstructing Womanhood: The Emergence of the Afro-American Woman Novelist* (New York: Oxford University Press, 1987), pp. 121–44.

19 Gates, p. x.

20 Frederick Douglass, *The Narrative of the Life of Frederick Douglass* (New York: Signet, 1968); Harriet Jacobs, *Incidents in the Life of a Slave Girl*, ed. Jean Fagan Yellin (Cambridge, MA and London: Harvard University Press, 1987).

21 See James Olney, '"I Was Born": Slave Narratives, Their Status as Autobiography and as Literature', *Callaloo*, 7 (Winter 1984), pp. 46–73. Reprinted in Davis and Gates, pp. 148–75.

22 Valerie Smith, *Self-Discovery and Authority in Afro-American Narrative* (Cambridge, MA: Harvard University Press, 1987), p. 34. See also *Invented Lives: Narratives of Black Women 1860–1960*, ed. Mary Helen Washington (Garden City, NY: Doubleday, 1987), pp. 3–15.

23 Adrienne Rich, 'When We Dead Awaken: Writing as Re-Vision', *College English*, 34 (October 1972), pp. 18–26. Morrison's words are quoted in Smith, *Publishers Weekly*, p. 51.

24 Fredric Jameson, *The Political Unconscious: Narrative as a Socially Symbolic Act* (Ithaca: Cornell University Press, 1981), p. 9.

25 Tate, p. 125.

26 Steven Mailloux, *Interpretive Conventions: The Reader in the Study of American Fiction* (Ithaca: Cornell University Press, 1982), p. 170.

27 See Helen Dudar, 'Toni Morrison: Finally Just a Writer', *Wall Street Journal*, 30 September 1987, p. 34. This is one of several newspaper articles to appear around the time of *Beloved*'s publication in which Morrison discussed the actual story upon which the novel is based.

28 See Sherley Anne Williams, 'The Blues Roots of Contemporary Afro-American Poetry', in *Afro-American Literature: The Reconstruction of Instruction*, ed. Dexter Fisher and Robert Stepto (New York: Modern Language Association of America), p. 73. In the novel, the statements of individual characters shape the 'call' to which other characters offer a 'response' by sharing their versions of the past. This pattern of call and response then shapes the collective story of slavery that binds the members of the community together. This pattern resonates with similar patterns found in the blues and other forms of African-American oral expression.

29 Frank Kermode, *The Genesis of Secrecy: On the Interpretation of Narrative* (Cambridge, MA: Harvard University Press, 1979), p. 144.

30 Toni Morrison, 'Rediscovering Black History', *New York Times Magazine*, 11 August 1974, p. 18.

31 Davis and Gates, p. xiii.

32 Mikhail Bakhtin, 'Discourse in the Novel', in *The Dialogic Imagination: Four Essays*, ed. Michael Holquist, trans. Caryl Emerson and Michael Holquist, (Austin: University of Texas Press, 1981), p. 421.

CHAPTER THREE

1 The epigraph to this chapter is taken from Toni Morrison, 'Rootedness: The Ancestor as Foundation', in *Black Women Writers (1950–1980): A Critical Evaluation*, ed. Mari Evans (Garden City, NY: Doubleday, 1984), p. 342.

2 Shlomith Rimmon-Kenan, 'Narration, Doubt, Retrieval: Toni Morrison's *Beloved*', *Narrative*, 4. 2 (May 1996), p. 116.

3 Rimmon-Kenan, p. 116.

4 Rimmon-Kenan, p. 116, quoting Jean Wyatt's formulation in 'Giving Body to the Word: The Maternal Symbolic in Toni

Morrison's *Beloved*', *PMLA*, 108 (1993), p.474.

5 James Phelan, 'Toward a Rhetorical Reader-Response Criticism: The Difficult, the Stubborn, and the Ending of *Beloved*', *Modern Fiction Studies*, 39 (1993), p.711.

6 Rimmon-Kenan, p.116.

7 Rimmon-Kenan, p.116.

8 Rimmon-Kenan, p.116.

9 Deborah Horvitz, 'Nameless Ghosts: Possession and Dispossession in *Beloved*, *Studies in American Fiction*, 17 (1989), p.157.

10 Toni Morrison quoted by Marsha Darling, 'In the Realm of Responsibility: An Interview with Toni Morrison', *Women's Review of Books*, March 1988, p.6.

11 Morrison herself very clearly expresses these ideas about memory in her interview with Darling, p.5.

12 Horvitz, p.157.

13 Although House gives it little attention, Denver's relation to Beloved might also be seen as part of this economy.

14 Walter Clemons notes that Morrison took the germ of Sethe's story from a newspaper account of an 1855 event: 'In 1855 a runaway slave from Kentucky named Margaret Garner was tracked by her owner to Cincinnati, where she had taken refuge with her freed mother-in-law. Cornered, she tried to kill her four children. Afterward, she was quite serene about what she had done.' See Walter Clemons, 'A Gravestone of Memories', *Newsweek*, 28 September, 1987, p.74.

15 Sethe's own need for a parent is expressed in a pained suspicion that her mother had been hanged for attempting to run away, an action that would have separated the woman not only from the horrors of slavery but also from her own daughter. Speaking to Beloved in a stream-of-conscious remembering, Sethe explains, 'My plan was to take us all to the other side where my own ma'am is. They stopped me from getting us there, but they didn't stop you from getting here. . . . You came right on back like a good girl, like a daughter which is what I

wanted to be and would have been if my ma'am had been able to get out of the rice long enough before they hanged her and let me be one. . . . I wonder what they was doing when they was caught. Running, you think? No. Not that. Because she was my ma'am and nobody's ma'am would run off and leave her daughter, would she? Would she, now?' (p.203).

16 In an interview with Walter Clemons, Morrison brought to his attention *Beloved*'s dedication, '*Sixty Million and more*', and explained that 'the figure is the best educated guess at the number of black Africans who never even made it into slavery – those who died either as captives in Africa or on slave ships'. Morrison notes, too, that 'one account describes the Congo as so clogged with bodies that the boat couldn't pass. . . . They packed 800 into a ship if they'd promised to deliver 400. They assumed that half would die. And half did.' And, the author wryly adds, 'A few people in my novel remember it. . . . Baby Suggs came here out of one of those ships. But mostly it's not remembered at all.' See Clemons, p.75. Of course, Beloved is the most important person in the novel who remembers the slave ships' horrors. However, Morrison does not reveal that fact here; she merely hints at it.

17 Although in 1807 Congress banned importations of slaves into the United States after 1 January 1808, the decree did not stop captured Africans from entering the country. In his classic work *The Suppression of the African Slave-Trade to the United States of America: 1638–1870* (New York: Russell and Russell, 1965), W.E.B. Du Bois notes that violations of the slave trade ban were especially prevalent in the Deep South and during the middle of the nineteenth century. In fact, Du Bois says, 'the slave trade laws, in spite of the efforts of the government . . . were grossly violated, if not nearly nullified, in the latter part of the decade 1850–1860' (p.183). Du Bois notes, too, that during this period, American ships

illegally but routinely carried African slaves not only to the United States but also to South American countries, especially Brazil (p.186). The first page of *Beloved* is set in 1873. Thus, the mysterious young woman, Beloved, could have entered the United States on one of the many American slave ships that sailed illegally in the late 1850s. Another possibility is that the girl was brought to the United States after the rest of the ship's cargo was delivered to another country, such as Brazil. The lines 'the others are taken   I am not taken' (p.212) could suggest that after the other slaves were unloaded in South America, Beloved was forced to accompany one of the ship's officers to the United States.

18 In *The Golden Bough*, James G. Frazer notes that several American Indian groups believed that the dead souls of their relatives returned to earth in the form of water turtles. See *The Golden Bough: A Study in Magic and Religion* (New York: Macmillan, 1940), pp.502–05. This concept fits with Morrison's use of the turtles in the scene in which Beloved decides that her lost loved ones are beneath the creek's surface.

19 I am indebted to William J. House for discussing psychological theories of human perception and memory with me.

20 The narrator says that all of Sethe's neighbours are eager to see the carnival, a show that advertises performances by people who have two heads, are twenty feet tall, or weigh a ton, and 'the fact that none of it was true did not extinguish their appetite a bit' (p.48). That Sethe and Denver attend this carnival immediately before meeting Beloved foreshadows their willingness, in fact their need, to believe that the mysterious girl is something other than an ordinary human. Neither the carnival world nor Beloved's status as a child returned from the dead is based on truth, but both provide much desired escapes from the pain of everyday reality.

21 Rimmon-Kenan, p.119.

22 See Margaret Atwood, 'Haunted by Their Nightmares', *The New York Times Book Review*, 13 September 1987, pp.49–50, Paul Gray, 'Something Terrible Happened', *Time*, 21 September 1987, p.34 and Clemons, pp.74–75.

23 Clemons, p.75.

24 Phelan, p.714.

25 Phelan, p.721.

26 Rimmon-Kenan, p.119.

27 Cathy Caruth, *Unclaimed Experience: Trauma, Narrative, and History* (Baltimore and London: Johns Hopkins University Press, 1996), p.4.

28 Criticism on the novel has focused largely on *Beloved*'s relation to memory and history. See especially Valerie Smith, '"Circling the Subject": History and Narrative in *Beloved*', in *Toni Morrison: Critical Perspectives Past and Present*, ed. Henry Louis Gates, Jr. and K.A. Appiah (New York: Amistad, 1993), pp.340–54 and Marilyn Sanders Mobley, 'A Different Remembering: Memory, History, and Meaning in Toni Morrison's *Beloved*', in *Toni Morrison*, ed. Harold Bloom (New York: Chelsea House, 1990), pp.189–99.

29 While some critics have compared Beloved to a succubus or vampire in passing, Trudier Harris alone focuses on Beloved as a demonic figure who feeds off Paul D and Sethe. According to Harris, Beloved enacts vengeance against those who would thwart her desire for her mother: against Sethe herself and against Paul D, who tries to exorcize the house. Harris depicts a contest between Paul D's masculine power and Beloved's feminine otherness, which is represented by her insatiable desire. In fact, Harris argues that Sethe is masculine insofar as motherhood is a 'symbol of authority almost masculine in its absoluteness'. Thus Beloved's life-threatening feeding aims to usurp Sethe's and Paul D's masculine sense of entitlement to 'power over life and death'. See Trudier Harris, *Fiction and Folklore: The Novels of Toni Morrison* (Knoxville: University of Tennessee Press, 1991), p.158. Although Harris does not treat Beloved's attacks as enactments

of sexual violence, she suggested that I do so.

30 One type included in sixteenth- and seventeenth-century Christian classifications of demons is the 'night terror, female demons that attack sleeping men, children and women in childbed to suck them of their vitality and blood'. Rosemary Guiley, *The Encyclopedia of Ghosts and Spirits* (New York: Facts on File, 1992), p.92. The vampire and the old hag are forms of the night terror.

31 In *American Folklore* (Chicago: University of Chicago Press, 1959), Richard M. Dorson writes that 'the shape shifting witches who straddle their victims in bed are English not African creations' (p.185) and Newbell Niles Puckett records the belief in these figures in *Folk Beliefs of the Southern Negro* (Chapel Hill: University of North Carolina Press, 1926). Regardless of their origins, the figures appear in African-American literature, notably in Charles W. Chesnutt's *The Conjure Woman* (1899): 'en dey say she went out ridin' de niggers at night, fer she wuz a witch 'sides bein' a cunjuh 'oman'. Charles W. Chesnutt, *The Conjure Woman* (Ann Arbor: University of Michigan Press, 1969), p.15.

32 Caruth defines trauma as an 'overwhelming experience of sudden catastrophic events in which the response to the event occurs in the often delayed, uncontrollable repetitive appearance of hallucinations and other intrusive phenomena', p.11. This repetition is a response to the sudden and 'unassimilated nature' of the event. In nightmares the trauma experience is made available to the consciousness that could not initially 'know' it (Caruth, p.4).

33 Cited in Caruth, p.61.

34 Caruth, p.59.

35 Caruth, p.4.

36 Caruth, p.7.

37 Although Morrison names Sethe's other children – Denver, Howard and Buglar – she never calls the dead girl anything but Beloved, a name that recalls the liturgy for marriage and burial. Thus

Morrison suggests that this character stands not only for a particular individual but also for the community that both mourns and celebrates individuals and community life.

38 See Darling, p.6.

39 Angela Davis, *Women, Race, and Class* (New York: Vintage, 1981), p.172.

40 Cited in Mae G. Henderson, 'Toni Morrison's *Beloved*: Re-Membering the Body as Historical Text', in *Comparative American Identities: Race, Sex, and Nationality in the Modern Text*, ed. Hortense J. Spillers (New York: Routledge, 1991), p.63.

41 See Sally Keenan, '"Four Hundred Years of Silence": Myth, History, and Motherhood in Toni Morrison's *Beloved*', in *Recasting the World: Writing after Colonialism*, ed. Jonathan White (Baltimore: Johns Hopkins University Press, 1993), p.56.

42 Caruth, who holds that trauma must be recognised as beyond knowing if 'witnessing' is to take place, argues for a hermeneutics that allows the effect of the 'not fully conscious address' and for a 'departure from sense and understanding' (Caruth, pp.24, 56). While Caruth provides a way of reading trauma, she does not discuss ways in which trauma victims might therapeutically retell their own stories. She does note, however, that trauma therapists such as Jodie Wigren view narrative completion – the process by which a survivor creates a meaningful story that includes the originally unknowable trauma – as integral to successful treatment (Caruth, p.117 n.8). My notion that the characters in Morrison's novel might have successfully confronted Beloved and their past memories relies on the idea that healing requires conscious meaning making about what is inherently incomprehensible.

43 Ernest Jones, *On the Nightmare* (New York: Liveright, 1951), p.243.

44 Jones, p.125.

45 Jones, p.98.

46 Cited in Jones, p.125. Freimark exhaustively catalogues instances of the

belief in sexual intercourse between mortals and supernatural beings. See Jones, p.124.

47 Guiley, p.92.

48 See Jones, p.119.

49 Lee Edelman, *Homographesis* (New York: Routledge, 1994), p.56.

50 Edelman, p.54.

51 Edelman, p.53.

52 Edelman, p.54.

53 Edelman, p.56.

54 Smith. p.348.

55 Smith, p.348.

56 Smith, p.346.

57 Mobley, p.193.

58 Keenan, p.68.

59 Of course, this dehumanisation also extends to enslaved black women, who are defined as commodities or 'broodmares'. While his nephews violate Sethe's body, schoolteacher sits nearby, filling a notebook with his definitions of the 'animal' and human characteristics of those enslaved at Sweet Home. His words relegate black people to subhuman status; thus, in Sethe's infanticide, he sees a 'mishandled' and rebelling 'creature', not a tragic manifestation of mother love (p.150).

60 Smith, p.350.

61 See *Female Sexual Abuse of Children: The Ultimate Taboo*, ed. Michele Elliot (Essex: Longman, 1993).

62 Susan Brownmiller, *Against Our Will: Men, Women, and Rape* (New York: Bantam, 1976) p.15. Morrison's fictional challenge echoes the work of black feminists such as Angela Davis who argue that the history of rape and lynching of blacks must be fully accounted for in any thorough and responsible study of rape.

63 See Kimberle Crenshaw's argument that Anita Hill's allegations of sexual harassment were rejected partly because of the absence of a narrative about the rape of black women and because of a dominant coding of the black female body as libidinous. Crenshaw asserts that rape is the primary trope of feminist resistance but that it has been mobilised for white women. Hill could not appropriate this trope, whereas Clarence Thomas could easily exploit the trope of anti-racist resistance – lynching. See Kimberle Crenshaw, 'Whose Story Is It, Anyway? Feminism and Antiracist Appropriations of Anita Hill', in *Race-ing Justice, En-gendering Power: Essays on Anita Hill, Clarence Thomas and the Construction of Social Reality*, ed. Toni Morrison (New York: Pantheon, 1992), pp.402–40.

CHAPTER FOUR

1 The epigraph to this chapter is taken from *Rhetorics of Self-Making*, ed. Debbora Battalgia, (Berkeley, CA: University of California Press, 1995), p.2.

2 Hazel V. Carby, 'The Multicultural Wars', in *Black Popular Culture*, ed. Gina Dent (Seattle: Bay Press, 1992), p.193.

3 Rafael Pérez-Torres' phrase, 'Knitting and Knotting the Narrative Thread – *Beloved* as Postmodern Novel', *Modern Fiction Studies*, 39 (1993), p.676.

4 William Faulkner, *Light in August* (New York: Vintage, 1987), p.81.

5 Toni Morrison, 'Unspeakable Things Unspoken: The Afro-American Presence in American Literature', *Michigan Quarterly Review*, 28 (1989), p.32.

6 In her analysis of the slave mother's role as reproducer in and of the slave system, Anne E. Goldman points out the 'conflation between reproduction and literary production in schoolteacher's use of Sethe's ink to record the taking of her milk by his nephews: his 'gaze collapses Sethe's milky maternal product into the inky literary one. . . '. See Anne E. Goldman, '"I Made the Ink": (Literary) Production and Reproduction in *Dessa Rose* and *Beloved*', *Feminist Studies*, 16 (1990), p.324.

7 Cynthia Davis asserts that 'power for Morrison is largely the power to name, to define reality and perception'. See 'Self, Society, and Myth in Toni Morrison's Fiction', *Contemporary Literature*, 13 (1982), p.323.

8 Likening Sethe to a 'Greek protagonist faced with a tragic dilemma', Terry Otten argues that the 'moral authority' of the

novel 'resides less in a revelation of the obvious horrors of slavery than in a revelation of slavery's nefarious ability to invert moral categories and behavior and to impose tragic choice'. See Terry Otten, *The Crime of Innocence in the Fiction of Toni Morrison*, (Columbia and London: University of Missouri Press, 1989), pp. 82–83.

9 Deborah Horvitz identifies the way in which Beloved's voice in these sections works as a kind of collective voice for all those women who suffered on slave ships, asserting that Beloved's 'sickening fear of her body exploding, dissolving, or being chewed up and spit out links each enslaved Beloved with her sister in captivity'. See 'Nameless Ghosts: Possession and Dispossession in *Beloved*', *Studies in American Fiction*, 17 (1989), p. 164.

10 Similarly, Horvitz suggests that the possessiveness inherent in this tortured mother-daughter relationship is 'reminiscent of the slave-master relationship'. See Horvitz, p. 161.

11 Missy Dehn Kubitschek argues that 'the beginning' the women go back to 'revoices not only God's creation of the world in Genesis but women's creation of other life, the sounds accompanying birth'. See *Claiming the Heritage: African-American Women Novelists and History* (Jackson: University Press of Mississippi, 1991), p. 174. While it is true that the bodily experience of women seems more closely tied to the articulation of this powerful, 'feminine' voice, it should also be remembered that the men of the community are equal participants in Baby Suggs's calling in the Clearing. Such communion between the sexes is consistent with the sense of community expressed in the novel: that 'to belong to a community of other free Negroes' means 'to love and be loved by them, to counsel and be counseled, protect and be protected, feed and be fed' (p. 177).

12 The church and its minister are otherwise absent in the novel, supplanted by the more organic religious rites inspired by Baby Suggs in the natural setting of the Clearing. The freedom from the physical restrictions of being 'indoors' permits the 'deeply loved flesh' of the 'congregation' to respond more intensely and uninhibitedly to the emotions elicited by Baby Suggs's calling. Further, in stripping this ceremony of Western convention, Morrison emphasises the importance of remembering the religion that had been practised in Africa and carried to America. Thus the fleeing Sethe instinctively draws on her memory of the 'antelope dance', in which the men and the women 'shifted shapes and became something other', to get her body and the 'little antelope' stomping inside it to the point where Amy rescues her (pp. 30–31).

13 Horvitz connects Beloved's fate to that of 'those African women who did not survive the Middle Passage', glossing 'disremembered' as 'meaning not only that they are forgotten, but also that they are dismembered, cut up and off, and not remembered'. See Horvitz, p. 165.

14 See Toni Morrison, 'Rootedness: The Ancestor as Foundation', in *Black Women Writers (1950–1980): A Critical Evaluation*, ed. Mari Evans (Garden City, NY: Doubleday, 1984), p. 341.

15 April Lidinsky, 'Prophesying Bodies: Calling for a Politics of Collectivity in Toni Morrison's *Beloved*', in *The Discourse of Slavery: Aphra Behn to Toni Morrison*, ed. Carl Plasa and Betty J. Ring (London and New York, Routledge, 1994), p. 191.

16 bell hooks, 'Postmodern Blackness', in *Yearning: Race, Gender, and Cultural Politics* (Boston, MA: South End Press, 1990), p. 28.

17 hooks, p. 28.

18 See, for example, Lilian Fultz's 'Images of Motherhood in Toni Morrison's *Beloved*, in *Double Stitch: Black Women Write about Mothers and Daughters*, ed. Patricia Bell-Scott (Boston, MA: Beacon Press, 1991), pp. 32–41. See also the article by Horvitz cited above.

19 Mae. G. Henderson argues that the privileging of 'the other in ourselves' distinguishes black women's writing,

operating through a 'dialectic of identity' that is illuminated by what she sees as the complementary discursive models of Hans-Georg Gadamer and Mikhail Bakhtin. See Henderson, 'Speaking in Tongues: Dialogics, Dialectics, and the Black Women's Literary Tradition', in *Changing Our Own Words: Essays on Criticism, Theory, and Writing by Black Women*, ed. Cheryl A. Wall (New Brunswick: Rutgers University Press, 1989), p.19.

20 Kristin Boudreau, 'Pain and the Unmaking of Self in Toni Morrison's *Beloved*', *Contemporary Literature*, 36 (1995), p.451.

21 Boudreau, p.450.

22 Horvitz writes that this conclusion 'paradoxically appears to belie the crucial theme of the book, that it is imperative to preserve continuity through story, language and culture', p.165. David Lawrence writes that 'While the painful heritage of slavery cannot simply "pass on", cannot die away . . . enslavement to that heritage, Morrison implies, must "pass on", must die away, in order to undertake the task of remembering and re-articulating the individual and the communal body'. David Lawrence, 'Fleshly Ghosts and Ghostly Flesh: The Word and the Body' in *Beloved, Studies in American Fiction*, 19 (1991), p.200. Rebecca Ferguson contends that, in spite of its claim, the narrative 'is passing the story on'. Rebecca Ferguson, 'History, Memory and Language in Toni Morrison's *Beloved*, in *Feminist Criticism: Theory and Practice*, ed. Susan Sellers and Linda Hutcheon (Toronto: University of Toronto Press, 1991), pp.123–24. And Karen E. Fields writes that *Beloved* 'is not a story to be retold in only one way'. Karen E. Fields, 'To Embrace Dead Strangers: Toni Morrison's *Beloved*', in *Mother Puzzles: Daughters and Mothers in Contemporary American Literature*, ed. Mickey Pearlman (New York: Greenwood, 1989), p.169.

23 The pervasiveness of the readings that I am challenging here is evident even in Morrison's own reflections on her work. In a *New York Times* article by Mervyn Rothstein, she suggests that the pain dramatised in *Beloved* unmakes rather than makes humanity: 'I don't know if that story came because I was considering certain aspects of self-sabotage, the ways in which the best things we do so often carry seeds of one's own destruction.' But in the same article she intimates that pain – whether self-propelled or derived from outside forces – can in fact be overcome: 'I wanted it to be our past, which is haunting, and her past, which is haunting – the way memory never really leaves you unless you have gone through it and confronted it head on.' See Mervyn Rothstein, 'Toni Morrison, in Her New Novel, Defends Women', *New York Times*, 26 August 1987, late ed., p.C17.

24 I am using the word 'unmake' as Elaine Scarry introduces it in *The Body in Pain*: 'Physical pain', Scarry writes, 'does not simply resist language but actively destroys it, bringing about an immediate reversion to a state anterior to language, to the sounds and cries a human being makes before language is learned.' See Elaine Scarry, *The Body in Pain: The Making and Unmaking of the World* (New York: Oxford University Press, 1985), p.4. More dramatically in *Beloved*, pain destroys not merely language but selfhood – which is founded, of course, on language. Morrison's novel, I want to suggest, owes less to European traditions of romanticised pain than to Scarry's insight that pain unmakes the world.

25 Scarry, pp.48–49.

26 See, for instance, Henry Louis Gates, Jr.'s discussion of rhetorical control in Frederick Douglass's *Narrative* in *Figures in Black: Words, Signs, and the "Racial" Self* (New York: Oxford University Press, 1987), pp.80–97.

27 Kubitschek notes the sustaining power of Baby Suggs's self-reliance without addressing its failure: 'Emphasizing preparedness rather than protection, Baby Suggs's method of mothering promotes,

through historical examples, the same self-valuing and self-reliance as her preaching.' See Kubitschek, p. 173.

28 If I have suggested that Baby Suggs voices an Emersonian version of self-reliance, here she resembles the sceptical Emerson of 'Experience', who discovers that scepticism regarding other selves might essentially lead to scepticism about one's own self. Emerson's suspicion that perhaps the world is a product of one's own mind, that 'perhaps there are no objects' in fact 'threaten[s] or insult[s] whatever is threatenable and insultable in us'. Emerson resolves the problem of scepticism by proposing an expediency of surfaces: 'We live amid surfaces, and the true art of life is to skate well on them.' See Ralph Waldo Emerson, 'Experience', in *Centenary Edition of the Complete Works of Ralph Waldo Emerson*, 12 vols. (New York: AMS Press, 1968), III, pp. 76, 59. Baby Suggs, too, resorts to an attentiveness to surfaces when she announces her intention to do nothing and to think of nothing but colours: 'What I have to do is get in my bed and lay down. I want to fix on something harmless in this world. . . . Blue. That don't hurt nobody. Yellow neither' (p. 179).

29 The rooster's name implies the cultural power of both class and the slaveholding system: 'Mister' is a term of respect, only a vowel away from 'master'. But in assigning this name to a barnyard animal (even the king of the livestock), Morrison suggests the arbitrary status of power and selfhood.

30 Emerson, III, p. 48.

CHAPTER FIVE

1 The epigraphs to this chapter are taken, respectively, from Isobel Armstrong, 'Foreword' to *The Discourse of Slavery: Aphra Behn to Toni Morrison*, ed. Carl Plasa and Betty J. Ring (London and New York: Routledge, 1994), p. xi and Walter Benjamin, 'Theses on the Philosophy of History', in *Literature in the Modern World: Critical Essays and Documents*, ed. Dennis Walder (New York: Oxford University Press, 1990), p. 362.

2 See Paul Gilroy, *The Black Atlantic: Modernity and Double Consciousness* (London and New York: Verso, 1993), pp. 217–22 and Homi K. Bhabha, *The Location of Culture* (London and New York: Routledge, 1994), pp. 15–18.

3 See Lynda Koolish, 'Fictive Strategies and Cinematic Representations in Toni Morrison's *Beloved*: Postcolonial Theory/Postcolonial Text', *African American Review*, 29 (1995), pp. 421–38 and Eleni Coundouriotis, 'Materialism, the Uncanny, and History in Toni Morrison and Salman Rushdie', *LIT: Literature Interpretation Theory*, 8 (1997), pp. 207–25.

4 Ruth Frankenberg and Lata Mani, 'Crosscurrents, Crosstalk: Race, "Post-coloniality" and the Politics of Location', in *Cultural Studies*, 7 (1993), p. 293.

5 Anne McClintock, *Imperial Leather: Race, Gender and Sexuality in the Colonial Contest* (New York and London: Routledge, 1995), p. 13.

6 See Chandra Talpade Mohanty's introduction to *Third World Women and the Politics of Feminism*, ed. C. T. Mohanty, A. Russo, and L. Torres (Bloomington: Indiana University Press, 1991), for a lucid discussion of the necessary inclusion of 'minority peoples or people of color in the U.S.A.' in definitions of the Third World.

7 Paul Gilroy, 'Living Memory: Toni Morrison Talks to Paul Gilroy', *City Limits*, 31 March–7 April 1988, p. 10.

8 In interview with Margaret Busby, *Bandung File*, Channel 4, 25 July 1989.

9 I borrow this term from Gayatri Spivak, who uses it to refer to the way 'metropolitan countries discriminate against disenfranchised groups in their midst' in order to distinguish the histories of these groups from other histories of post-coloniality (Gayatri Chakravorty Spivak, 'Who Claims Alterity?', in *Remaking History*, ed. Barbara Kruger and Phil Mariani, DIA Art Foundation Discussions in Contemporary Culture no. 4 [Seattle: Bay Press, 1989], p. 274). Michele Wallace has applied Spivak's term to

African-American culture, which, she says, as a 'product of "internal colonization", constitutes an important variation on postcolonial discourse' (*Invisibility Blues: From Pop to Theory* [London and New York: Verso, 1990], p.2).

10 See Jerry Phillips's essay 'Educating the Savages: Melville, Bloom, and the Rhetoric of Imperialist Instruction', in *Recasting the World: Writing after Colonialism*, ed. Jonathan White (Baltimore: Johns Hopkins University Press, 1993), pp.25–44, for a discussion of this issue.

11 Bill Ashcroft, Gareth Griffiths, and Helen Tiffin, *The Empire Writes Back: Theory and Practice in Post-Colonial Literatures* (London and New York: Routledge, 1989), p.175.

12 Sherley Anne Williams, *Dessa Rose* (London: Macmillan, 1987), p.5.

13 Ashcroft, Griffiths, and Tiffin, p.51.

14 Donna C. Stanton, 'Difference on Trial: A Critique of the Maternal Metaphor in Cixous, Irigaray, and Kristeva', in *The Poetics of Gender*, ed. Nancy K. Miller (New York: Columbia University Press, 1986), p.175.

15 Bhabha, summarized in Ashcroft, Griffiths, and Tiffin, p.52.

16 Deborah Gray White, *Arn't I a Woman? Female Slaves in the Plantation South* (New York: W.W. Norton, 1985), p.70.

17 Barbara Omolade, 'Hearts of Darkness', in *Desire: The Politics of Sexuality*, ed. A. Snitow, C. Stansell, and S. Thompson (London: Virago, 1984), p.365.

18 Jacqueline Jones, *Labor of Love, Labor of Sorrow: Black Women, Work, and the Family from Slavery to the Present* (New York: Basic Books, 1985), p.20.

19 Hazel V. Carby, 'Ideologies of Black Folk: The Historical Novel of Slavery', in *Slavery and the Literary Imagination*, ed. Deborah E. McDowell and Arnold Rampersad (Baltimore: Johns Hopkins University Press, 1989), pp.137–38.

20 Mae G. Henderson, 'Toni Morrison's *Beloved*: Re-membering the Body as Historical Text', in *Comparative American Identities: Race, Sex and Nationality in the Modern Text*, ed. Hortense J. Spillers (New York: Routledge, 1991), p.74.

21 Henderson, p.73.

22 Henderson, p.74.

23 Jessica Benjamin, 'Master and Slave: The Fantasy of Erotic Domination', in Snitow, Stansell, and Thompson, p.96. Benjamin's argument is made within the context of object relations psychoanalytic theory. Her point that a very young child has no conception of the mother as an autonomous being with needs of her own is redolent of the relationship between Sethe and Beloved.

24 Henderson argues that Morrison's representation of 'maternal delivery . . . becomes a means of "deliverance" from the dominant conception of history as a white/paternal metaphor' (p.76). While I would not disagree with this, it seems to me that Morrison's text does not conclude with this maternal metaphor 'as a primary metaphor of history and human culture'. Rather, I regard the text's closing scenes as provoking questions about the dangers of such all-embracing metaphors; Morrison implicitly challenges the very process of remythologising in which she has engaged.

25 Omolade, pp.374–75.

26 See Jennifer Fitzgerald, 'Selfhood and Community: Psychoanalysis and Discourse in *Beloved*', *Modern Fiction Studies*, 39 (1993), pp.669–87 and Jean Wyatt, 'Giving Body to the Word: The Maternal Symbolic in Toni Morrison's *Beloved*', PMLA, 108 (1993), pp.474–88.

27 Peter Nicholls, 'The Belated Postmodern: History, Phantoms, and Toni Morrison', in *Psychoanalytic Criticism: A Reader*, ed. Sue Vice (Oxford and Cambridge, MA: Polity Press, 1996), p.50.

28 Wyatt, p.485.

29 See Sigmund Freud, 'From the History of an Infantile Neurosis', *The Standard Edition of the Complete Psychological Works of Sigmund Freud*, trans. and ed. James Strachey *et al*, 24 vols. (London: The Hogarth Press,

1953–74), XVII, pp. 1–123.

30 Linda Ruth Williams, *Critical Desire: Psychoanalysis and the Literary Subject* (London: Edward Arnold, 1995), p. 130.

31 Nicholls, p. 52.

32 Nicholls, p. 51.

33 Nicholls, p. 51.

34 Nicholls, p. 56.

35 Toni Morrison, *Playing in the Dark: Whiteness and the Literary Imagination* (Cambridge, MA and London: Harvard University Press, 1992), p. v.

36 Henderson, p. 63.

37 Jean Laplanche and Serge Leclaire, 'The Unconscious: A Psychoanalytic Study', *Yale French Studies*, 48 (1972), p. 128. Cf. John Forrester, *The Seductions of Psychoanalysis: Freud, Lacan, and Derrida* (Cambridge: Cambridge University Press, 1990), p. 199 on 'Freud's theory that it was a way of remembering that was traumatic, rather than what was remembered'.

38 David F. Krell, *Of Memory, Reminiscence, and Writing: On the Verge* (Bloomington and Indianapolis: Indiana University Press, 1990), p. 106.

39 Cf. Henderson, p. 64: 'Morrison seeks to repossess the African and slave ancestors after their historic violation'. See also Henderson, pp. 80–81 on Sethe's ability to '"relive" or re-enact the past'.

40 Dominick LaCapra, 'History and Psychoanalysis', in *The Trials(s) of Psychoanalysis*, ed. Françoise Meltzer (Chicago and London: University of Chicago Press, 1988), p. 18.

41 This particular view of the postmodern is to be distinguished from that of Fredric Jameson who has argued consistently that post-modernity is characterised by a 'waning' of a thematics of time and memory ('memory has been weakened in our time', as he puts it in *Postmodernism, or the Cultural Logic of Late Capitalism* [London and New York: Verso, 1991], p. 364). For a critique, see my 'Divergences: Modernism, Postmodernism, Jameson and Lyotard', *Critical Quarterly*, 33. 3 (Autumn 1991), pp. 1–18.

42 Freud, XVII, p. 45 n. 1. Cf. the letter to Fliess of 15 October 1895, in *The Origins of Psycho-Analysis: Letters to Wilhelm Fliess, Drafts and Notes: 1887–1902* (London: Imago, 1954), p. 127: 'Have I revealed the great clinical secret to you . . .? Hysteria is the consequence of presexual *sexual shock*. Obsessional neurosis is the consequence of presexual *sexual pleasure* later transformed into guilt.' Freud goes on to observe that 'the relevant events become effective only as *memories*'.

43 *Écrits: A Selection*, trans. Alan Sheridan (London: Tavistock, 1977), p. 48.

44 Jean Laplanche and J.-B. Pontalis, *The Language of Psychoanalysis*, trans. Donald Nicholson-Srnith, with an introduction by Daniel Lagache (London: Karnac Books, 1988), p. 113. Cf. Laplanche, *New Foundations for Psychoanalysis*, trans. David Macey (Oxford: Blackwell, 1989), p. 112: 'This theory postulates that nothing can be inscribed in the human unconscious except in relation to at least two events which are separated from one another in time by a moment of maturation that allows the subject to react in two ways to an initial experience or to the memory of that experience.'

45 Forrester, p. 206.

46 Andrew Benjamin, *Art, Mimesis and the Avant-Garde* (London and New York: Routledge, 1991), p. 197. Cf. Lacan, p. 48: '. . . the effect of full speech is to reorder past contingencies by conferring on them the sense of necessities to come, such as they are constituted by the little freedom through which the subject makes them present'.

47 Laplanche and Pontalis, p. 114.

48 Laplanche, p. 118.

49 Michel Foucault, *Language, Counter-Memory, Practice: Selected Essays and Interviews*, ed. Donald F. Bouchard, trans. Donald F. Bouchard and Sherry Simon (Ithaca: Cornell University Press, 1977), p. 172.

50 See Ned Lukacher, *Primal Scenes: Literature, Philosophy, Psychoanalysis* (Ithaca and London: Cornell University Press, 1986), p. 35: 'Deferred action demands that one recognize that while

the earlier event is still to some extent the cause of the later event, the earlier event is nevertheless also the effect of the later event. One is forced to admit a double or "metaleptic" logic in which causes are both causes of effects and the effect of effects.'

51 Jacques Derrida, *Mémoires for Paul de Man*, rev. ed., trans. Cecile Lindsay *et al* (New York: Columbia University Press, 1989), p. 58: 'Memory stays with traces, in order to "preserve" them, but traces of a past that has never been present, traces which themselves never occupy the form of presence and always remain, as it were, to come.' Cf. Jacques Derrida, *Margins of Philosophy*, trans. Alan Bass (Brighton: Harvester Press, 1986), p. 21. The same point is stressed by Lyotard in *Heidegger and 'the jews'*, trans. Andreas Michel and Mark Roberts (Minneapolis: University of Minnesota Press, 1990), p. 13: 'It will be represented as something that has never been presented'. Krell, p. 6, observes of Merleau-Ponty's elaboration of a similar idea in *The Phenomenology of Perception* that it 'heralds the passing of an epoch of mnemic metaphysics. It marks the inception of a memory beneath the traditional ontotheological uses of recollection, a memory no longer in thrall to presence.'

52 Andrew Benjamin, 'Translating Origins: Psychoanalysis and Philosophy', in *Rethinking Translation: Discourse, Subjectivity, Ideology*, ed. L. Venuti (London: Routledge, 1992), p. 30. This logic is perhaps inscribed in the etymology of the verb 'to remember', from the Latin *rememorari*, 'call to mind again, remember *again*'; Morrison's 'rememory' is not, as is sometimes thought, a coinage, but an archaism that the *OED* defines as 'remembrance'.

53 See *The Naked Lunch* (London: Corgi, 1974), p. 247: '"Possession" they call it [. . .] Sometimes an entity jumps in the body [. . .] As if I was usually there but subject to goof now and again [. . .] *Wrong! I am never here* [. . .] Never that is *fully* in possession . . . .'. Thomas

Pynchon's *Gravity's Rainbow* (1973; Harmondsworth: Penguin, 1987) provides one definitive exploration of the 'interiorization' of control: 'All these things arise from one difficulty: control. For the first time it was inside, do you see. The control is put *inside*. No more need to suffer passively under "outside forces"' (p. 30).

54 For Beloved as the force of desire, see p. 58: 'A touch no heavier than a feather but loaded, nevertheless, with desire. Sethe stirred and looked around. First at Beloved's soft new hand on her shoulder, then into her eyes. The longing she saw there was bottomless. Some plea barely in control.' The implications of the last phrase become clear as Beloved becomes increasingly demanding (p. 240): 'when Sethe ran out of things to give her, Beloved invented desire'.

55 For the temporal relation trivialised as 'echo', see, for example, Peter Ackroyd, *Hawksmoor* (1985) and *Chatterton* (1987).

56 Cf. *Beloved*, p. 244: 'Like Sweet Home where time didn't pass'.

57 *Beloved*, p. 86: 'Her heavy knives of defense against misery, regret, gall and hurt, she placed one by one on a bank where clear water rushed on below.' But we have already had a forewarning (p. 57) of the conflict to come between Sethe and Beloved: 'In lamplight, and over the flames of the cooking stove, their two shadows clashed and crossed on the ceiling like black swords.'

58 As Laplanche and Pontalis explain, p. 211, Freud uses 'incorporation' to define the 'Process whereby the subject, more or less on the level of phantasy, has an object penetrate his body and keeps it "inside" his body. Incorporation constitutes an instinctual aim and a mode of object-relationship which is characteristic of the oral stage. . .'. 'Introjection' (a term that Freud borrowed from Ferenczi) is 'closely akin to identification' and while 'close in meaning to incorporation [. . .] does not necessarily imply any reference to the body's real boundaries

(introjection into the ego, into the ego-ideal, etc.)' (Laplanche and Pontalis, p. 229).

59 Jacques Derrida, 'Fors: The Anglish Words of Nicolas Abraham and Maria Torok', trans. Barbara Johnson, in Abraham and Torok, The Wolf Man's Magic Word: A Cryptonomy, trans. Nicholas Rand (Minneapolis: University of Minnesota Press, 1986), pp. xvi–xvii. Cf. pp. xxi–xxii: 'By resisting introjection, it prevents the loving, appropriating assimilation of the other, and thus seems to preserve the other as other (foreign), but it also does the opposite. It is not the other that the process of incorporation preserves, but a certain topography it keeps safe, intact, untouched by the very relationship with the other to which, paradoxically, introjection is more open.'

60 Nicolas Abraham and Maria Torok, 'Introjection – Incorporation: Mourning or Melancholia', in Psychoanalysis in France, ed. S. Lebovici and D. Widlocher (New York: International University Press, 1980), p. 8. See also Maria Torok, 'Maladie du deuil et fantasme de cadavre exquis', in Abraham and Torok, L'Ecorce et le noyau (Paris: Flammarion, 1987), pp. 229–51.

61 Abraham and Torok, Wolf Man's Magic Word, p. 81: 'For the crypt is already constructed, and the Ego cannot quit the place where it had once been; it can only withdraw into seclusion and construct a barrier separating it from the other half of the Ego.'

62 Elisabeth Roudinesco, Jacques Lacan and Co.: A History of Psychoanalysis in France, 1925–1985 (London: Free Association Books, 1990), p. 599.

63 Derrida, 'Fors', p. xvii.

64 Gloria Naylor and Toni Morrison, 'A Conversation', Southern Review, 21 (1985), 584 (my emphases).

65 Naylor and Morrison, p. 585.

66 Naylor and Morrison, p. 585.

67 Naylor and Morrison, p. 585.

68 Note how the struggle between them is permeated with images of orality and ingestion. The image of Beloved as pregnant reverses the phantasmal moment earlier in the novel when Sethe's water seems to break for the second time when she first sees Beloved (p. 51).

69 Interview with Salman Rushdie, The Late Show, BBC2, June 1992.

70 Bloomsbury Theatre, London, 6 June 1992.

71 Nicolas Abraham, 'Notes on the Phantom: A Complement to Freud's Metapsychology', trans. Nicholas Rand, in Meltzer, pp. 75–80. See also the use made of this idea in Jacqueline Rose, The Haunting of Sylvia Plath (London: Virago, 1991).

72 Abraham, p. 76.

73 Abraham, p. 76.

74 Cf. Abraham, pp. 77–78: 'The phantom's periodic and compulsive return lies beyond the scope of symptom-formation in the sense of a return of the repressed; it works like a ventriloquist, like a stranger within the subject's own mental topography.'

SELECT BIBLIOGRAPHY

Works cited

Elizabeth Abel, 'Black Writing, White Reading: Race and the Politics of Feminist Interpretation', *Critical Inquiry*, 19 (1993), pp. 470–98

Marilyn Judith Atlas, 'Toni Morrison's *Beloved* and the Reviewers', *Midwestern Miscellany*, 18 (1990), pp. 45–57

Margaret Atwood, 'Haunted by Their Nightmares', rev. of *Beloved, New York Times Book Review*, 13 September 1987, pp. 49–50

Pamela E. Barnett, 'Figurations of Rape and the Supernatural in *Beloved*', *PMLA*, 112 (1997), pp. 418–27

P. S. Bassett, 'A Visit to the Slave Mother Who Killed Her Child', [1856], *The Black Book*, comp. Middleton Harris, [ed. Toni Morrison], (New York: Random House, 1974), p. 10

Bernard W. Bell, '*Beloved:* A Womanist Neo-Slave Narrative; or, Multivocal Remembrances of Things Past', *African American Review*, 26 (1992), pp. 7–16

Homi K. Bhabha, *The Location of Culture* (London and New York: Routledge, 1994)

Kristin Boudreau, 'Pain and the Unmaking of Self in Toni Morrison's *Beloved*', *Contemporary Literature*, 36 (1995), pp. 447–65

A. S. Byatt, 'An American Masterpiece', rev. of *Beloved, Guardian*, 16 October 1987, p. 13

Barbara Christian, 'Fixing Methodologies: *Beloved,*' *Cultural Critique*, 24 (Spring 1993), pp. 5–15

Walter Clemons, 'A Gravestone of Memories', rev. of *Beloved, Newsweek*, 28 September 1987, pp. 74–75

Eleni Coundouriotis, 'Materialism, the Uncanny, and History in Toni Morrison and Salman Rushdie', *LIT: Literature Interpretation Theory*, 8 (1997), pp. 207–25

Stanley Crouch, 'Aunt Medea', rev. of *Beloved, New Republic*, 19 October 1987, pp. 38–43

Marsha Darling, 'In the Realm of Responsibility: A Conversation with Toni Morrison', *Women's Review of Books*, March 1988, pp. 5–6

Jacqueline de Weever, *Mythmaking and Metaphor in Black Women's Fiction* (New York: St. Martin's Press, 1991)

Thomas R. Edwards, 'Ghost Story', rev. of *Beloved, New York Review of Books*, 5 November 1987, pp. 18–19

Rebecca Ferguson, 'History, Memory and Language in Toni Morrison's *Beloved*', *Feminist Criticism: Theory and Practice*, ed. Susan Sellers and Linda Hutcheon (Toronto: University of Toronto Press, 1991), pp. 109–27

Karen E. Fields, 'To Embrace Dead Strangers: Toni Morrison's *Beloved*', *Mother Puzzles: Daughters and Mothers in Contemporary American Literature*, ed. Mickey Pearlman (New York: Greenwood, 1989), pp. 159–69

Jennifer Fitzgerald, 'Selfhood and Community: Psychoanalysis and Discourse in *Beloved*', *Modern Fiction Studies*, 39 (1993), pp. 669–87

Lilian Fultz, 'Images of Motherhood in Toni Morrison's *Beloved*', *Double Stitch: Black Women Write about Mothers and Daughters*, ed. Patricia Bell-Scott (Boston, MA: Beacon Press, 1991), pp. 32–41

Paul Gilroy, 'Living Memory: A Meeting with Toni Morrison', *Small Acts: Thoughts on the Politics of Black Cultures* (London: Serpent's Tail, 1993), pp. 175–82

—— *The Black Atlantic: Modernity and Double Consciousness* (London and New York: Verso, 1993)

Anne E. Goldman, '"I Made the Ink": (Literary) Production and Reproduction in *Dessa Rose* and *Beloved*', *Feminist Studies*, 16 (1990), pp. 313–30

Paul Gray, 'Something Terrible Happened', rev. of *Beloved*, *Time*, 21 September 1987, p. 34

Trudier Harris, *Fiction and Folklore: The Novels of Toni Morrison* (Knoxville: University of Tennessee Press, 1991)

—— 'Toni Morrison: Solo Flight Through Literature into History', *World Literature Today*, 68 (1994), pp. 9–14

Mae G. Henderson, 'Toni Morrison's *Beloved*: Re-Membering the Body as Historical Text', *Comparative American Identities: Race, Sex, and Nationality in the Modern Text*, ed. Hortense J. Spillers (New York: Routledge, 1991), pp. 62–86

Kristine Holmes, '"This is flesh I'm talking about here": Embodiment in Toni Morrison's *Beloved* and Sherley Anne Williams' *Dessa Rose*', *LIT: Literature Interpretation Theory*, 6 (1995), pp. 133–48

Deborah Horvitz, 'Nameless Ghosts: Possession and Dispossession in *Beloved*', *Studies in American Fiction*, 17 (1989), pp. 157–67

Elizabeth B. House, 'Toni Morrison's Ghost: The Beloved Who is Not Beloved', *Studies in American Fiction*, 18 (1990), pp. 17–26

Sally Keenan, '"Four Hundred Years of Silence": Myth, History, and Motherhood in Toni Morrison's *Beloved*', *Recasting the World: Writing after Colonialism*, ed. Jonathan White (Baltimore: Johns Hopkins University Press, 1993), pp. 45–81

Olga Kenyon, *Writing Women: Contemporary Women Novelists* (London and Concord, MA, 1991)

Lynda Koolish, 'Fictive Strategies and Cinematic Representations in Toni Morrison's *Beloved*: Postcolonial Theory/Postcolonial Text', *African American Review*, 29 (1995), pp. 421–38

Missy Dehn Kubitschek, *Claiming the Heritage: African-American Women Novelists and History* (Jackson: University Press of Mississippi, 1991)

David Lawrence, 'Fleshly Ghosts and Ghostly Flesh: The Word and the Body in *Beloved*', *Studies in American Fiction*, 19 (1991), pp. 189–201

Charles Lewis, 'The Ironic Romance of New Historicism: *The Scarlet Letter* and *Beloved* Side by Side', *Arizona Quarterly: A Journal of American Literature, Culture, and Theory*, 51. 1 (Spring 1995), pp. 32–60

April Lidinsky, 'Prophesying Bodies: Calling for a Politics of Collectivity in Toni Morrison's *Beloved*', *The Discourse of Slavery: Aphra Behn to Toni Morrison*, ed. Carl Plasa and Betty J. Ring (London and New York: Routledge, 1994), pp. 191–216

Carl D. Malmgren, 'Mixed Genres and the Logic of Slavery in Toni Morrison's *Beloved*', *Critique: Studies in Contemporary Fiction*, 36. 2 (Winter 1995), pp. 96–106

Sylvia Mayer, '"You Like Huckleberries?": Toni Morrison's *Beloved* and Mark Twain's *Adventures of Huckleberry Finn*', *The Black Columbiad: Defining Moments in African American Literature and Culture*, ed. Werner Sollers and Maria Diedrich (Cambridge, MA and London: Harvard University Press, 1994), pp. 337–46

David L. Middleton, ed. *Toni Morrison's Fiction: Contemporary Criticism* (New York and London: Garland, 1997)

Marilyn Sanders Mobley, 'A Different Remembering: Memory, History and Meaning in Toni Morrison's *Beloved*', *Toni Morrison*, ed. Harold Bloom (New York: Chelsea House, 1990), pp. 189–99

Richard C. Moreland, '"He Wants to Put His Story Next to Hers": Putting Twain's Story Next to Hers in Morrison's *Beloved*', *Modern Fiction Studies*, 39 (1993), pp. 501–25

Gloria Naylor and Toni Morrison, 'A Conversation', *Southern Review*, 21 (1985), pp. 567–93

Peter Nicholls, 'The Belated Postmodern: History, Phantoms, and Toni Morrison', *Psychoanalytic Criticism: A Reader*, ed. Sue Vice (Oxford and Cambridge, MA: Polity Press, 1996), pp. 50–67

Terry Otten, *The Crime of Innocence in the Novels of Toni Morrison* (Columbia and London: University of Missouri Press, 1989)

Linden Peach, *Toni Morrison* (Basingstoke and London: Macmillan, 1995)

Rafael Pérez-Torres, 'Knitting and Knotting the Narrative Thread – *Beloved* as Postmodern Novel', *Modern Fiction Studies*, 39 (1993), pp. 689–707

Nancy J. Peterson, 'Introduction: Canonizing Toni Morrison', *Modern Fiction Studies*, 39 (1993), pp. 461–79

James Phelan, 'Toward a Rhetorical Reader-Response Criticism: The Difficult, the Stubborn, and the Ending of *Beloved*', *Modern Fiction Studies*, 39 (1993), pp. 709–28

Shlomith Rimmon-Kenan, 'Narration, Doubt, Retrieval: Toni Morrison's *Beloved*', *Narrative*, 4. 2 (1996), pp. 109–23

Ashraf H. A. Rushdy, 'Daughters Signifyin(g) History: The Example of Toni Morrison's *Beloved*', *American Literature: A Journal of Literary History, Criticism, and Bibliography*, 64 (1992), pp. 567–97

Valerie Smith, '"Circling the Subject": History and Narrative in *Beloved*', *Toni Morrison: Critical Perspectives Past and Present*, ed. Henry Louis Gates, Jr. and K. A. Appiah (New York: Amistad, 1993), pp. 340–54

—— *Self-Discovery and Authority in Afro-American Narrative* (Cambridge, MA: Harvard University Press, 1987)

Claudia Tate, ed., *Black Women Writers at Work* (New York: Continuum, 1984)

Danille Taylor-Guthrie, ed., *Conversations with Toni Morrison* (Jackson: University Press of Mississippi, 1994)

Richard Todd, 'Toni Morrison and Canonicity: Acceptance or Appropriation?', *Rewriting the Dream: Reflections on the Changing American Literary Canon*, ed. W.M. Verhoeven (Amsterdam: Rodopi, 1992), pp. 43–59

Molly Abel Travis, 'Speaking from the Silence of the Slave Narrative: *Beloved* and African-American Women's History', *Texas Review*, 13 (1992), pp. 69–81

Caroline M. Woidat, 'Talking Back to Schoolteacher: Morrison's Confrontation with Hawthorne in *Beloved*', *Modern Fiction Studies*, 39 (1993), pp. 527–46

Cynthia Griffin Woolf, '"Margaret Garner": A Cincinnati Story', *Massachusetts Review*, 32 (1991), pp. 417–40

Jean Wyatt, 'Giving Body to the Word: The Maternal Symbolic in Toni Morrison's *Beloved*', *PMLA*, 108 (1993), pp. 474–88

Toni Morrison

Novels

——, *Beloved* (London: Vintage, 1997/New York: Knopf, 1987)

——, *Jazz* (New York: Knopf, 1992)

——, *Paradise* (New York: Knopf, 1998)

——, *Song of Solomon* (New York: Knopf, 1977)

——, *Sula* (New York: Knopf, 1973)

——, *Tar Baby* (New York: Knopf, 1981)

——, *The Bluest Eye* (New York: Holt, Rinehart, and Winston, 1970)

Criticism

——, *Playing in the Dark: Whiteness and the Literary Imagination* (Cambridge, MA and London: Harvard University Press, 1992)

——, 'Rootedness: The Ancestor as Foundation', *Black Women Writers (1950–1980): A Critical Evaluation*, ed. Mari Evans (Garden City, NY: Doubleday, 1984), pp. 339–45

——, 'The Site of Memory', *Inventing the Truth: The Art and Craft of Memoir*, ed. William Zinsser (Boston, MA: Houghton Mifflin, 1987), pp. 103–24

——, 'Unspeakable Things Unspoken: The Afro-American Presence in American Literature', *Michigan Quarterly Review*, 28 (1989), pp. 1–34

Edited Works

——, ed., *Race–ing Justice, En–gendering Power: Essays on Anita Hill, Clarence Thomas and the Construction of Social Reality* (New York: Pantheon, 1993)

——, [ed.], *The Black Book*, comp. Middleton Harris (New York: Random House, 1974)

——, and Claudia Brodsky Lacour, ed., *Birth of a Nation'hood: Gaze, Script, and Spectacle in the O.J. Simpson Case* (New York: Pantheon, 1997)

Suggested Further Reading

This includes essays and articles not cited in the text that readers of *Beloved* may nonetheless find useful.

James Berger, 'Ghosts of Liberalism: Morrison's *Beloved* and the Moynihan Report', *PMLA*, 111 (1996), pp.408–20

Susan Comfort, 'Counter-Memory, Mourning and History in Toni Morrison's *Beloved*', *LIT: Literature Interpretation Theory*, 6 (1995), pp.121–32

Gary W. Daily, 'Toni Morrison's *Beloved*: Rememory, History and the Fantastic', *The Celebration of the Fantastic: Selected Papers from the Tenth Anniversary International Conference on the Fantastic in the Arts*, ed. Donald E. Morse *et al* (Westport, CT: Greenwood, 1992), pp.141–47

Jane E. Hindman, '"A little space, a little time, some way to hold off eventfulness": African American Quiltmaking as Metaphor in Toni Morrison's *Beloved*', *LIT: Literature Interpretation Theory*, 6 (1995), pp.101–20

Marianne Hirsch, 'Maternity and Rememory: Toni Morrison's *Beloved*', *Representations of Motherhood*, ed. Donna Bassin *et al* (New Haven: Yale University Press, 1994), pp.92–110

Sharon P. Holland, 'Bakulu Discourse: The Language of the Margin in Toni Morrison's *Beloved*', *LIT: Literature Interpretation Theory*, 6 (1995), pp.89–100

Linda Krumholz, 'The Ghosts of Slavery: Historical Recovery in Toni Morrison's *Beloved*', *African American Review*, 26 (1992), pp.395–408

Susan Janet McKinstry, 'A Ghost of An/Other Chance: The Spinster-Mother in Toni Morrison's *Beloved*', *Old Maids to Radical Spinsters: Unmarried Women in the Twentieth-Century Novel*, ed. Laura L. Doan *et al* (Urbana: University of Illinois Press, 1991), pp.259–74

Barbara Hill Rigney, '"A Story to Pass On": Ghosts and the Significance of History in Toni Morrison's *Beloved*', *Haunting the House of Fiction: Feminist Perspectives on Ghost Stories by American Women*, ed. Lynette Carpenter and Wendy K. Kolmar (Knoxville: University of Tennessee Press, 1991), pp.229–35

Caroline Rody, 'Toni Morrison's *Beloved*: History, "Rememory", and a "Clamor for a Kiss"', *American Literary History*, 7. 1 (Spring 1995), pp.92–119

ACKNOWLEDGEMENTS

The editor and publishers wish to thank the following for their permission to reprint copyright material: the *Guardian* (for material from 'An American Masterpiece'); *New York Review of Books* (for material from 'Ghost Story'); Random House (for material from *The Black Book*); Chelsea House (for material from *Toni Morrison*); Houghton Mifflin (for material from *Inventing the Truth: The Art and Craft of Memoir*); Modern Language Association (for material from *PMLA*); The University of Wisconsin Press (for material from *Contemporary Literature*); Routledge (for material from *The Discourse of Slavery: Aphra Behn to Toni Morrison*); Polity Press (for material from *Psychoanalytic Criticism: A Reader*); Johns Hopkins University Press (for material from *Recasting the World: Writing After Colonialism*).

Every effort has been made to contact the holders of any copyrights applying to the material quoted in this book. The publishers would be grateful if any such copyright holders whom they have not been able to contact, would write to them.

Carl Plasa is a Lecturer in English in the Centre for Critical and Cultural Theory, University of Wales, Cardiff. He has published a number of articles on nineteenth- and twentieth-century literature and co-edited *The Discourse of Slavery: Aphra Behn to Toni Morrison* (Routledge, 1994). He is currently completing a monograph on race and identification from Shakespeare to Tsitsi Dangarembga, to be published by Macmillan in 1999.

INDEX